"*Aggiornamento* is back! Paul Turner has updated the first volume of Adrien Nocent's *The Liturgical Year* in a discrete, respectful, and informed manner, enabling the author's reflections on the feasts and seasons as well as on the Lectionary to connect effectively with the concerns and interests of present-day readers. I look forward to the next two volumes."

Patrick Regan, OSB
Author of *Advent to Pentecost*

"Though originating in the postconciliar period, Adrien Nocent's volumes remain one of the church's finest commentaries on the Lectionary and contain remarkable up-to-date insights for our times. Thanks to the emendations and annotations of Paul Turner, one of today's finest liturgical scholars, these volumes will enrich the thoughts of parish liturgists, presiders, homilists, musicians, lectors, theology students, and participants in the church's liturgy."

Stephen J. Binz
Author of *Conversing with God in Advent and Christmas*

"Adrien Nocent was truly a remarkable scholar, well ahead of his time! . . . He weaves the paschal mystery, eschatology, and living liturgy daily into a core tool for interpreting Advent, Christmas, and Epiphany in a fresh way. In this reissue, Fr. Paul Turner sensitively respects Nocent's own voice as he bridges the time after the Council to the present age. . . . This work needs to be on every priest's, liturgist's, musician's, and assembly member's 'go to' shelf."

Joyce Ann Zimmerman, CPPS
Institute for Liturgical Ministry, Dayton, Ohio

"In 1977 when Adrien Nocent's book appeared in English translation, I was studying the liturgical year with him at Sant'Anselmo. I remember how moved I was to read his deep reflections after having experienced the new lectionary with its three-year cycle of readings at that point only a couple of times. Now, having experienced the three-year cycle more than a dozen times, I am still moved by his writings. I am delighted that his book has been updated by Paul Turner and is coming into print again."

Michael S. Driscoll
University of Notre Dame

The Liturgical Year

Volume One

ADVENT, CHRISTMAS, EPIPHANY

by

Adrien Nocent, OSB

Translated by

Matthew J. O'Connell

Introduced, Emended, and Annotated by

Paul Turner

LITURGICAL PRESS
Collegeville, Minnesota

www.litpress.org

Nihil Obstat: Reverend Robert C. Harren, J.C.L., *Censor deputatus.*
Imprimatur: ✠ Most Reverend John F. Kinney, J.C.D., D.D., Bishop of Saint Cloud, Minnesota, August 8, 2013.

Cover design by Ann Blattner. Illustration by Frank Kacmarcik, OblSB. Saint John's Abbey, Collegeville, Minnesota. Used with permission.

Available in three volumes, *The Liturgical Year* is the authorized English version of Célébrer Jésus-Christ, L'année Liturgique, published by Jean-Pierre Delarge, 10, rue Mayet, 75006 Paris, France. The English translation of *The Liturgical Year* was first published by Liturgical Press in four volumes in 1977.

1   2   3   4   5   6   7   8   9

Library of Congress Cataloging-in-Publication Data

Nocent, Adrien.
    [Célébrer Jésus-Christ. English]
    The liturgical year : Advent, Christmas, Epiphany / by Adrien Nocent, OSB ; Translated by Matthew J. O'Connell ; Introduced, Emended, and Annotated by Paul Turner.
        volumes   cm
    Includes bibliographical references.
    ISBN 978-0-8146-3569-8 (v. 1 : pbk. : alk. paper) —
    ISBN 978-0-8146-3594-0 (v. 1 : e-book)
    1. Church year.   I. Title.

BV30.N6213   2013
263'.9—dc23

                                                    2013011152

Contents

The Advent Mystery

The Christmas Mystery

Abbreviations

AAS   *Acta Apostolicae Sedis*

CCL   *Corpus Christianorum, Series Latina.* Turnhout, 1953–

CL   *Constitution on the Sacred Liturgy*

CSEL   *Corpus Scriptorum Ecclesiasticorum Latinorum.* Vienna, 1866–

LH   *Liturgy of the Hours*

PG   *Patrologia Graeca*, ed. J. P. Migne. Paris, 1857–66

PL   *Patrologia Latina*, ed. J. P. Migne. Paris, 1844–64

SC   *Sources Chretiennes.* Paris, 1942–

TPS   *The Pope Speaks.* Washington, 1954–

Series Introduction

When the postconciliar lectionary first fell into the hands of priests, musicians, and parish liturgists in 1970, few could fully grasp the significance of the event. The vast selection of readings, the nimble choice of responsorial psalms, and the blossoming of the liturgical year would become clearer only in time.

One of the first companions to the revised lectionary was composed by Adrien Nocent, a Belgian monk who became a consultor for the Sacred Congregation for Divine Worship in 1969. In 1964 he had served as a consultor for the Consilium for the Implementation of the Constitution on the Sacred Liturgy of the Second Vatican Council. He was the secretary for the Consilium's Study Group 17, which worked on the revision of Holy Week, and, among other responsibilities, was part of Study Group 11, which revised the Lectionary for Mass. He drew up the preliminary schemas for Advent, the Sundays after Epiphany, and the Sundays following Pentecost.

For Nocent, a commentary on the lectionary could not be a mere commentary on a book but an exploration of the dialogue between the Word of God and humanity in every culture and time. The Church had been through only one complete three-year cycle of the lectionary when Nocent was writing this book. He shared his vision of this project for eager readers, students, and worshipers.

On the occasion of the fiftieth anniversary of the Constitution on the Sacred Liturgy, Liturgical Press is proud to reissue Nocent's work. I was deeply honored at the invitation to contribute annotations—honored because when I was in the seminary, *The Liturgical Year* was the main resource I consulted to prayerfully approach my participation in the Sunday Mass; honored because as a young priest, I used *The Liturgical Year* to help prepare my homilies; honored because as a liturgical catechist, my brain had been hardwired to Nocent's approach to the lectionary: Start with the gospel, then look at the first reading, then the psalm, and be ready to discard the second reading from your treatment of the Sunday lectionary.

Readers today may criticize Nocent's approach as too "thematic" in content. He presumes that each Sunday carries a theme and that he knows what it is. In reality, there is no single theme, and the second reading deserves its place in the sun. Still, in practice, Nocent's ability to explain the layout of the lectionary is still vital. Although a specialist in liturgy, he reveals himself as a most capable biblical exegete; although a man of philosophical depth, he constantly returns to the question of relevance: What does this passage have to say to us today? I have added a few annotations where I thought the reader needed a bridge between Nocent's day and our own, but I have kept these at a minimum to let the author's voice speak.

I have also refrained from changing too much of Matthew J. O'Connell's fine original translation. He wrote before issues of gender-inclusive language became important, however, and I felt that the book could not be reissued without attention to this detail. The greatest number of changes I introduced to the translation have to do with this concern. I have also emended O'Connell's work where I thought it needed greater clarity due to the length of sentences, obscure vocabulary, or theological imprecisions. Otherwise, again, I wanted his voice to win.

Nocent's seven-volume work in French, which had been rearranged into four volumes in English, is now redistributed again into three. All the material is here, along with Nocent's desire to share his profound faith and scholarship. I am confident that you, the reader, will meet a friend, a spiritual father, and a compelling mentor in Adrien Nocent.

Paul Turner

Preface

I began this work only after a good deal of hesitation. A simple revision of some older book in the light of the new lectionary seemed hardly worthwhile.* On the other hand, I could not but ask whether there was any point to publishing, in our day, several volumes on the liturgical year. The very name "liturgical year" seemed terribly dated, with its overtones of simple spirituality and love of the old texts and rituals dear to earlier generations. Would I be doing anything more than disturbing the dust on antiques now lodged in a museum that is often closed and is in any case inaccessible to the crowds of today's faithful?

After inquiries of my own among the young, the faithful of all ages, and priests and religious, and after careful inquiry on the part of the publisher, it became clear that the treasures contained in the new lectionary will be a source of confusion rather than a help unless they are presented in a simple straightforward way. To many, the connection between the various readings and other elements of a celebration is not always clear, nor is the broad overall theme of a liturgical season. More importantly, many do not see these celebrations as being in any way relevant to their life in the modern world. There seemed to be room, then, for a simple presentation of the liturgical year as envisaged in the reform that the Second Vatican Council initiated; in such a presentation I would try to meet the needs expressed to me in various pastoral circles.

My purpose explains the threefold division of each volume. First come biblico-liturgical reflections on the particular phase of the liturgical year. Has this celebration, connected as it is with the history of salvation, anything to do with us today? Next, I take up the structure and themes of the season. How are the readings and celebrations of the season organized? How are we to read the Scripture texts that the liturgy inserts into a specific context? Finally, there are suggestions

* The author refers to older books in general, not a specific earlier work of his.

from the past. In order to widen our field of vision and to supply material for celebrations of the word, may we not draw upon the local churches of the past and share their experience of the liturgical seasons as these gradually took shape in the life of these churches?

These volumes make no claim to be complete. Their aim is simply to offer lines of thought and subjects for reflection to the faithful and their pastors, to those in charge of various groups, and, above all, to those who wish to experience the Church's liturgy more fully. At no point have I felt I was being unfaithful to scientific standards or to a method that should never be set aside, even in pastoral work. My work is intended to be readable, but as the notes will suggest at times, it is also based on strict scholarly principles without which any work, even if it be pastoral or "spiritual," will lack objectivity and solidity.

I have not thought it advisable to supply a bibliography. The reformed liturgical year has not yet been studied as a whole. There do exist collections providing essays on each Sunday or feast, but these are well known and will be of help to any who wish to undergird their celebrations with a more profound liturgical and spiritual theology. There are also a good many articles on the new lectionary and its composition, good points, and limitations, but citation of these would be out of place in a work that does not aim to give readers a complete inventory of studies done on the new liturgy or to guide them in future study of their own. This work, like every other, must be faithful to its own purpose and corresponding structure.[†]

My desire is to serve as many as I can of those faithful who wish to experience the greatest treasure and most vital stimulus the Church has to offer them: the presence of the Lord in her word and her Eucharist.

Adrien Nocent, OSB

[†] For the benefit of today's readers, a bibliography has been supplied in volume 3 of this series.

Introduction to the Liturgical Year

Does the "Church Year" Have a Meaning?

"Church year" and "liturgical year" are very ancient phrases and may be suspect today. Suspect, among other things, of expressing ideas that are outdated and unrealistic, having nothing to do with the expectations of our present-day world. Suspect, too, as representing the escapism of those who are frightened by the dogmatic and moral upheaval going on in contemporary religious life and are looking for security.* These people take comfortable refuge in a "contemplation" based supposedly on solid theology but in fact on neo-romantic yearnings; they turn their back on the volcano and gaze toward a distant, peaceful, soothing horizon. Their prayer is a retreat, a way of building up psychological security, a dam against the mounting flood of the sexual revolution, a source of tranquility for tense neurotics. Such at least are the attitudes attributed to an inoffensive group living out what they call the "liturgical year."

And yet the Second Vatican Council, with open enthusiasm, set about revitalizing the celebration of the liturgy and making it a genuine response to the needs of contemporary people. The Council regarded the liturgy as the summit and source of the Church's activity, and the source of sanctification as well.[1]

For the vast majority of people this represented a discovery. In their eyes, the liturgy had previously been the preserve of sacristans and rubricists; to a few others, the liturgy had had a higher status, as being a field of research on which the sciences of paleography, history, and archeology were brought to bear. After the Council a bishop was heard to say that he had been converted to the liturgy—once they had made the sacraments part of it! And, in fact, some theologians (not always just the ones unknown to the general public) go on

---

* Nocent is describing the world of the early 1970s, but many of his concerns remain current.

1

teaching the theology of the sacraments without the least reference to the liturgy; in their view, the liturgy has no authority as a theological source.

The situation in the past was not unfairly described by saying that, to some, the liturgy was a kind of religious luxury reserved for distinguished persons who seemed beyond the reach of ordinary life's many problems.

Now, almost miraculously, the Church took the liturgy in hand at the Second Vatican Council. It did not touch on disputes over technical matters and details but did affirm the ontological (as distinct from the merely moralistic) value of the liturgical celebration as being "the summit of the Church's activity." The Church did so because it saw in that celebration the saving mysteries of Christ made present here and now and rendered visible through signs. "Summit of the Church's activity, and source of sanctification"!† What a brilliant light radiated from these words! They became the starting point for a renewed spiritual life that would be centered upon reality and protected against all abstractionism. Such at least was the objective proposed for the reform of the liturgy. Many believed in the reform and its aims, especially such individuals as bore the responsibility for Catholic communities.

Was it all a delusion? Have we been the victims of a collective hallucination? For, as we now realize, it was not quite such a simple matter as it seemed. The immense enthusiasm seems to have faltered somewhat, and there are those who think that the reform has petered out.

At the very moment when the rich values of tradition were being rediscovered and seemed capable of inspiring the masses, new problems arose to absorb the attention of our contemporaries. In consequence, the renewal seemed hardly to have begun when it risked being overwhelmed by a psychological and philosophical tidal wave. Desacralization, secularization, secularism, the claims of psychoanalysis, a new anthropology, problems of languages, the demand for total commitment on the part of the Church, the call for a politically oriented worship—all these stormed the temple whose façade had been remodeled only shortly before.

---

† Nocent is paraphrasing *Sacrosanctum Concilium*, paragraph 10.

The Paradox of a Secularized Liturgy

Contemporary Christians do not think they have lost their faith when a toothache drives them to the dentist rather than to St. Apollonia. Workingmen are much less likely to pray to the patron saint of their trade than to set up a union when they want to improve their working conditions. The hot-tempered man who feels himself in danger of committing a criminal act knows that it is time to get his thyroid gland examined. Experience shows that when a person obsessed with sex prays and meditates, he often only strengthens the hold of the obsession; such activities are more likely to intensify rather than alleviate the problem. In a land beset by persistent drought, people turn, not to Rogation Day processions, but to the building of an artificial lake that will serve when the rain fails.

We must not be blind to this phenomenon. People today will not accept a liturgy that is offered as a sacred moment apart, detached from life and everyday affairs, as if the created order and the world of technology were evil and heavenly blessing had to be pronounced on everything—the world, times, places—before it could be used. They may understand and know from experience the world's limitations, but they will not therefore be resigned to celebrating a liturgy that is cut off from the world and represents a flight from the world, a kind of transcending of the world so as later to bring back to it a sanctification that will render it fit to share in the praise of God. People are convinced that the world itself provides the material for the building of something new and great, that the liturgy is not "the sacred" and the world "the profane," and that worship is not meant to be an action and a moment "apart from the world" so as to sanctify the world.

In short, hardly has the renewal of the liturgy begun in the West when we see the irresistible growth of a secularization that is seemingly incompatible with one type of worship.

A Report of the Theological Commission on Worship (Geneva, 1963) states that the term "worship" has lost its meaning for contemporary people and rouses no interest anymore. But in that same year the report on the sessions of the Fourth World Conference on Faith and Order (Montreal) claims that Christian worship is profoundly compatible with human life today.[2] However, the Conference also shows itself aware that a new attitude is abroad in the world:

> The Churches carry on their worship today in a world that is proud of
> its technological success, but at the same time is deeply troubled. In
> ways old and new our world shows itself opposed or indifferent to
> Christian worship and apathetic to the Good News of Jesus Christ.
> Sometimes simply ignorant of humanity's transcendent destiny, some-
> times full of seeming contempt for it, the modern world seems willing
> to accept absurdity, once daily worries have been overcome or, on the
> other hand, material security is wholly lacking.[3]

But the Conference is realistic; it states:

> In these circumstances we must very carefully examine the worship of
> the Churches. The Churches must ask themselves whether or not the
> liturgical language, images, and symbols they use are intelligible to our
> contemporaries, and whether or not preachers are able to explain the
> Christian heritage in language that is meaningful to people of today.[4]

This is undoubtedly what the Second Vatican Council attempted to
do. But is such a task feasible on the whole? Is it enough to concede
the adaptations that science and politico-social ideas seem to call for?
The danger of such a procedure is that we may reach an illusory
answer by papering over a house that is full of holes; it can only be
a stage in a longer process, a temporary solution dictated by necessity.
The real need is to work from inside and start taking into account the
real circumstances in which people find themselves. In the last analysis, what is needed is greater confidence in the capacity of the Church
to find embodiment in human values, a full acceptance of all earthly
things that are good, and an effort to become a guiding force in
peoples' daily lives.

In short, we are confronted here with one application of the law of
incarnation that Christ willed should reign. In this sense the Church
becomes a missionary, and the vocation that is inseparable from her
being requires of her a "secularization" that will take various forms
in various times and places. In thus "secularizing" herself, the Church
will be in continuity with the prophets, who were so careful to avoid
absorption in worship and, above all, any connection with the kind
of cultic institution that would dispense humanity from genuine faith
and love.

But there is danger of great confusion here, since the road of secularization is not easy and simple. Observers have criticized the snobbery typical of much closet secularization, where the latter is seen

simply in intellectual terms (and not always with all desirable clarity). They have sometimes attacked it on good grounds:

> The abusive, unthinking, commercialized use of "secularization" and related words is disagreeable and wearying. Thinking people do not thus deal with realities profoundly rooted in their being, nor do they attack, in such a blanket, confused, and partisan fashion, a set of values intimately connected with God.[5]

And yet there is a real problem behind it all. For how can we settle for a liturgy that has no connection with a person's temporal activities? The problem is by no means new, of course; the liturgical reform has certainly been aware of it. But what remedy is to be applied in this scandalous situation? Are we to consider temporal activity something untouchable and adjust the liturgy to it? Are we to insert the liturgical signs among the signs proper to temporal life, with its program that is geared to earth and time?

Such an approach is harsh and simplistic. No matter—the mentality it presents is in fact widespread. It is not always officially expressed, but it corresponds to an instinct of our contemporaries. At the very moment when the liturgy and its incomparable values were being rediscovered, humanity and its world were also being exalted.

Consequently, it is difficult for our contemporaries to think of Christianity simply as something given and imposed on them by God. Rather, the individual and the world think they have the right to question God and to receive an answer. In other words, the new-found consciousness of human and worldly values does not dispose people to accept readily the values of a ready-made liturgy, a sort of "take-out" affair that needs only to be adjusted a bit (what all parties would agree to call "adaptation"). Such a liturgy would be incapable of confronting or challenging people, and consequently it would lose its whole justification. For many people think they have the right to challenge God in turn. This is why they instinctively reject the whole idea of a "sacred time," texts imposed by authority, and a prefabricated ritual, no matter how traditional. As some people would put it, don't we moderns have our own "scriptures," written by our daily lives? Shouldn't we be reading, during the liturgy of "the world," the records jotted down in our diaries? Should they, have they the right to, oblige us to certain prayer formularies and specific themes for celebration? And so on, until the challenge becomes a claim to exercise an unlimited creativity.

Given these conditions, how can we possibly ignore these various reactions (some of them quite justified) and offer the reader a commentary on the texts of the liturgical year universally used by the Roman Catholic Church?

Spiritual Worship

As we pointed out above, the term "worship" is no longer acceptable to many, or at best they have little use for it. They have little use for it because they have a false idea of it. In fact, many Christians really have a pagan idea of worship, and many theological books only keep them locked up in their misconceptions. To think of worship as an act in which the spirit is raised to God in order to honor him and to acknowledge our dependence on him is to have but a partial vision of it and a very rudimentary and textbookish theology.

The Second Vatican Council, profiting by the studies that preceded it, has given us access to a much richer and more vibrant reality. The Council sees Catholic worship as a dialogue of God with humanity. In this dialogue God takes the initiative; he solicits and expects our response in the form of praise and prayer but also in the form of questions. Here we have the biblical attitude as represented in chapter 19 of the book of Exodus, where the *Qahal*, or "called community," is described. God gathers his people in order to speak to them through Moses. The people listen and then answer; their response takes the form of praise and petition and culminates in the offering of sacrifice.

We must bear in mind the dynamic character of this divine intervention that initiates dialogue. For God, the word is a form of action; in his word he gives himself as a savior, and his very word is already a saving gift. Our response, therefore, cannot be simply an empty rite; it too must be the offering of life. That is what St. Paul is telling the Romans when he exhorts them to offer their bodies as a living sacrifice that is holy and acceptable to God (Rom 12:1-2). This is spiritual worship. Spiritual worship embraces life in its entirety: all that is interior to a person, one's orientation to others and to the community, one's openness to the world's needs and to the world's progress.

We might be tempted to think that Paul is here establishing a clear break between conceptions proper to the New Testament and conceptions proper to the Old, the latter being much more "cult-bound." But this view is certainly extreme; in fact, it is even inaccurate. The book of Joshua already suggests a service of Yahweh that is not simply cultic but embraces the whole of life through the fulfillment of the law (Josh 24:21-24).[6] Later on, the prophets even challenged the value of the cultic institutions. "Obedience is better than sacrifice, / to listen, better than the fat of rams" (1 Sam 15:22). And recall the well-known words of Hosea: "For it is loyalty that I desire, not sacrifice, / and knowledge of God rather than burnt offerings" (6:6). Christ would make these themes his own in an emphatic way in Matthew 9:13 and 12:7. In the Old Testament there was an increasing spiritualization of worship, but after the Exile came a new wave of institutionalization, as feasts, days, Sabbaths, seasons, and holy places took on increasing importance; thus, for example, the Sabbath, a day of rest (Exod 20:8), became a day of worship (Book of Jubilees 2, 30-31).

The New Testament has a resolutely spiritualist vision of worship, as we have already pointed out. Worship means the offering of the person (1 Cor 16:15; Rom 16:5; Heb 9:14-28; 1 Pet 2:5; Rev 14:4). But it also means that the Christian's entire life is placed at the service of evangelization, faith, and familial love. In 2 Corinthians 9:11-12, St. Paul writes: "You are being enriched in every way for all generosity, which through us produces thanksgiving to God, for the administration of this public service is not only supplying the needs of the holy ones but is also overflowing in many acts of thanksgiving to God." The Letter to the Philippians (4:18) contains the same theology: the charitable offering of the Philippians is a sacrifice that God finds pleasing and acceptable. In a sterner way, the Letter of St. James confirms this spiritualization of worship with its aspect of gift: "Religion that is pure and undefiled before God and the Father is this: to care for orphans and widows in their affliction, and to keep oneself unstained by the world" (1:27).

We noted above, and shall not delay on it here, that the handing on of the faith and the preaching of the gospel are also a worship and a liturgy. The whole apostolic life of Paul is a sharing in the sacrificial offering of Christ (Col 1:24; 2 Cor 4). Paul thinks of himself as the liturgical minister of Jesus Christ among the Gentiles, as priest of God's gospel, and the goal of his work is to help the Gentiles become a pleasing sacrifice that is consecrated by the Holy Spirit (Rom 15:15-16).

The Letter to the Hebrews thinks of Jesus' redemptive action in cultic terms; herein lies the originality of the letter (see especially Heb 5–10).

Worship, then, as seen by the Scriptures, is spiritual and leads toward a future. Christ is its high priest (Heb 2:17; 7:1-14, 23-28); he transcends the whole created order, thus showing the limitations of all cultic paraphernalia and filling the world with his light and power.

Now, these are the realities that lay hold of our everyday life through the mediation of the signs, words, and gestures that make up the liturgy.

There is now no separation of sacred and profane, although the world has not yet achieved the full dimensions of the kingdom. It is because the world has not yet done so that the Church and its sacraments are indispensable as means of laying hold of the world and building the kingdom.[7]

To think of the liturgy in the way we have been indicating is to orient oneself toward the future. The Christian must use the world as building material for a new world. If we take the world as it is, without fearing it, we open it to God's action and our own action; we offer it the possibility of being reshaped in accordance with God's original plan for it. But the world is not simply something to be rebuilt, and it is not rebuilt simply because the Church pours out upon it the transforming gifts of heaven. Rather, it takes an active part in its own rebuilding. Christians, therefore, do not condemn the world as such, though they do condemn its present sinful limitations. Thereby, they commit themselves to the creation of that future in which the material world itself will be redeemed.

Worship gathers up all these aspects. Worship is God's descent, but it is also the individual's ascent, using the created world to reach its God, while offering one's daily life and loving service of others, spreading the Good News, with eyes fixed on the future, and helping the world in its entirety to evolve toward oneself (and thus toward one's God).

Is St. Paul an Opponent of the Church Year?

A superficial reading of the Letter to the Galatians might lead us to see in St. Paul a convinced foe of Christian feasts: "[B]ut now that you have come to know God, or rather to be known by God, how can you turn back again to the weak and destitute elemental powers?

Do you want to be slaves to them all over again? You are observing days, months, seasons, and years. I am afraid on your account that perhaps I have labored for you in vain" (4:9-11).

Christ had said that the Sabbath was made for humans, not humans for the Sabbath (Mark 2:27).

In a similar vein St. Paul tells the Colossians, in connection with yearly and monthly feasts and Sabbaths: "These are shadows of things to come; the reality belongs to Christ" (2:17).

Texts such as these do not seem to encourage the celebration of a liturgical year. How, then, has the Church been able to celebrate days and years? Has she fallen back into the fault of which St. Paul speaks? In the beginning the Church celebrated each Sunday; then, in the mid-second century, she chose one Sunday for the special celebration of the Pasch—and chose that Sunday for its relation to the full moon! Then, out of the Easter Vigil developed the fifty days of Easter Time as well as a Lent that gradually reached its present form. Christmas and Epiphany were established, and later on at Rome, Advent.

But the basic issue in this whole development is our deliverance— that is the object of all these joyous feasts. If the liturgical celebration were a burden, if it were the yoke of the Mosaic law in a new form, then humans would be made for the Sabbath. In fact, however, the Sabbath is made for humans, and all the feasts point to our salvation. This is why every day is a feast day for the Christian. The celebration of feasts such as Sunday does not mean that certain days are now not profane like the others, nor does the phrase "keep Sunday holy" mean to make sacral a day that otherwise would be profane. The fathers emphasized rather the deeper theological dimension of "feast" and insisted that for the Christian every day is a Sabbath. There is a classical text of St. Justin on the subject:

> The new law bids you celebrate an unbroken Sabbath. You, on the other hand [i.e., Trypho and the Jews], remain inactive for a single day and think yourselves pious on that account. . . . Anyone who is an adulterer, a thief or a liar should change. That is how he will properly celebrate the joyous Sabbaths of God.[8]

Reflecting on Paul's attitude toward feasts, Origen writes:

> I think this is what Paul had in mind when he called the feast that is held on days set apart from the others "part of a feast" [Col 2:16]; he

hinted by this phrase that the life that is continually being lived according to the divine word is not a "part of a feast" but an entire and continual feast.[9]

The early Church and the patristic writers kept their eyes on the reality of salvation as received in the community that is Christ's Body, and therefore they thought like Origen in this matter. We must bear in mind that until the fourth century the dominant reality was the Pasch of the Lord; that is what was being celebrated. Whether the "Every day" of Acts 2:46 is to be taken literally or loosely, the Christians of the first generation were certainly zealous about the breaking of bread and prayer (Acts 2:42). Each day they broke bread in their homes and praised God (Acts 2:46-47); each day the Lord added to their community those who were being saved (Acts 2:47); each day they preached the Good News of Jesus Christ (Acts 5:47). The vivid experience of deliverance, and of new life begun in them and progressively reaching out to embrace the whole world, was the basis for the "feast," the Christian's daily celebration.

However, precisely because a person enters into the celebration with the whole of one's human reality, it was natural to make one or other day the special time for prayer and the gathering of the community; such a day, as we might expect, would be the day on which the resurrection of Jesus had occurred. But this observation by itself is not enough, it seems to me. Precisely because a person enters into the celebration completely, it is not enough to celebrate the feast of the resurrection each day, no matter how conscious one may be of the daily passage of the Lord through one's life. For one needs special moments; one's basic psychology requires it. People need special actions that will enable them to express, to lay hold of in a more personal and reflective way, the reality of their deliverance. Christians indeed live always and at every moment in the end-oriented time of salvation and are no longer enslaved by time as measured in days and years; nonetheless, it is normal that a certain recurrence and repetition should enable them to enter more deeply into their own joy and to unite themselves more fully to the deliverance bestowed upon them.

The liturgical year, therefore, is not an iron yoke; it is not an accumulation of memories that have nothing to do with life and that one listens to patiently, as one might listen to an old man who buries himself in the past and repeats the same stories over and over again. On the contrary, the liturgical year brings home both the reality of one's new life and the profound value of one's daily existence.

The Liturgical Year: Reality or Psychological Stimulus?

We may ask whether the liturgical year with its Sundays and feasts represents only a psychological need. Does it have stimulus value but no real content?

For an answer to this basic question we must have recourse to Scripture and the Jewish liturgy. Here is how practicing Jews think: "Do not flee the world of space; use spatial realities for your action— but concentrate your love on eternity alone."[10] This would represent at least one Jewish approach to our present question. For the Jew, God is involved in history; but for God, the past, present, and future coexist. God is the One who was and is and will be. The Jewish liturgy is envisaged as an act that allows a being whose existence is transitory to come into contact with him who always is; the One who always is comes into contact with one whose existence is transitory.

If Jews at worship were concerned only with past history, their worship would be indistinguishable from the Hellenistic cults. In fact, two attitudes that Jews regard as supremely important and that, in their eyes, correspond to the real order set their worship apart from other cults. They are contemporary with what was but also contemporary with what will be. "To commemorate is not to stand afar off from what happened in the past; on the contrary, it is to eliminate the distance between present and past." To commemorate is to give the past a new existence; it is to think that each of us is contemporaneous with historical events whose consequences we still endure or whose effects we still prolong in time.[11] At the same time, the Jewish liturgy is oriented toward a future. The Passover meal is not an imaginary commemoration of the Exodus from Egypt; rather, each participant thinks of himself or herself as now freed from slavery. And they are not thinking in terms of poetry or abstract theology; they mean a real deliverance right now. On the other hand, at the Passover meal a place is reserved for the prophet Elijah, showing hope and expectation of fulfillment.

Is the Church year simply a psychological stimulus? A kind of imaginative instruction in the faith? Patristic tradition, at least, thought of it quite differently. For the fathers, the liturgical year is not an edifying commemoration of the past but a making real in the present for the sake of a future. But, we may ask, was not the fourth century a period that tried to sacralize everything? Did it establish its celebrations in the same spirit that animated the liturgies of the earlier centuries? Some writers sense in the Christian feasts of that period sacralizing, and thus paganizing, tendencies.[12]

Now it is a fact that we find in the fathers a tendency to imitate at least the vocabulary of contemporary religions. They did this, most of the time, in order to be understood. We can also reproach them for being excessively distrustful of the world. And yet, there is nothing in them of a false kind of sacralization. They had an innate sense of God's involvement in history; events, in their mind, formed a continuous web. To convince ourselves of this, we need only recall their interest in typology: in the typological view, world history as directed by God is not made up simply of successive events or "stories" but forms a unity. A "type" is not simply an example; it is also a starting point that reaches its corresponding end point in the "antitype." For example, the crossing of the Red Sea is not an illustration but a type of baptism; that is, it is the starting point, and our baptism is the continuation of this beginning as we move toward the complete "crossing" in which we shall meet the Lord.

In this view, then, we are part of a history that we both continue and bring to completion. We begin to glimpse what the world meant to the fathers. In their eyes, every celebration meant an actual presence of the mystery of Christ, who continues the history of the Old Testament in the New and in the ongoing present. We find St. Leo the Great affirming this in categorical fashion and without any effort to be poetic about it: "Although the series of bodily actions is now past, as ordained in the eternal plan . . . nevertheless we adore the virgin birth that brings us salvation."[13]

What St. Leo writes with regard to the Nativity, he repeats in greater detail for the Epiphany: "For, although this day passed, the power of the work revealed on this day did not also pass away."[14]

St. Leo's intention is to emphasize the effectiveness of the liturgical celebration as a means of dispensing the past mysteries of Christ, which we must receive in our own today. He writes:

> Beloved, the remembrance of what the Savior did for humankind is most useful to us, provided that what we venerate in faith we also re-

ceive and imitate. For in the communication of the mysteries of Christ to us, there is present both the power of grace and the encouragement that teaching gives, so that we may follow by our deeds him whom we confess in the spirit of faith.[15]

In the mind of St. Leo, "the remembrance of what the Savior did" is not a simple recall of the past but a remembering that enables us to share in the mysteries of Christ. The sharing is based on grace, teaching, and example. We have here a doctrine dear to St. Leo, who likes to insist that the sacrament (that is, the efficacious sign that gives the action of Christ a here-and-now existence) is for us both an example and a grace.

Two classic passages from the sermons of St. Leo confirm what we have been saying about him. One passage relates to the annunciation:

> The astonishing conversation of the angel Gabriel with Mary and the conception that is the work of the Holy Spirit and that is as marvelous in the promise of it as in Mary's believing acceptance of it do not take place simply in our memories but before our very eyes, as it were.[16]

The same teaching of the actualization of a past mystery in a present "remembrance" is affirmed of the redemption. This actualization St. Leo calls a "sacrament of redemption" (*sacramentum redemptionis*)[17] and explains elsewhere what he means by these words:

> All that the Son of God did and taught for the reconciliation of the world we not only know through the narration of past events; we also experience the effects of it in virtue of these present deeds [the sacraments].[18]

These texts and numerous others have served as the basis for a theology of the liturgy. Dom Odo Casel, a German monk of Maria-Laach, was a chief pioneer in the elaboration of this theology. His rediscovery was, however, more intuitive than scientifically and exegetically, or even theologically, well founded. It would be out of place for us here to offer a positive and negative critique of his views; in any event, others have done this.[19] But despite some principles that are open to criticism or even simply unacceptable, the pioneers managed to shape a theology of the liturgy that has now been presented to the Church in Vatican II's Constitution on the Sacred Liturgy.

The Liturgical Year:
Actualization of the Past for the Sake of the Future

The Constitution on the Sacred Liturgy offers us a first-rate theology of the liturgy. Three sections give the essentials of this theology.[20] First, there is the redemptive work of Christ; then, the redemptive work as continued by the Church and accomplished in the liturgy; finally, the presence of Christ in the liturgy. These passages have been the subject of so many commentaries that there is no point in our giving the whole text of them. We shall try, in our own way, to explain the vital meaning of the liturgical celebration of the mysteries of salvation and to do so in a simple fashion.

If we are to understand the liturgy, we must take as our starting point the incarnation of the Word and the later coming of the Spirit. Until the Word became incarnate, a person's experience of God was of a philosophical kind: a prayerful reflection, an intellectual and psychological approach to God, with the more or less profound effects this might have on the person's private and social behavior. The Old Testament, in its steadfast monotheism, shows the beginnings of a mediation through signs, for example, the sign of fire, which indicates the presence of the Lord (Exod 3:2-4; 19:18).

With the incarnation, however, the manner in which a person comes into saving contact with God is radically changed, and the flesh becomes the instrument of salvation.[21]

As soon, however, as we say "incarnation," we are bound to take past, present, and future into account.

The past: Christ focuses upon his own person all the expectations and the whole typology of the Old Testament. Moreover, as soon as we think of the incarnation, we recall the whole series of events making up the history of a world that awaits reconstruction and renewal. The Christ who is born according to the flesh represents the fulfillment of the Old Testament types, which are neither simple prophecies nor simple examples but the starting points of events that are fulfilled in Christ and continue to be fulfilled in the Church. This is the case, for example, with the Exodus and Passover.

The present: Through signs, the first and foremost of which is the Church, we are in contact with Christ, who continues to be present. When Jesus tells his disciples, "[I]t is better for you that I go" (John 16:7) and when he promises them the Paraclete (John 14:16-19), he is emphasizing the continuity of his presence among us. It is good for us that he has gone. Indeed, it was necessary that he go if he was to take the glorified body that would give him an unlimited presence in time and space. Now, through signs, we are in contact with the glorious body of Christ.

Our experience of God is thus a sacramental experience—not a primarily contemplative experience, but an experience by real contact with the real person of Christ in his glorified body and by means of signs. It is, then, an experience that is, so to speak, materialist, being both our own and intrinsically bound up with the incarnation. Only because the body of Christ is glorified is it possible for us to enter into contact, here and now, with all his mysteries, mysteries that absorb into themselves their preparation and beginnings in the Old Testament.

Only because God has become incarnate can we be, as we are, in the presence of two facts. On the one hand, for Christ as for every other person, his actions are limited in space and time; think, for example, of his death on Calvary. On the other hand, since Christ is God, none of his actions are limited in space and time; in him there is neither before nor after. Consequently, at the Last Supper he could render already present what would be effectively done later, on Good Friday. For the same reason it is possible for us, in the eucharistic celebration, to make actual a past event that happened only once: the death of Christ and the whole paschal mystery.

If we apply what has just been said to all the mysteries of salvation, we can see how immensely rich the reality of the liturgical year really is. The celebration of Christmas is not a simple remembering; rather, it actualizes for us the whole mystery of the incarnation. Similarly, to await the incarnation is not a mere poetic fiction, since in awaiting the sign that is the celebration of Christmas, we await the moment when the incarnation of the Lord will be actualized for us. The expectation that characterizes Advent is thus a genuine, not a simulated, expectation of what Christmas makes real.

The future: This dimension is there because Christ is in his glory and the sending of the Spirit creates in the Church a tension toward the full realization of the divine plan of salvation. Experiential contact with the glorious body of Christ is contact with the whole of the Old Testament and with the mysteries of salvation that are made present now for the sake of a future which I experience in hope and of which

I already have a pledge. I experience sacramentally the past, the present, and the future. Thus, in our liturgical experience of God, we are always constructing a future. We are not simply being drawn toward a future; we are building it together with Christ, who is present through us. The entire world has the task of reconstructing itself in view of a future until God's plan is perfectly fulfilled and Christ comes to gather in the mature fruit of his entire work of paschal reconciliation.

The Presence of the Lord

If we can speak so emphatically of the intrinsic value of the liturgical year, it is because we celebrate it together with Christ himself. The special nature of the Church year is entirely due to the fact that the Lord himself presides over it and that he celebrates his mysteries with the Church for the glory of the Father. The Second Vatican Council laid heavy stress on the various ways in which Christ is present in the liturgical celebration.[22] The highest form of this presence is the real presence in the Eucharist, and it is the source and summit of all liturgical celebration because it is the presence of the paschal mystery. On the other hand, each eucharistic celebration, while having the paschal mystery as its basis and background, derives its particular features and coloring from the celebration of the Liturgy of the Word. The eucharistic celebration on Christmas is different from, as well as the same as, the eucharistic celebration of the day when the Pentecostal Spirit was sent. The celebration of the word gives each eucharistic celebration its special coloring.

We must emphasize, moreover, the presence of the Lord in the celebration of the word as such, just as in the celebration of the Liturgy of the Hours. The Constitution on the Sacred Liturgy asserts the fact but does not risk an explanation of it. Pope Paul VI seems to have been struck by the rediscovery of this presence of the Lord in the proclamation of the Word. The Bible, by itself a dead book, becomes alive and actual when it is proclaimed in the liturgical assembly. The Constitution on the Sacred Liturgy simply teaches that the Lord himself is still proclaiming his gospel even today,[23] but the pope seems to go further.

In his encyclical *Mysterium fidei*, in which his chief purpose is to insist on the permanence of the real eucharistic presence, Pope Paul VI takes the opportunity to say that there is more than one "real" presence and that we must not exclude all presences but the eucharistic one. This statement is all the more important since it is made in a context where the main point is to insist on the reality and value of the eucharistic presence. The pope writes: "This presence of Christ in the Eucharist is called 'real' not to exclude the idea that others are 'real' too, but rather to indicate presence par excellence."[24] This statement represents a step forward and is a very valuable clarification. But we must still try to penetrate its meaning more fully.

The writer who seems to have done this with the greatest depth and clarity is S. Marsili.[25] According to Paul VI, there are several modes of real presence. What distinguishes them is not the realness of the presence but the mode of it; this diversifies them and gives each its own "level," as it were, but all are real. The real eucharistic presence presupposes both a "transubstantiation" and a permanence in the sign; other presences, for example that of Christ in the proclamation of the Word, do not have these distinguishing marks.

The important thing is that the presence of the Lord in the proclamation of the Word is not analogical and figurative, as when someone reads the works of a poet at an intellectual gathering and titles the reading "The Abiding Presence of. . . ." In the proclamation of the Word there is a real, active presence of the Lord. This notion is still unfamiliar and has not become part of the instinctive habits of mind of our contemporaries, whose attention is still focused exclusively on the real eucharistic presence. This latter presence does, of course, still represent the supreme form of the Lord's presence.

This last point needs to be emphasized. It is the most important of all, for it gives the celebrations of the liturgical year their full coherence and value.

The
Advent
Mystery

Biblico-Liturgical Reflections on the Advent Season

1. WAITING IN HOPE

Is There a Christian Way of Hoping?

The subject is a complicated one, but it is also of basic importance. For how is it possible to really live without looking forward to someone and something? Would it be possible to breathe without hope? Could Christians be prisoners turning around in a circle, knocking their heads on the walls of their cell, whether it be of legalism or of some ready-made affair called "the spiritual life"? Does not the Christian, like every other person (though perhaps more than any other), have the duty of cultivating a stern yet joyous discontent with the human condition? Perhaps that is what distinguishes the Christian's hope: though it is fierce and implacable, stern and eager, it is also, paradoxically, full of joy. But isn't that very description just bad poetry and ecclesiastical drivel?

As a matter of fact, hope is an aspect of faith and inseparable from love. The connection with love, however, is not specifically Christian. Anyone who loves another, precisely because she loves him, has unquestioning confidence in him and with great hope expects everything from him. Péguy, in one of his brilliant theological intuitions, saw hope as a little girl who goes off to school between her two big sisters, faith and love, holding each by the hand. He explains his meaning in his *Le porche de la deuxième vertu*: In the eyes of those who see the three sisters passing, little hope is being guided by the other two; in fact, however, little hope is pulling forward the two who seem to be leading her.

If Péguy is correct, then we must recognize that the distinction between these three fundamental attitudes of faith, hope, and love is not easily to be made. The books of the Old Testament show hardly any awareness of a distinction between what would later be called the three theological virtues. The Hebrew texts show how close in meaning are the three terms, whose roots too are closely connected. Some of the terms used seem to mean the fact of hoping, but the meaning is not an exclusive one, and sentiments of faith and love mingle with it.

St. Paul will speak of the three virtues as distinct but closely interwoven (1 Tim 1:3; 1 Cor 13:13; Gal 5:5-6). There is no hope without faith and love. On the other hand, one believes and loves because one hopes; hope gives strength to faith and love, while faith and love give rise to hope.

Our world is a sad place; it seems to be without hope, precisely because its crisis is a crisis of faith and love. But the crisis is an old one. The whole drama of the Old Testament is focused on hope and its fluctuations. The problem experienced there can shed light on ours.

Through his prophet, who is a human-divine concretization of hope, God gradually led his people to hope for more than earthly blessings. And yet, what he promises them is a land flowing with milk and honey (Exod 3:8)! It will take centuries before Israel as a people realizes what the hope of salvation entails. To some extent this hope will materialize in the "remnant" that will be saved and become a leaven of renewal (Amos 9:8; Isa 10:19). The basic content of that renewal is revealed by divinely inspired prophets; its outlines are sketched as they stimulate the hope of peace and salvation, light and God's full victory over sin. Their efforts are focused on an objective not easily attained: to push the people of God toward a hope in ultimate righteousness before God.

Is knowing God important? This knowledge becomes the object of hope, but we must give the word "know" the full meaning it has in the Semitic languages. The point is not a metaphysical knowledge but an experiential knowledge: to know God is to touch him, to see him (Isa 11:9). The renewal sought is primarily a renewal of one's heart (Ezek 36–37). At this point there is quite naturally a call for a perfect, disinterested worship, what we might readily call selfless contemplation (Pss 63; 84).

However, the people of the Old Testament (in contradistinction to the divinely inspired revelation in the Old Testament) stopped short while still on their journey; their hope was still in the means to which they could attach themselves. The result was disillusionment, painful yet often beneficent. The whole tireless work of the prophets had to be done before the people of God finally put their hope in God himself (Isa 60:19, etc.). They had to learn that only the Lord and his reign were worth waiting and hoping for (Pss 96–99).

This was not all just words. There were some in Israel who were sincere, who really believed what God said and wanted to live accordingly. These really wanted to find salvation in God (Wis 5:9); they had a burning desire for immortality (Wis 3:4), and gradually their hope was purified. But the hope by and large remained an earthly, and often even a material, hope. And so we see willing without real willing, hope without real hope, love without real love—all the unexpected, contradictory movements so deeply rooted in a person's psyche at every stage of human history. God should be the only important one in the life of his peoples; suffering and death should count for nothing (Pss 73; 49:16); but how difficult it is to look for God alone while expecting everything from his hand!

But is the Old Testament a genuine experience for us as well? Do we really hope for salvation? The ideal we would like to see the Church realize; hope in the realization of this ideal; the vision of what holiness should be; pride in theology for its own sake; detailed and barren criticism of the Church as an institution; hope for the earthly achievement of the ideal of holiness that we dream up for ourselves— all these are subtle barriers to true hope!

Is there, then, a Christian way of hoping? Has Christianity really made a contribution to the idea and reality of hope? The answer is clearly and irremediably disillusioning for anyone who does not believe.

The reason is that, for the believer, his personal hope is inseparably connected with the hope of the entire Church and that when united to the hope of the Church, it is oriented in two directions: toward Christ and toward the renewal of the world.

Christ? We await during Advent the actualization of his incarnation and then we celebrate Christmas, but we still hope and wait for his second coming. This is a hope the nonbeliever cannot share, for it is contrary to what hope should normally be. This Christian hope is indeed a strange thing; no human society has ever been able to walk this road, because it seems contradictory and turns any sane philosophy topsy-turvy. Why? Because Christians hope for what they already possess! In the inscription of Pectoris we read: "(You hold) the Fish in your hand."[1]

"Fish" in Greek is *ichthys*, and *ichthys* is the monogram of Christ. Therefore, we hold Christ in our hand. But this is either simple stupidity or it is true; if it isn't true, the whole of Christianity is nothing but mystical poetry without real value. It is true enough, of course, that Christians haven't much faith in the privilege that is theirs: with and in Christ they are dead and risen (Rom 6:1-7; Col 3:1); they already possess in an invisible but real fashion what the baptismal ritual, in the oldest of its prayers, calls the "beginnings of their own glory," which is invisible[2] but present and real (2 Cor 3:18–4:6). This is why, according to St. Paul, every Christian possesses the firstfruits of the world to come (Rom 8:11-23).

Christian hope is thus compounded of certainty: that is, we hope for what we already possess. The powerful dynamism that inspires this hope of a reality we already possess and grasp, though we do not see it, is an intense light for faith and a joyful spur to love. We cannot explain in any other way the attitude of the martyrs and the saints. As for ourselves, our glory resides in the Christ whom we possess, and it is so great (2 Cor 4:17) that it shines through our present life (1 Pet 1:8).

Purged of anxiety, calm, sure, joyous: such is Christian hope—in theory. In fact, we see around us sad-faced Christians who claim, with a pride not wholly devoid of snobbery, that they live in anxiety. They lack the deliberately maintained good humor that is a sign of the genuine hope of those who already possess it. We Christians are in an unusual position: we already possess it, "as though we were looking on the invisible God," but we still await the face-to-face encounter with him who is promised to us and whom we now possess. Our hope thus consists in waiting for the successive realities that we can already touch and that we already share.

Let the Mirror Be Broken!

How, in the last analysis, can we explain this specifically Christian hope, which consists in waiting for what we already possess?

I think it is possible to express this hope in very concrete terms (though I shall avoid trying to persuade the reader of the theology behind my view). Without realizing it, we hope now for the disappearance of the signs and sacraments through which we lay hold of God and our happiness. At the very moment when we celebrate that happiness, and for the very reason that the celebration thrusts us into the future, we eagerly wait for the disappearance of the whole regime of liturgy and sacrament. We hope that the veil will be rent and the mirror broken. We see now "as in a mirror" (1 Cor 13:12). We long and hope and wait for the mirror to be broken. To bring that great moment closer to us is one of the purposes of every liturgical celebration. It is in this way that our hope grows more abundant (Rom 15:13), since all of God's promises to us have been fulfilled in Jesus Christ (2 Cor 1:20).

If the preceding remarks on hope seem to us nothing but preacher's jargon, we show that we have not yet begun to live the Christian life nor understood the meaning of our baptism. And that is precisely the situation of the vast majority of the baptized! They live as if they were dead, and their hope seems inspired by bitterness; they hope because they do not see what else they can do. They have not yet been enlightened as to the real object of their hope. They have to stop fixing their hopes on the here and now, on success in this life, on the glory of the institutional Church, or on the splendid flowering of science. Their hope is in fact a stunted, ill-natured thing; it is sour. In its place they need a hope that can embrace people and the whole of this world that is passing away and destined for renewal.

Many Christians think they cherish a Christian hope. In fact, however, their hopes are limited to themselves. It is difficult to stop hoping only for one's personal future or for the world's future because one is part of that world. Many hopes are ultimately self-centered. The Church realizes full well how difficult Christian hope is. That is why over the centuries she has fashioned a special liturgy that, beyond other liturgies, is a liturgy of hope, of waiting in hope. But liturgy is never simply a moralizing exhortation, never simply a set of consoling words to restore the energetic outlook and make the patient endure by helping to forget the toothache.

The purpose of liturgy is to put the Christian in contact with a reality that, though spiritual, is fully real. Each year, then, the Church puts Christians into a situation where their hope can come alive and grow strong: she bids them hope, along with the whole of the Old Testament, for the coming of deliverance. The deliverance has already been accomplished; now they can celebrate it as a deliverance that is present to them through signs, and as they celebrate it, they can reach out for, and make their way toward, that moment when all signs shall vanish. The element of waiting that is part of Christian hope finds sacramental expression as the Christian relives in the present the Old Testament past, lives the incarnation as an event of today, and waits for the return of Christ and the breaking of the mirror on the last day.

Such is the rich life of the Advent season. We must now indicate its major elements and explain the waiting and the present hope that characterize it.

The Hope of a Sinful People

Hope is impossible unless we sincerely acknowledge what we are, what we ought to be, and what we will have to make of ourselves. The Church and each of us, her members, must be courageous enough to face up to our real condition, in order that we may bring to life once more the energies latent in hope. The prophet Isaiah is not afraid to use harsh words that we do not like to hear these days. He confronts the people of God as their judge and, within the space of a few verses, levels two relentless charges against them.

First of all, he says, the people of God has sinned gravely: God has made the Israelites his sons, but that people does not know God and has departed from him. "An ox knows its owner, / and an ass, its master's manger; / But Israel does not know, / my people has not understood" (Isa 1:3). Punishment has been to no avail, and the Lord does not know how to chastise them and make them understand their own state of soul (Isa 1:5-6). The seriousness of Israel's situation is reflected in the devastation of the land, which looks like Sodom after it had been overthrown; the physical scene brings home the perverse moral condition of the people (Isa 1:7). Happily, though, a small remnant remains and carries responsibility for the salvation of the people (Isa 1:9).

The second accusation is just as harsh: The people think they can have recourse to their liturgical practices and everything will be fine! No, the important thing is justice toward the neighbor. Without such honest dealing, Israel will continue to be punished (Isa 1:10-18). Prayer must become honest and pure, for only then can it be acceptable to God.

Then the light of hope shines: "Come now, let us set things right, / says the LORD: / Though your sins be like scarlet, / they may become white as snow; / Though they be red like crimson, / they may become white as wool" (Isa 1:18).

Isaiah repeats the theme in another form: the contrast between the faithful wife and the adulterous wife.[3] The consequences for the city of her sin are evident: she has become the haunt of murderers, and every dweller in the city thirsts for power. But the vision is not one of total darkness, for God will win out over his enemies and then the city will be called "city of justice, faithful city" (Isa 1:26). Then comes the marvelous vision of chapter 2, which we should read here:

> In days to come,
> The mountain of the LORD's house
>   shall be established as the highest mountain
>   and raised above the hills.
> All nations shall stream toward it.
>   Many peoples shall come and say:
> "Come, let us go up to the LORD's mountain,
>   to the house of the God of Jacob,
> That he may instruct us in his ways,
>   and we may walk in his paths."
> For from Zion shall go forth instruction,
>   and the word of the LORD from Jerusalem.
> He shall judge between the nations,
>   and set terms for many peoples.
> They shall beat their swords into plowshares
>   and their spears into pruning hooks;
> One nation shall not raise the sword against another,
>   nor shall they train for war again.
> House of Jacob, come,
>   let us walk in the light of the LORD! (Isa 2:2-5)

Thus, the faithless city becomes the eschatological center for the gathering of the nations in peace and unity. Such is the hope-filled vision set before a people that acknowledges its sinful state.

But there is a serious danger, always present, never wholly exorcized: the danger of religious formalism that gives rise to a false hope, the danger of hope that is not grounded in conversion. Isaiah seems haunted by this danger. There must be no acts of worship to which nothing corresponds in a person's heart;[4] God is fed up with rote prayers.

Here we are, in darkness, without faith, unable to see. Here we are, irresolute and stupefied, blind and sightless, our eyes shut and our heads covered (Isa 29:10). But once again salvation is on the way, and Isaiah paints a splendid picture of eschatological salvation in the latter part of chapter 29 (vv. 17-24). "On that day the deaf shall hear / the words of a scroll; / And out of gloom and darkness, / the eyes of the blind shall see" (Isa 29:18).

Hopeful Waiting in Time of Conversion

No hope is possible unless we turn to the Lord and wait for him to come to us. This is a theme frequently found in the gospel readings for Advent as well as in the Old Testament readings.

In the conversion that makes hope possible, we can distinguish three elements: conversion, watchfulness, and God's initiative.

The Old Testament offers the conversion of Ephraim as a model for us.[5] The conversion in this instance was radical:

> On that day people shall turn to their maker,
>   and their eyes shall look to the Holy One of Israel.
> They shall not turn to the altars, the work of their hands,
>   nor shall they look to what their fingers have made. (Isa 17:7-8)

Here conversion is a turning to God, an abandonment of one's own outlook, of the prayers learned by heart and the meaningless gestures of contrition, of the easy worship that is meant to protect a person against God. Here conversion means leaving everything else and advancing toward God (Isa17:7). John the Baptist will be constantly summoning people to conversion; such will be his basic role and the image we will rightly have of him.[6]

Conversion can be triggered by reflection on what would have happened if we had been attentive to the Lord: "If only you would attend to my commandments, / your peace would be like a river, / your vindication like the waves of the sea" (Isa 48:18).[7] The searing vision of lost time, of all that has been missed and destroyed, can lead to hope, conversion, and waiting upon God. Henceforth we must walk uprightly and without stumbling toward the day of Christ, when we shall have in full measure the justice won for us by Jesus Christ.[8] To do God's will in imitation of Christ, and to do it without any of the bigoted hope we find so insufferable in pseudo-Christians who shift all their crosses onto the shoulders of others—that is what conversion means.[9] That is the authentic turnabout required by the waiting in hope of which conversion is the indispensable condition. One who refuses to change one's way of life does not possess authentic hope.

More is required, however, than a first, easy act of turning (heroic though we may think it!). We must also persevere. The conversion that gives rise to hope requires vigilance. To be always waiting means that we hope and never rest, simply because we are always expecting the fulfillment of our desires. We must keep watch, therefore, because we know not the day nor the hour of the Lord's coming.[10]

The convert thus faces a great deal of work, which John the Baptist,[11] echoing Isaiah,[12] describes as smoothing the rough ways, filling in the valleys, and preparing the Lord's paths.

The hope that springs from conversion also implies faith. Jesus had harsh words for his people: John the Baptist came to them, but they did not accept him or believe what he told them, but the prostitutes and tax collectors did believe him.[13] Hope, faith, and love—all are required if we are to turn to God.

God's Compassion for Us

A single cry, and God bestows his favor upon us;[14] as soon as he hears he answers. And straightway our eyes are opened and we discover our true condition: "You shall defile your silver-plated idols / and your gold-covered images" (Isa 30:22). Then the Lord covers us with blessings: "[T]he LORD binds up the wounds of his people / and heals the bruises left by his blows" (Isa 30:26).

Compassion is a response dear to the Lord. In the missionary discourse of Matthew's gospel, from which the gospel for Saturday of the First Week of Advent is taken, we hear Jesus voicing his pity for the crowd and telling us that he and his disciples are sent "to the lost sheep of the house of Israel."[15] The Lord comes to save us, and our God himself is our salvation.[16] The saving action of God is, in the concrete, identical with his coming, his two comings. What we now hope for in a confused fashion is his coming to meet and save us once and for all.

Waiting in the Spirit

The special characteristic of Christian hope is the unique dynamism that the Holy Spirit instills into it.

We may regard as a special grace of the Holy Spirit in our time the keen, restless desire of our contemporaries for the end and fulfillment of history. They seem to share the chief concern of the early Church in this respect. The present generation seems convinced that the time is short (1 Cor 7:29); it is deeply sensitive to the present moment of history. This twofold outlook fits in very well with the mind-set of the liturgy for the Advent season: a grasp of the provisional nature of the present time and a grasp of the end of time that is coming. Such a grasp is not possible, however, without special attention to the work of the Spirit.

We must recall here the purpose for which the world was created and the manner in which it was created. A careful reading of Genesis shows how God willed to create the world as a unity. At the beginning of God's action, the *ruah*, or breath, which is a type of the Spirit, presided over the process of creating a unified world. Thus, sub-human creatures were created to serve one another and human beings and, in the last analysis, to glorify God. Since they were incapable of expressing their own submission to the Lord, they did it through the mediation of Adam, whose being is bound up with theirs. In Genesis, Adam is summoned to give these lower creatures their names as a sign of his authority over them.

Adam himself is also created as a unity, with his body the outward manifestation of his soul. He is the image of God and, as such, is closely united to God. Sin will consist precisely in the breaking of the unity. Once sin has occurred, God's plan is to reconstruct a world that is united in every respect, as he had willed in his original plan. As the Spirit had presided over the creation of the world, so he will preside over its re-creation.

At the various stages of Old Testament history, we see the Spirit given to leaders—prophets, judges, kings—so that the people might be reshaped and renewed. The failure of the various covenants leads God to make a definitive effort at reconstruction through the incarnation of the Word, which takes place by the power of the Spirit. Here we have the first and long-awaited coming of God among us. Henceforth people are the object of God's good will (Luke 2:14). When the fullness of time comes (Gal 4:4), the Spirit overshadows the Virgin Mary, and by his power she is found with child (Matt 1:18).

This Spirit is closely bound up with the Word who enters Mary's womb at the annunciation. The collect for December 20, which speaks of the Virgin as the dwelling place of divinity, emphasizes the fact that she both received the ineffable Word and was filled with the light of the Holy Spirit. Thus, her response, "May it be done," led to the coming into her of the Word and of the Spirit who is present in the incarnate Word. At the very moment of the incarnation, which the Spirit effects, the mystery of Easter begins. All that is done here will eventually lead by the Spirit to the glory of the resurrection, of which the collect for the Fourth Sunday of Advent speaks. At the beginning of the Letter to the Romans, St. Paul writes: "[Christ was] established as Son of God in power according to the spirit of holiness through resurrection from the dead" (Rom 1:4). Thus the Spirit shows himself already at work in this first coming of Christ. He continues his action in the Eucharist (which is the Passover of the Church), as we are reminded in the prayer over the offerings on the Fourth Sunday of Advent: "May the Holy Spirit, O Lord, sanctify these gifts laid upon your altar, just as he filled with his power the womb of the Blessed Virgin Mary."

When the fathers speak of the time or age of the Church, they think of it as the time of "the Spirit's dispensation." This idea emerges especially in the liturgy of Advent.

To sum up: What we await is the gathering of all peoples, and we find the Holy Spirit at work during this time, doing what is special to him: creating unity.

A Twofold Expectation

There is a further point that arises frequently in the Advent liturgy, an idea we shall have to delve into more deeply in another chapter. It is the idea that the Advent hope looks to a double coming.

> We proclaim the coming of Christ—not just a first coming but another as well that will be far more glorious than the first. The first took place under the sign of patient suffering; the second, on the contrary, will see Christ wearing the crown of God's kingdom.
>
> Almost everything about our Lord Jesus Christ is twofold. He has two births: one from God before the ages, the other from the Virgin at the end of the ages. He has two comings: the one is hidden and resembles the falling of the dew upon a fleece; the other—the future one—on the contrary, will be manifest. At his first coming, he was wrapped in linens and laid in a manger; at the second, light shall be his robe. In his first coming he endured the Cross, heedless of its shame; at his second coming he will be in glory and surrounded by an army of angels. Let us therefore not stop at his first coming but look forward to the second. We hailed him at his first coming with the words, "Blessed

is he who comes in the Lord's name!" and shall hail him in the same way at his second coming. For we shall go out to meet the Lord and his angels, and, prostrating ourselves before him, we shall cry, "Blessed is he who comes in the Lord's name!"[17]

Although there was no Advent liturgy in the East in the fourth century, St. Cyril of Jerusalem was well aware that the liturgy cannot separate two events that it must render actual and contemporaneous with us. We must accustom ourselves to these complex superimpositions in which the various levels and stages illuminate one another. We can glimpse here how different an exegetical reading of the Bible is from a liturgical reading of it. In a liturgical celebration we cannot proclaim Genesis without glimpsing the presence of Revelation as well. In each and every reading we read the whole Bible, from the first book to the last, and all of it in the light of the paschal mystery. That is why, as we shall see, the liturgical theology given us on the first three Sundays of Advent relates to the second coming of Christ as well as to the first; both comings are envisaged in the chants and readings.

In order, however, to better grasp the specific nature of the Christian hope that found expression in the seventh century in the Roman liturgy of Advent, we must enter more deeply into the meaning of the expectation voiced in Scripture and the liturgy.

2. THE HOPE AND EXPECTATION OF THE AGES

Advent is a special season in the Church's life, and during it we find her laying heavier stress than at other times on a basic Christian need: a living faith. Living faith alone gives coherence to Christian life, and it alone gives the Christian real access to what the Church herself calls "the summit toward which the activity of the church is directed."[1] But if we live our faith and our Christian life as modern people, shaped by the cultural ambience of our age and concerned to meet the concrete and very complicated demands that contemporary life makes of us, can we really enter into the mysteries of the Church? Or must we first cut ourselves off from our normal surroundings and set aside our everyday questions and anxieties?

In order to give an honest answer to this question, we must first give a synthetic overview of the biblico-liturgical theology of Advent as the Church of today understands it.

The Church is part of a longer history; she represents a new stage of it that will last until the final day. It should not surprise us, therefore, to find her using the Old Testament as the starting point for her various celebrations. In the Old Testament she discerns attitudes and events that are fulfilled in the New Testament and that continue to be actualized in our liturgical gatherings today and to require acceptance by each of us. Consequently, distant though the hopes and fears of the Old Testament people may seem to be from the questions that concern us here, it is with those hopes and fears that we must begin.

The Expectation of Israel

Expectation, waiting, was characteristic of the Israelite people throughout their history. Even a cursory reading of the Old Testament will see in its pages countless traces of a never-failing hope in a deliverer and in the salvation he brings.

It is less easy, however, to discern in this firm belief the nature of the one for whom the Israelites clamor so loudly and the role they expect him to play.

The Old Testament in its entirety looks for the coming of the Messiah, but we must be careful to see how people thought of the Messiah. To foretell the coming of a Messiah is not to foretell the coming of a human-God, especially not one who possesses, so to speak, the theological dimensions that the teaching of Christ, the light of his Spirit, and the Church's long tradition have enabled us to grasp. To project the Christian understanding of the Messiah back into a past that was not yet transformed by the blood of Christ and illumined by Pentecost would be to fail to see the slow process of purification through which Israel's thought had to pass. Contemporary exegetes think they can now make out the progressive stages of Israel's belief in its deliverer. Israel hoped for a Messiah, but its hope was not bold enough initially to glimpse the Messiah as we now know him to have been and as he is for all ages: a King not only of Israel but of the universe, a universal King and a God.

At the same time, it would be a mistake to think that Israel's hope was focused solely on a nationalist goal and limited to the material world. To think this would be to misunderstand the Semite, who does not neatly separate the spiritual from the material as we do. In a Semite's eyes, the material is the sign of the spiritual; the material universe is a gift of Yahweh. The world is a sign of spiritual realities and at the same time an outflow of God's superabundant riches. Spiritual values and material values are thus closely connected, the latter being an emanation, as it were, and a sign of the former.[2]

It would also be an error to separate the hope and expectation of salvation for the people as a whole from the hope and expectation of a personal salvation. That kind of distinction is unknown in the world of the Bible, where knowledge is not ruled by metaphysics but is focused on a human being in the concrete: a person who is body and soul and is closely linked to the community and the world in which one lives and with which one is in ontological continuity.[3]

What believing Israel waited for was to win out over sin and walk intimately with God. Without explicitly identifying this God with the Messiah, but in the last analysis implicitly assuming their identity, the people of the Old Testament hoped that their God would come. They even knew that their God had already come and yet was still coming and that these "comings" were a preparation for the final great coming. God "is always coming"!

The reference here is to the theophanies that gave vitality to Israel's hope and made it eager for the day of the final encounter, "the day of Yahweh." The "comings," the "days of Yahweh," were what set in motion the long history of Israel, which stretches from the Fall to the day when God will establish his kingdom on earth. The very name of Yahweh, which means "I am" in Exodus (3:13-15), signifies the only God, God with us, but it also signifies the God who is there, who intervenes on his appointed "days," and by his interventions keeps the world moving toward his "day." The very name of Yahweh has an eschatological meaning.[4] Yet even then he often came into the midst of his people, as the prophets and the psalmist were well aware. The refrain of Psalm 46, for example, expresses this conviction: "The LORD of hosts is with us" (vv. 8, 12). Concretely, all the important events of Israel's history, and all the blessings, catastrophes, and chastisements, were regarded by God's prophets as "days of Yahweh," as "comings" of their God. "The LORD of hosts is with us: / the God of Jacob is our stronghold" (Ps 46:8).

The "comings" of Yahweh, the "days of Yahweh," the "visitations of Yahweh" are pretty much equivalent expressions. They all point to the ceaseless activity of God in the history of his people. Nothing happens that does not have God for its first cause: "Does disaster befall a city, / unless the LORD has caused it" (Amos 3:6). This theme of the day of Yahweh is important; we find its real fulfillment in the Gospel theme of Jesus' "hour."

Israel loved to recall the "days" that had shaped and continued to shape its history. The "day of Midian," for example, on which Gideon had won a great victory, was always remembered in the history of Israel (Isa 9:3), since the victory was seen as indisputable proof of Yahweh's personal action in the midst of his people. Isaiah writes, "See, the name of the LORD is coming from afar" (30:27); and later, when the Israelites are carrying the burden of exile: "Be strong, do not fear! / Here is your God; / he comes with vindication; / With divine recompense / he comes to save you" (35:4). Yahweh's coming is thus close at hand; the prophets—and Amos, perhaps, even more than the others—usually think of the day as imminent. Yahweh comes—but for the sake of retribution. He is a judge, and "human pride shall be abased, / the arrogance of mortals brought low, / And the LORD alone will be exalted on that day. / The idols will vanish completely" (Isa 2:17-18). This is a judgment of Yahweh that allows Israel to pick itself up and continue its journey.

In a text that has become classical, Zephaniah foretells the terrible intervention by his God:

Near is the great day of the LORD,
  near and very swiftly coming.
The sound of the day of the LORD! Piercing—
  there a warrior shrieks!
A day of wrath is that day,
  a day of distress and anguish,
  a day of ruin and desolation,
A day of darkness and gloom,
  a day of thick black clouds,
A day of trumpet blasts and battle cries
  against fortified cities,
  against lofty battlements.
I will hem the people in
  till they walk like the blind,
  because they have sinned against the LORD;
And their blood shall be poured out like dust,
  and their bowels like dung.
Neither their silver nor their gold
  will be able to save them.
On the day of the LORD's wrath,
  in the fire of his passion,
  all the earth will be consumed.
For he will make an end, yes, a sudden end,
  of all who live on the earth. (1:14-18)

Thus Yahweh multiplies his days and his comings in order to give new life and vigor to his people. That is how the hope of Israel is strengthened. Because of his interventions, Yahweh is a God who is always there, ready to help, to repay, and, in a manner sometimes harsh, to set his people on the right path again. "On the foundation of the past, hope looks forward to the future in the experience of the present moment."[5]

But at the End of Days . . .

These many comings of Yahweh will end with his decisive "coming," his decisive "day." After the visitations of Yahweh that are connected with concrete historical events in the life of his people, there will be a coming that is both imminent and yet unspecified in its relation to time, despite its definite character. It is described in vague terms such as "in those days," "at that time," "at the end of days." Prophets and the psalmist give enthusiastic descriptions of this day of God's decisive coming to triumph over sin and death. The prophets look upon it as the day of the new covenant that God will freely initiate, despite the incurable sinfulness of his people and their complacency in their infidelity. His coming will be an encounter at which sins will be forgiven and a people sickened by their own evildoing will be made new again. On this point Ezekiel is the most explicit of the prophets:

> I will take you away from among the nations, gather you from all the lands, and bring you back to your own soil. I will sprinkle clean water over you to make you clean; from all your impurities and from all your idols I will cleanse you. I will give you a new heart, and a new spirit I will put within you. I will remove the heart of stone from your flesh and give you a heart of flesh. I will put my spirit within you so that you walk in my statutes, observe my ordinances, and keep them. You will live in the land I gave to your ancestors; you will be my people, and I will be your God. I will deliver you from all your impurities. I will summon the grain and make it plentiful; I will not send famine against you. (36:24-29)

Psalm 130 echoes the prophet:

> My soul hopes in the Lord
> more than watchmen for daybreak.
> Let Israel hope for the LORD.
> For with the LORD there is mercy,
> in him is plentiful redemption.
> It is he who will redeem Israel
> from all its iniquities. (vv. 6-8)

According to the prophet Daniel, the Messiah's role will be to purify:

> Seventy weeks are decreed
>   for your people and for your holy city:
> Then transgression will stop and sin will end,
>   guilt will be expiated,
> Everlasting justice will be introduced,
>   vision and prophecy ratified,
>   and a holy of holies will be anointed. (9:24)

But there will be only one Servant, the Servant of Yahweh, whose mission will be to bear the sins of his brothers and sisters and to establish a lasting covenant:

Yet it was our pain that he bore,
  our sufferings he endured.
We thought of him as stricken,
  struck down by God and afflicted,
But he was pierced for our sins,
  crushed for our iniquity.
He bore the punishment that makes us whole,
  by his wounds we were healed. . . .

Because of his anguish he shall see the light;
  because of his knowledge he shall be content;
My servant, the just one, shall justify the many,
  their iniquity he shall bear. (Isa 53:4-5, 11)

Then the earth will at last be at peace. Isaiah's vision recalls the first days of paradise:

Then the wolf shall be a guest of the lamb,
  and the leopard shall lie down with the young goat;
The calf and the young lion shall browse together,
  with a little child to guide them.
The cow and the bear shall graze,
  together their young shall lie down;
  the lion shall eat hay like the ox.
The baby shall play by the viper's den,
  and the child lay his hand on the adder's lair.
They shall not harm or destroy on all my holy mountain;
  for the earth shall be filled with knowledge of the LORD,
  as water covers the sea. (Isa 11:6-9)

To sum up Israel's expectation in a few words, we might say that it is an ardent, restless longing for a definitive, transforming encounter with God, one that makes sin and guilt passé.

The Expectation of the Church

There is seemingly an impassable gulf between the outlook of Israel and our own. If Christians were to enter into the feelings of the Israelites as they waited for the Messiah, they would be putting themselves into a situation that is unreal for them. Undeniably, in the not too distant past, a spirituality filled with good intentions did endeavor to lead us along paths where we felt ill at ease. But there can be no question, really, of our cultivating an expectation of the Messiah such as the Israelites had; we are not called to practice a spirituality based on fiction or to celebrate a liturgy that would in the last analysis be simply playacting! There is no basis in tradition for this kind of thing, and it is difficult to see how it could help make the mysteries of salvation real in us.

In other words, Christians cannot adopt the psychological viewpoint proper to a time in history when the Messiah had not yet come. They can indeed examine and try to grasp the psychological state of a people who were waiting for a savior-king as the agent of their full development, but they are not justified in trying to live as though that were really their own state; nor has the Church any reason for asking them to make such an artificial journey back in time. We must therefore reject any spirituality of Advent that is based on such an attempt and tries to make us pray as if God had not yet sent his Son among us and as if we had not yet received him. That would be a perverse and destructive misinterpretation of what the Church's liturgy is and is meant to be.[6]

Why, then, should we recall the hope Israel had? Why does Advent remind us of the expectations cherished by the patriarchs, the prophets, and the whole of Israel? Isn't it because their expectation and waiting are an anticipation of ours?

But the expectation of Israel was directed to more than the coming of a Messiah whose person and true role became clear only in a long, slow evolution. More radically, Israel's messianic expectation took concrete form in the hope of an encounter with God that would eliminate sin and all its obscene implications; with sin totally abolished, God could and would embrace his people and all people in loving peace.

For us, the Christ, or Anointed One, has already been born; we have received the Messiah, and everyone has seen the kind of salvation he brings. We know that in principle we are already within the kingdom, although we also know that God's reign over sin and Satan has not yet reached its full form and is still developing. Our definitive encounter with God has not yet taken place, and we see him now only in mystery and "as in a mirror." The face-to-face meeting is still in the future and will come on the last day when Christ returns; now we wait for it.

Christians always look toward this hour of their personal encounter with God; it is also the hour when the world in its entirety will acquire the dimensions of holiness that the Lord intended it to have when he created it. It is in relation to that future that Christian expectation becomes the prolongation of Israelite expectation. We may even say that ancient Israel's longing and waiting finds its completion in the longing and waiting of Christianity for the completion of salvation from sin and guilt and the glorious return of Christ.

There is thus no opposition between Israel's waiting and ours; on the contrary, there is continuity between them and progression from the one to the other. The coming of the Messiah does not cause an unbridgeable break between the two phases in the long waiting, rather it intensifies the ardent longing of the Christian. The Lord's birth does not put an end to Israel's waiting but gives it its full meaning, intensifies it even more, and fills it with an impatient longing for the Lord's definitive coming in his fully established kingdom. With the same fervor as the people of Israel, we follow them in their hopes but make these hopes even richer and bolder. Therefore, we can sing with Israel: "The Lord is close at hand; come, let us worship him"; "Tomorrow . . . the sinfulness of earth will be destroyed. The Savior of the world will be our king."[7]

We can see from this the spirit in which we may seek a better understanding of Israel's expectation. There is to be no fictional re-creation of the past, for we are dealing with two successive moments, not with a single identical one. We celebrate the same waiting and longing but at a higher and more perfect level. Speaking of the Old and New Testaments, St. Irenaeus wrote, "God called his people from secondary concerns to primary, from types to realities, from things temporal to things eternal, carnal to spiritual, earthly to heavenly."[8]

The coming of Christ, his atoning sacrifice on the cross, and his resurrection were the beginning of eternal life and complete salvation. Yet history continues on in our time and in our midst. Far from stopping the course of history, Christ's coming gave it a new impulse, and the world is moving toward its fulfillment. The Church of our time celebrates her expectation of the end, but her hope is rendered patient and serene because it rests on a past in which God has already shown his wonderful deeds. The *mirabilia*, or "marvelous acts," that God freely accomplished in Old Testament times in order to guide humanity's hopes toward the kingdom are a pledge that has been confirmed by the first coming of Christ and by the new marvels that Christ performed and that foretell and prepare for the definitive kingdom that will be established at his second coming when "sin and death will be no more."

When the Church of our time applies to her own situation the words of prophet and psalmist, she does not apply them from without to her present circumstances, as though they were images intended to illustrate and explain these circumstances. The point is rather that the prophecies, types, and psalms acquire their full meaning only in Christ and now in his Church. Moreover, they will find their complete fulfillment only when Christ returns at the end of time. The passages borrowed from the Old Testament show that God's plan is a single plan continuously operative in the history of the world, in the history of Israel, and in our own history. We can say of the Psalter, as we can of every book of the Old Testament, that it contains in germ a reality that will develop fully in the future. In a single phrase that reality is redemption from sin—the Passover mystery.

The liturgy of Advent, then, does not require the Christian to indulge in fiction. It is in a fully real way that the believer of today shares Israel's hope: the hope of forgiveness, the hope of meeting God. The Christian, like the Israelite of Isaiah's time, can with complete truthfulness sing the words of the entrance antiphon for the First Sunday of Advent: "To you, I lift up my soul, O my God" (Ps 25:1). But for Christians, Christ's coming deepens their desire for the eternal vision of God, and thus this entrance antiphon has an even greater depth of meaning and poignancy for them, while it also expresses a limitless confidence based on the first coming of Christ into our world.

The gospel of the first Sunday brings home to us the full scope of Advent, for it concerns the parousia, or return of Christ on the last day. Here is where our expectation and that of Israel coincide. For us, the Messiah has already come within earthly time; we do not still await that first coming, and it would be foolish for us to try to live, along with Israel, an experience that cannot be ours. On the other hand, with a fervor deepened by Christ's first coming, we can and do await with Israel of old the world's encounter with its Deliverer at his second coming. Israel's expectation bridged the gulf between the Fall and the birth of Christ; ours bridges the distance between the coming of the Lord within historical times and his second coming at the end.

The Israelite of old and the Christian today hope for the same thing. Both are summoned to "awake from sleep" and to "throw off the works of darkness and put on the armor of light." That is the point of the epistle for the first Sunday.[9]

We have noted how the fervor of our hope for encounter with our God has been greatly intensified by the fact of Christ's first coming. Thus our waiting and longing, while linking us to the Chosen People of old, also separates us from them by the fact of the Messiah's birth in time.

There is a further difference between the two hopes, Israel's and ours. Just before his earthly pilgrimage ended, Jesus the Messiah gave us a special bread to eat and a special cup to drink: a divine food, our sustenance on the journey toward the promised land, a Eucharist closely bound up with his death. It is of this food that St. Paul says: "For as often as you eat this bread and drink the cup, you proclaim the death of the Lord until he comes" (1 Cor 11:26). The Eucharist, then, creates in the Christian a state of restless longing for the Lord's return. The Lord himself, through his sacrificial, atoning death for sin and his resurrection, which are present in the Eucharist, nourishes in each Christian and in the world at large the hope of his return; it is he who hastens the maturation process so that the hour of his coming and of our definitive encounter with him may come at last.

We shall have occasion later on to speak again of these essential aspects of Catholicism. What we have already said, however, is enough to help us understand both the longing expectation of Israel and what our own should be as a prolongation of Israel's and by contrast with it.

We cannot understand Advent if we eliminate any of the perspectives we have been analyzing. All make up a single complex totality, and the meaning of the whole is falsified if we isolate one aspect and focus exclusively on it. Two realities must be kept in view and not separated: Israel's waiting, which was a preparation for the historical coming of the Messiah, and our own waiting, which is grounded in the Lord's birth and looks ever more intently for God's complete sovereignty over the world and the full establishment of his reign of holiness and peace.

The two Advent prefaces give an excellent synthesis, in prayer form, of the season's two themes, which overlap and fit perfectly together in God's plan. "For he assumed at his first coming the lowliness of human flesh, and so fulfilled the design you formed long ago, and opened for us the way to eternal salvation, that, when he comes again in glory and majesty and all is at last made manifest, we who watch for that day may inherit the great promise in which now we dare to hope."

Thus does the first preface, at the beginning of the eucharistic prayer, present the two comings of Christ. The second preface bases its description rather on the concrete facts of history. "For all the oracles of the prophets foretold him, the Virgin Mother longed for him with love beyond all telling, John the Baptist sang of his coming and proclaimed his presence when he came. It is by his gift that already we rejoice at the mystery of his Nativity, so that he may find us watchful in prayer and exultant in his praise."

The World's Waiting

Let us return to the question we started with. Does this whole liturgy, however rich and beautiful it may be, afford any answer to the world's distress?

We have the right to ask whether or not a sound theology of Advent as experienced and "acted out" in our liturgical life can answer the agonizing problems of the modern world and give meaning to our existence as we seek our human development.

The generations now alive have had too brutal an experience of the world's frailty not to be ready to downgrade any effort to rebuild that world. The collapse of value systems and of institutions recognized as essential for human life has led people to believe that the end has come, that there is no more hope. The experience of two World Wars* has made them think in apocalyptic terms and see the end of the world as imminent; our present experiences and the uncertainty of peace stimulate the same kinds of thoughts.

Admittedly, the same thoughts have filled people's minds at every great crisis in history. What is peculiar to our age is a despair, a sense of futility, a keen awareness of the uselessness of human efforts to ensure earthly progress. A philosophy is now abroad that springs from the sudden, violent accumulation of catastrophes that humanity has brought upon itself. It is perhaps here that we have the most serious of the illnesses now afflicting the human race. It is very important

---

* One can only imagine how Nocent would have incorporated the events of a terrorist age in these comments.

that a clinical analysis be made of the situation, since it is one that endangers important spiritual values.

The illness is complicated and even paradoxical. As perhaps never before, people have been discovering more and more ways of raising the living standard, doing away with many forms of material drudgery, and thus making possible a broader and richer use of humanity's intellectual faculties as well as a greater scope for its spiritual energies. At the same time, however, there is a contrary movement; people have become deeply impressed by the uncertainty of their very existence and have developed a philosophy of despair. Literature and the arts are full of this agonizing awareness. Many, especially among the young—all allowances made for faddism—are obsessed by the brutal discovery of what they regard as a life doomed to failure.

Since, then, we are headed for final annihilation, why try to develop a civilization, a science, or an art? In a way, what we have here once again is the attitude St. Paul branded onto the Thessalonians.[10] It would be a mistake, however, to see a perfect parallel between today and St. Paul's day. The modern attitude is due, in fact, either to a type of atheism or to an erroneous or incomplete theology.[†]

Heidegger's philosophy is still alive and active among us. His atheism admittedly has a certain grandeur about it. People may be locked into dread because they are fettered to a world whose very existence is a precarious thing. But they do not therefore have the right, says Heidegger, to give way to discouragement and apathy. On the contrary, having discovered nothingness, they must take hold of themselves, confront their lot without flinching, scorn the nothingness they have discovered, look for ways to improve the lot of their brothers and sisters, and raise the level of a civilization they know to be hopelessly doomed to annihilation. Such is the tough, stoic attitude of a proud cynic.

Many believers are ready, perhaps unwittingly, to adopt such an outlook without any significant modifications. In their view, when faced with Christ and his word of salvation, people must recognize the nothingness of this present life and the ineffectiveness and worthlessness of all human actions, even those done for religious motives. The kingdom of God is simply given to people, and the latter may

[†] Again, Nocent would have found plenty to say about the rise of atheism in the early twenty-first century.

not for a moment believe that their actions or their virtues prepare for it in any way; there is no connection at all between the virtuous acts people do and the kingdom that is offered to them. Only faith counts—faith in the risen Christ.

On the basis of that faith, salvation is bestowed upon us, and we can only accept it; it can in no way be brought to pass within history. Christians do not work for their salvation in time and in this world, for in the world and time there can be no acquisition of authentic values and no real progress. Consequently, Christians share with pagans a pessimistic view of the world. There is nothing to do but to reject the world, since in it there can be no progress, spiritual or even simply human, that has any relation to the kingdom of God.

Catholics indeed believe that their faith and their works do have a relation to the kingdom of God and to eternity. Despite this, many of them ask whether there is any point in seeking human progress when the world itself is passing away. A certain kind of philosophy and its distrust of technological progress is one of the most distressing signs of a tendency that explains to some extent the unbelief of scientists. In responding to a questionnaire on the reasons for contemporary unbelief, Teilhard de Chardin wrote as follows:

> To those who are not extremely familiar with it, Christianity quite certainly gives the impression . . . of not making up its mind frankly to accept, in their general application and in their spirit, the views on cosmic developments that are universally accepted everywhere except in Christianity. It seems to delight in belittling human hopes and pointing out the weaknesses of our society. It despises or fears progress and discovery; in short, it in no way hallows or magnifies the loftiest and most intensely felt aspirations of modern man.[11]

There is a type of Christianity that admittedly does justify such a criticism. For if we judge by the outlook of one category of Christians (often people very concerned to be authentically Christian), there is no reason for desiring the advancement of our civilization, since Christian hope has nothing to do with the present world. These people appeal to Scripture and Tradition in attempting to justify their rejection of progress: the world is passing and is destined to give way to the kingdom when Christ returns.

I see a usefulness in thus summarizing several views that see no relation between human progress and God's plan, either because they deny that there is any divinely established order, or because, while admitting such an order, they see no continuity between a person's actions, even virtuous ones, and a person's eternal destiny in God's final kingdom, or, finally, because in the name of Scripture and Tradition they set up an extreme opposition between the present world and the world to come.

Far from having digressed from our subject, we are now at the very heart of it. We wait for the Lord, and we cherish a sure hope that we shall someday go to meet him. But what should our attitude be to the present world? Do our actions have anything to do with the coming of the kingdom? These are questions of central importance for understanding the Advent that is our lives.

First, let us recall a point made earlier: our culture has become used to compartmentalizing spiritual and material values. If we are to find an answer to the questions we ask in our distress, we must set aside attitudes like that, which are alien to the biblical view of reality. Salvation is meant for the whole of our being, body and soul, and it embraces the whole of creation, including subhuman reality. As we wait, therefore, for the definitive establishment of the kingdom, we may not totally separate the spiritual and the fleshly, soul and body, spiritual values and material values. The world that is to come will restore full value to all these orders of reality and restore a balance in which they are in perfect harmony each with the others.

The contemporary rediscovery of Scripture, of the fathers who comment on Scripture, and of the liturgy, which actualizes the Scriptures and enables us to "live" them, is helping us develop broader, more balanced, and less fragmented views on the relations between these different orders: the divine, the spiritual, the human, the fleshly.

In his book *Catholicism*,[12] Henri de Lubac has gathered numerous statements of the fathers of the Church on how creation is to be understood and how it is affected first by sin and then by redemption.

The fathers are not interested in a scientific explanation of the events recorded in Genesis; their purpose is not to reject or accept the views of the writer of Genesis on creation, in the name of scientific discoveries. Their theological interpretation is not dependent on a scientific knowledge of the world but looks rather to the spirit in which God created the world. He created Adam in his "image and likeness." God himself is the model for humankind, and the latter derives its unity from the one divine image that is reproduced in each individual.

But humanity is in turn the center of creation, and everything about it is created for its sake. Subhuman creatures share in the unity that humankind possesses by God's will, and Adam was put into the world as a cosmic personage; that is, an ontological bond unites him to the rest of creation. He is God's steward; his mediation makes it possible for mute subhuman creatures to express their acceptance of the divine will. Consequently, there is a close bond between the world and people, within each person, between human and subhuman creatures, and among subhuman creatures themselves. The world was created as a completely unified reality, a unity deriving from the fact that it is a reflection of God. The fathers are unanimous in subscribing to this vision of the world.

They are no less unanimous in seeing Adam's sin as the cause of the dislocation that now marks the world. Adam's sin fragmented the world; a world in which there was no "mine and yours" has become an aggregation of individuals violently at odds with one another. The fragmentation of the world is the most evident consequence of sin. Origen sums it all up in a few words: *Ubi peccata ibi multitudo* ("Where there is sin, there is fragmentation").[13]

Thus, God has his own conception of humankind, which he created as a unity in which a human is called to give subhuman creatures their names (or, in Western terms, to dominate them). To this conception correspond God's efforts, after the Fall and throughout the Old Testament, to renew his intimate relationship with his creation.

The Bible brings before us a drama that begins with the first sin and portrays the unwearying, stubborn effort of a Creator-God to begin his creation anew, rescue it from the fragmentation caused by sin, and restore it for good to the unity that derives from its being his image. The story of Noah and the ark shows how God sought unity for his creation: as he saves people by enclosing them in the ark, he also saves, along with humanity, a pair from each species of animal. His creation will survive in the form he willed for it; it will be a totality, a whole made up of many parts. The theme of the covenant could be studied with a view to seeing at every point how God aims to restore his creation to a unity that embraces human and subhuman creatures.

The fathers of the Church go on to show how the incarnation of God, the cross, and the resurrection affect the material universe. In a single word St. Paul sums up the effect of Christ's activity on the material world when he speaks of redemption as a "restoration" or "recapitulation" of the world. The old Adam, a cosmic personage, was united to the world around him—even the material world—that was to contribute marvelously to the development of the natural human. This first Adam is followed by the new Adam, Christ; like the old Adam, he too is a cosmic personage. His mission is to gather into unity the whole created world, that is, humanity and the rest of creation, through the victory of the cross.

How is it possible, in view of God's really taking our flesh to himself, to maintain the impossibility of a connection between human progress and his plan? Christ's mission is to renew God's image in all things; every created thing can appeal to him as the living exemplar in whose likeness it has been made. God's activity in the Old Testament was but a preparation for the decisive moment of the incarnation and for the new period in which the whole of creation would, amid "groans" (cf. Rom 8:22), gradually reach its deliverance at the moment when it would experience a resurrection and become identified on the last day with God's kingdom.

It is at this point in our effort to gain a vital understanding of the link between human progress and God's plan that we must turn to the liturgy as the Church understands it and as the faithful ought to understand it.

We have briefly sketched God's intervention in the history of the Old and New Testaments. We have done so because this same intervention of God is still being exercised now, today. The liturgy of the Church is far more than ceremony, pomp, and rubrics. Its only real purpose is to render present in our world, to re-actualize for the world of today, God's action in the old covenant and his sending of his Son to die for us and rise from the dead as the foundation of the new covenant. In other words, the Catholic liturgy has for its purpose to continue the gathering of creation into the unity whose basis is the divine likeness, and it does so by raising up before the eyes of the world the sign of the new and everlasting covenant: the cross of Christ.

There we have the essential function of the eucharistic celebration: to actualize for us the redemptive work of Christ.

The new Adam, the one St. Paul calls the Head of the Mystical Body, intends his redemption not simply for the spiritual element in humans but for the whole of their being, body and soul; he comes to save the whole human person. Moreover, he wills to save not only the whole human person but the whole of creation over which humans are to rule. The entire universe is part of the Mystical Body of Christ, and since the redemptive actions of Christ are actualized for us in the Mass and in the rest of the liturgy, we must think that the whole of creation, like the Mystical Body, is growing and developing.

The re-actualization of the historical events of our salvation, with the mysteries of Christ's life as the climax, is a leaven at work in the world. The new covenant has been given to us only so that we may advance toward a definitive fulfillment. The Eucharist is the goal of the whole Old Testament and of God's efforts to restore the world, but it is also a starting point for a journey leading to the Lord's return at the end of time. In other words, all that is summed up in the term "sacred history" is made real here and now in the eucharistic celebration, and we really, truly, actually experience the whole of that history.

The cross of Christ is the goal of all the history that came before it. We may say that the whole of the Old Testament is a movement toward the historical life of Christ on earth. This life in turn is in its entirety a movement toward the cross; the historical event of the cross looks to its representation or actualization by the eucharistic celebration, and the actualization then initiates a progressive movement toward the return of Christ and the inauguration of the eternal kingdom.

We cannot limit the re-actualization to the Eucharist and the sacraments. The tradition of the Church shows quite clearly that we cannot restrict the representative effectiveness of the liturgy solely to the sacramental order and that we must not subscribe to the narrow definition of liturgy that would make it coextensive with the sacraments.[14] In addition to the sacramental re-presentation that takes place in us and acts in us and influences the whole of creation through us as long as we do not prevent it, there is another way in which our salvation is actualized for us and for the created universe, human and subhuman. This other way is the living celebration of the liturgical mystery.

We Catholics do not reflect enough on this when we participate in the liturgy. And yet, especially at the celebration of the Eucharist, we are commissioned, with and in Christ, to embrace the world and the whole of creation. We are to bear witness that creation in its entirety is the workplace of God. We may say, in consequence, that human thought, art, technology, progress are all moving in the same direction as God and Christianity. For all these things are bringing the world to its maturity and preparing it for its renewal. Would it be an overstatement to claim that Christianity cannot be its full self unless it welcomes progress, not simply with a benevolent smile but with an ardent embrace?

Thus, for Catholics who reflect on what they are doing, every participation in the Mass and the rest of the liturgy will be seen as a contribution not only to the spiritual development of the world but also to the advancement of the material universe as it moves toward its fulfillment. It has often and rightly been said that the incarnation of Christ sanctified matter by restoring to it its dimension of truthful sign. All matter has now become a sign, a symbol of higher realities. We need but think of the sacraments and the new significance they give to matter: water, oil, bread, wine, fire—all of them material signs whose function it is to prolong in time the incarnation of the Christ, who continues to work in our world.

By means of the liturgy, then, we must rediscover the meaning God gives the world, the meaning he gives to work and progress. There is no question, of course, but that both Scripture and Tradition contrast the present world and the world to come. Recall the First Letter of St. John:

> Do not love the world or the things of the world. If anyone loves the world, the love of the Father is not in him. For all that is in the world, sensual lust, enticement for the eyes, and a pretentious life, is not from the Father but is from the world. Yet the world and its enticement are passing away. But whoever does the will of God remains forever. (1 John 2:15-17)

But, given what we have been saying about God's plan and its understanding by the fathers, we must not be simplistic in our interpretation of this passage and of similar words spoken by Christ; we must not reduce them to a mistrustful moralism. The scriptural tradition does indeed contrast two worlds: the present world and the world to come. It does not, however, reject creation, since creation is God's handwork and continues to be it even after the Fall. What the Scripture is focusing on is what the evil one is doing in the world.

St. John makes this quite clear when he writes that "the whole world is under the power of the evil one" (1 John 5:19).

There is no doubt that the effort to incarnate Christianity in people's temporal life can and does present dangers. What we have been saying up to this point may lead some to think that by their effort Christians can build a paradise on earth and that the apparent slowing down of the advance of Christianity is due simply to the fact that Christians have not made those efforts. But a Christian life that includes an intimate sharing in the Church's liturgical life will not fall victim to that kind of confusion. When Catholics receive a sacrament, they know that they now possess a power that can raise the world to new heights. But their very reception of the sacrament also shows them how they are to conceive such a re-creation of the world.

They know that after the incarnation and redemption the world cannot again be fragmented and that we, along with the rest of creation, are saved in principle. This truth is the source of their optimism and hope, but they do not let it blind them to reality. They know that the ever-active power of redemption must work against Satan, who continues to be present in the world and can turn human progress into an instrument of warfare against God, against redemption, and against the authentic reconstruction of the world.

When they leave the liturgical celebration, Catholics have just borne witness to two facts, *sin* and *death*, which have ravaged the world and caused the death of Christ. When they finish the celebration in which the sacrifice of the cross has been actualized for us, they go forth with the assurance that the world is redeemed and the entire universe lifted up and that the world is advancing in accordance with the same divine will that decreed its redemption. But they do not forget that this progress on the world's part can only be along the road of the cross.

Catholics, then, should seek progress; they should devote themselves to lessening the social and economic disorder around them; they should be on the lookout for ways of alleviating people's suffering; they are conscious, as St. Augustine was, that we cannot preach the gospel to people who are starving. At the same time, however, Catholics leaving Mass also know that their mission is to display the cross to the world. They must do all they can to lessen the sufferings of others, but they also have the mission of persuading others to accept suffering as a means of becoming victors over suffering itself and death.

Catholics, then, do not dream of an earthly paradise or imagine that the struggle will have a definitive happy ending in this world. Sin, suffering, and death will continue to be the world's lot, and Christian hope must not be confused with human success. Redemption, which is rendered constantly present in the world through the liturgy, does indeed have the last word to say in our world, but it does not therefore suppress suffering and death; instead, it makes of them instruments enabling people to better identify themselves with the cross of Christ.[15]

Yves de Montcheuil sums up nicely what we have been saying thus far:

> Although living in a sense outside this world and touching an abiding reality, the true Christian cannot be excused from working to transform the world so that someday the dawn of the heavenly city may break over it. Christians must also realize, however, that the full light of heavenly day will never shine on any earthly creation. Therefore they must keep at a task they know can never be successfully completed, and yet not scorn it or, at the other extreme, let themselves be seduced by the recurring protean myth of possible success. They must set their heart on what lies beyond this world, and yet they have no right to lose themselves in the foretaste of it that is given to them here below. There can be no living of true Christianity unless the various elements of the latter are kept in balance or, more accurately, in tension.[16]

This passage sums up exactly what the liturgy tells us about human progress and God's outlook on the world. Redemption actualized over and over again in the liturgy renders the world more worthy of human efforts and more disposed for genuine progress. But the world that is thus moving toward its fulfillment should be the object of our interest only insofar as our relations to it are in perfect conformity with God's plan.

Such, then, should be our attitude during the Advent that is our earthly lives, lived as they are in the long interim between the birth of Christ and his return at the end of time.

Is the answer to our distress and that of the world now complete? Yes, it is complete objectively and as far as God is concerned. But it will satisfy only those who believe and have entered upon the way of the paschal mystery, those who, enlightened by faith, have come to see that the answer is contained in the mystery of death and resurrection. It is a hard answer, and yet it is, even humanly, a satisfying one for those who have had the sacramental experience of Christ and realized how the Lord of glory made our humanity his own in order to transform it in the fire of suffering. The Church has no other answer to give. If she is to avoid being mistaken for simply another political organization, she must endeavor to transmit to her children and to the world only the one treasure that is hers: the death and resurrection of Christ, as an efficacious sacrament unto holiness and as a model to be imitated.

3. WAITING FOR THE COMINGS OF THE LORD

A point made earlier must be repeated and applied here: There would be no purpose in reading this chapter if we did not have faith. What we shall be saying would seem ridiculous or, at best, lacking in any real content. Catholic liturgy says nothing except to those who believe, but for them it can lead to deep peace in the possession of God.

Every liturgical celebration has three dimensions: it recalls the past, in the present, for the sake of what is to come. Advent provides a splendid opportunity to see the intricate interconnection of these three dimensions. Consequently, it is the ideal season for entering fully into a living theology of the Roman Catholic liturgy.

The Two Dimensions of Expectation

The liturgy of Advent gradually took shape in the Church beginning in the fourth century. Toward the end of this century we find in Gaul and Spain a period of preparation for the feast of Christmas. The feast itself had just been established at Rome as a kind of Christianization of the pagan celebration of the victorious sun: *Natale solis invicti* (birth of the unconquered sun) or celebration of the winter solstice, when the sun triumphed over the winter mists.* The Church of Rome saw in the natural occurrence a symbol of Christ victorious over the dark powers of evil and took the occasion to celebrate on December 25 the birth of Christ according to the flesh. She saw in this birth the beginning of the mystery of humankind's deliverance from sin and guilt that will culminate in the Pasch of the Lord. It seemed natural, therefore, to prepare for the celebration, just as for the celebration of the Pasch. We will have to ask, however, why it

---

* Nocent dwells considerably on this theory about the origins of Christmas; however, the view has been challenged. See Thomas J. Talley, *The Origins of the Liturgical Year* (New York: Pueblo Publishing Company, 1986), 91–99. Also Paul F. Bradshaw and Maxwell E. Johnson, *The Origins of Feasts, Fasts, and Seasons in Early Christianity* (Collegeville, MN: Liturgical Press, 2011).

took so long for this period of preparation to be introduced into the Church of Rome, where it appeared, in fact, only in the middle of the sixth century.

Preparation for the incarnation of Christ supposes a certain faith-inspired outlook or, to put it another way, a specific understanding of the celebration of Christmas. Christmas did not have the same importance in everyone's eyes. St. Augustine, for example, saw in this feast a simple "memorial."[1] From his point of view, the celebration was only a recalling, even though the recall possessed a special spiritual efficacy. In this case the liturgy could not awaken an authentic expectation in its participants, since the event had already taken place and only the memory of it was now being celebrated. We can appreciate the effects of a past event, even if the event remains purely in the past. But how can we prepare actively for its celebration and be filled with a joyous impatience to encounter the event in its concrete reality?

St. Leo has quite a different understanding of the celebration of Christmas. For him it is a "sacrament" and possesses an actuality because it is the first moment in the carrying out of the Easter mystery and is closely bound up with the latter.[2] This is why Christmas is efficaciously present across time and space. On the Vigil of Christmas the Eastern martyrology proclaims, "A Pasch, a three-day festive holiday."[3]

Against this background we can better understand why the Church decided to introduce a period of preparation for the liturgical actualization of Christ's birth. The Council of Saragossa (380) obliged the faithful to gather daily from December 17 to January 6. In the sixth century, St. Gregory of Tours mentions a penitential period lasting from November 11 to Christmas, during which people fasted three days a week; this is the period that would later be called "St. Martin's Lent."[4] In the sixth century, the tendency was to make Advent as long as Lent.

At Rome, it was only toward the middle of the sixth century that an Advent liturgy was celebrated; the season lasted six weeks. On the sixth Sunday, however, there was no liturgy; the introduction of the Ember Days meant that the liturgy was celebrated during the night between the fifth Saturday and the sixth Sunday, the latter then having no proper liturgy of its own. Under St. Gregory the Great, the number of Sundays was reduced to four.

Advent, then, as a special season, came into existence during the period from the fourth century to the middle of the sixth. But while elsewhere it was generally a time of fasting and only gradually developed its special liturgy, at Rome it was seen as liturgical from the beginning and related to the feast of Christmas (first celebrated in 336).

This very summary sketch could give a false impression of the theology at work. As a matter of fact, from the time that Christmas became a feast of major importance in the Roman liturgy, Advent had a twofold significance: it was a preparation for the Lord's birth (this aspect was emphasized especially outside Rome), and it was a time of waiting for the parousia. So interwoven are the two themes that it is difficult to say whether the readings and prayers were chosen to prepare the faithful for Christmas or for the parousia. Reference to the parousia was not missing from the non-Roman liturgies, which had begun to celebrate Advent before Rome did, but it became prominent only after Rome had created its own Advent liturgy. There are still two questions to be asked concerning the celebration of Advent at Rome.

We know that there is evidence of a celebration of Advent beginning in the fourth century elsewhere than at Rome. How are we to explain the fact that Rome, which had instituted the feast of Christmas, lagged so far behind in introducing the celebration of Advent? Furthermore, how are we to explain the Roman emphasis on the two objects of Advent expectation?

It is difficult, perhaps impossible, to give definitive answers to these questions, but we can at least offer plausible hypotheses while resisting the temptation to make certainties out of them.

It is possible that Rome viewed Christmas simply as a feast preparatory to the paschal feast. For the Romans, Christmas was a kind of inchoative Pasch; Easter alone was to be dignified by a preparatory season (which from the fourth century on included the catechumenate). Easter alone was to be celebrated in a way worthy of the feast that actualizes the heart of the whole mystery of salvation.

But the biblical and instinctively theological sensibilities of the faithful enriched the feast of Christmas by introducing a time of expectation that focused on a twofold object, as we have already said. Christmas was celebrated in close relation to the paschal mystery, being regarded as the beginning of Christ's triumph over evil. The fathers of the Church, especially St. Leo, linked the Lord's coming to

Bethlehem with his second coming in glory at the end of time. In their eyes, despite the lowly state of the Lord in the crib, Christmas is a victory feast, connected both with the redemptive triumph of the cross and with the final triumph of Christ at his return.

Quite naturally, then, the preparation for the feast of Christmas took on the same rich dimensions and twofold perspective as the feast itself. *Adventus* was a term borrowed from the pagans and meant "coming"; it was extended from the feast or event itself to the preparation for it and acquired the meaning "expectation." In other words, "advent" meant first of all the Lord's birth and the anniversary of it, then the time of preparation for the event, and finally the expectation of, or time of waiting for, the second coming of Christ.[5]

Expectation of the Second Coming

The books of the New Testament are filled with the confident thought of the Lord's coming on the last day; a Christian messianism underlay the theology that the Church lived from the very beginning of its existence. Christ himself often refers to his return, and it was quite natural that the writings closely concerned with him should reflect the promise of that coming, which was always present in the minds of his apostles and disciples.

With the passage of time, the theology and even the very imagery connected with the second coming would be seriously distorted. The catastrophes accompanying the end of the world, and the proximity of that end, would become the chief focus of interest, and the return of the Lord would be cast into the shadow. In modern times, spirituality seemed to have simply lost sight of the end of the world and of Christ's return and to have concentrated on the individual's encounter with the sovereign Lord and just Judge at the moment of death. Apocalyptic descriptions and paintings of the final judgment and second coming betrayed an erroneous theology.

It is far easier for us today to obtain a proper understanding of the biblical mentality. This, along with the themes of the Advent liturgy, can help Christians grasp the real meaning of the events we await and the concrete meaning of the waiting itself. But the ground must first be cleared, for Christians have developed attitudes that make it difficult for them really to focus their attention on the end of the world and the return of Christ.

To begin with, it is difficult for us to rid ourselves of a very commercialized and individualistic vision of the history of salvation. Despite the sociological jargon we use and despite our preoccupation (philosophical at best, but most often purely verbal) with the salvation of the community, we tend to see the problem solely from the viewpoint of the individual. The end of the world means *my* end; the judgment is the judgment to be passed on *me*; and the encounter with the returning Christ is *my* encounter with him.

Such a conception of the retribution that Christ brings can hardly rouse enthusiasm. A theology of hope and a real life of hope cannot be focused on individuals, as though they existed as isolated monads. In fact, individuals cannot accept salvation unless others and the world itself are involved. Only an outlook that is as hopeful for the future of the world as it is for others and for the individual can win a person's enthusiastic assent and become the basis for a whole style of life.

Here, of course, we have entered the domain of faith. We made this point at the beginning of the chapter and must repeat it here: Without faith, all that we have been saying and shall be saying is meaningless. There can be no efficacious liturgical celebration without faith. But we must also repeat something else said earlier: The properly Christian outlook on the future and renewal of the world is of concern even to those "outside" who are allowed to gain a right understanding of it through the scriptural and theologico-moral presentation of Advent.

"He Will Gather His Elect from the Four Winds"

Christ did not mince words in predicting his return. This is evident from a well-known passage of St. Mark's gospel:

> But in those days after that tribulation,
>   the sun will be darkened,
>   and the moon will not give its light,
>   and the stars will be falling from the sky,
>   and the powers in the heavens will be shaken.
> And then they will see "the Son of Man coming in the clouds" with great power and glory, and then he will send out the angels and gather [his] elect from the four winds, from the end of the earth to the end of the sky. (Mark 13:24-27)

St. Mark is here utilizing a messianic prophecy of the prophet Daniel:

> As the visions during the night continued, I saw coming with the clouds
>> of heaven
> One like a son of man.
> When he reached the Ancient of Days
>> and was presented before him,
> He received dominion, splendor, and kingship. (Dan 7:13-14a)

The theme of gathering is basic. It is interesting to see that just as on the day of the Fall the world that had been created in God's likeness was fragmented, so (in the imagery of the apocalypses) the whole world is shaken by the Lord's return. The first action of the Son of Man will be to "gather his elect from the four winds." The image will be very familiar to the early Christians; we find it, for example, in the attractive prayer of blessing in the *Didache*.[6]

Isaiah foretells the gathering of the nations in the temple at Jerusalem for an age of happiness and peace:

> He [the Lord] shall judge between the nations,
>> and impose terms on many peoples.
> They shall beat their swords into plowshares
>> and their spears into pruning hooks;
> one nation shall not raise the sword against another,
>> nor shall they train for war again. (Isa 2:4-5; *LH*, Monday, first week;
>> Mass, first Sunday [A])

Isaiah also sees the remnant of God's people surviving all the trials and being reunited on Mount Zion (Isa 4:2-6; *LH*, Tuesday, first week).

St. Matthew puts on Christ's lips a prediction of a gathering for the banquet in God's kingdom: "I say to you, many will come from the east and the west, and will recline with Abraham, Isaac, and Jacob at the banquet in the Kingdom of heaven" (Matt 8:5-11; Mass, Monday, first week). Jesus is here foretelling the fulfillment of Isaiah's prophecy.

In the "apocalypse" of Isaiah (cc. 24–27), there is a prediction of the great universal banquet:

> On this mountain he will destroy
>> the veil that veils all peoples,
> The web that is woven over all nations;
>> he will destroy death forever. (Isa 25:6-9; Mass, Wednesday, first week)

The Golden Age

The theme of gathering into unity is a favorite of Isaiah's. He gives it fine expression in his well-known poem on the golden age:

> Then the wolf shall be a guest of the lamb,
>   and the leopard shall lie down with the kid;
> the calf and the young lion shall browse together,
>   with a little child to guide them.
> The cow and the bear shall be neighbors,
>   together their young shall rest;
>   the lion shall eat hay like the ox.
> The baby shall play by the cobra's den,
>   and the child lay his hand on the adder's lair. (Isa 11:1-10; Mass,
>   Tuesday, first week, and second Sunday [A])

What is being foretold here is the restoration of creation to unity, as envisaged in God's first plan, according to which all creatures serve one another for the glory of the Father.

Second Isaiah describes him whom God has chosen and sanctified so that he might bring about this gathering into unity. Prisoners will be liberated and captives released; the Lord will make justice and praise spring up before all the nations (Isa 61:1-11; Mass, third Sunday [B]).

The prophet Baruch offers a similar vision of the gathering of God's people: "Up, Jerusalem! stand upon the heights; / look to the east and see your children / gathered from the east and the west / at the word of the Holy One" (Bar 5:1-9; Mass, second Sunday [C]).

According to Jeremiah, the new form for oath taking will be: "'As the Lᴏʀᴅ lives, who brought the descendants of the house of Israel up from the land of the north'—and from all the lands to which I banished them; they shall again live on their own land" (Jer 23:5-8; Mass, December 18).

The gathered people will pray and worship together. According to Isaiah, the Lord's house will be called "a house of prayer for all peoples" (Isa 56:1-8; Mass, Friday, third week).

If we refer back to what was said earlier on the unity of creation and on the disappointment of God, who then decides to renew the world and even sends his Son to establish a new paschal covenant, we will be struck by the way the liturgical texts of Advent focus on the idea of the regathering of the nations. The theme is both paschal and eschatological. God's plan of renewal will surely succeed, and that is a key element in Christian hope during the time of waiting.

St. Cyprian emphasizes the aspect of patient perseverance that must characterize our hope in what we do not yet see:

> Our Lord and Teacher has a salutary warning for us: "The one who endures to the end will be saved." And again: "If you continue in my word, you are truly my disciples, and you will know the truth, and the truth will make you free." We must therefore endure and persevere, dear brothers and sisters, so that, having been given the hope of truth and freedom, we may be able to attain that truth and that freedom. What makes us Christians, after all, is faith and hope; but if faith and hope are to reach fruition, we must be patient.
>
> It is not a present but a future glory that we seek, as Paul the Apostle reminds us: "In this hope we were saved. Now hope that is seen is not hope. For who hopes for what he sees? But if we hope for what we do not see, we wait for it with patience." Waiting and patience are necessary if we are to complete what we began and if we are to obtain what, by God's inspiration, we believe in and hope for.[7]

In the same spirit, the Liturgy of the Hours has taken as an Advent reading a passage from Vatican II's Dogmatic Constitution on the Church, which speaks of the eschatological nature of the pilgrim Church.

> The church, to which we are all called in Christ Jesus, and in which by the grace of God we attain holiness, will receive its perfection only in the glory of heaven, when the time for the renewal of all things will have come (Acts 3:21). At that time, together with the human race, the universe itself, which is so closely related to humanity and which through it attains its destiny, will be perfectly established in Christ (see Eph 1:10; Col 1:20; 2 Pet 3:10-13).
>
> Christ when he was lifted up from the earth drew all humanity to himself (see Jn 12:32 Greek text). Rising from the dead (see Rom 6:9) he sent his life-giving Spirit upon his disciples and through him set up his body which is the church as the universal sacrament of salvation. Sitting at the right hand of the Father he is continually active in the world in order to lead people to the church and through it to join them more closely to himself; by nourishing them with his own body and Blood, he makes them sharers in his glorious life. The promised and hoped for restoration, therefore, has already begun in Christ. It is carried forward in the sending of the holy Spirit and through him continues in the church in which, through faith, we learn the meaning of our earthly

life while, as we hope for the benefits which are to come, we bring to its conclusion the task allotted to us in the world by the Father, and so work out our salvation (see Phil 2:12).

Already the final age of the world is with us (see 1 Cor 10:11) and the renewal of the world is irrevocably under way; it is even now anticipated in a certain real way, for the church on earth is endowed already with a sanctity that is true though imperfect. However, until the arrival of the new heavens and the new earth in which justice dwells (see 2 Pet 3:13) the pilgrim church, in its sacraments and institutions, which belong to this present age, carries the mark of this world which will pass, and it takes its place among the creatures which groan and until now suffer the pains of childbirth and await the revelation of the children of God (see Rom 8:19-22).[8]

A Constructive Judgment

The Christian expectation is not only of a gathering on the last day but of a judgment as well. Consequently, the expectation is accompanied by vigilance.

When Jesus shows his intention of returning among people to gather the fruit that has been ripening there for him, he speaks of two purposes for his return: he returns to judge as well as to renew the world at the stage of maturation it will have achieved. In the Gospel of St. Matthew, return and retribution are connected: "For the Son of Man will come with his angels in his Father's glory, and then he will repay everyone according to his conduct" (Matt 16:27).

Later on, in a more detailed description, we see the Son of Man coming in his glory to the assembled nations and separating the sheep from the goats (Matt 25:31-46). St. Mark also points out, though in a more allusive way, the judgment that will come with Christ's return: "Whoever is ashamed of me and of my words in this faithless and sinful generation, the Son of Man will be ashamed of when he comes in his Father's glory with the holy angels" (Mark 8:38).

But we must avoid too narrow an understanding of the judgment. The judgment is in fact only a necessary moment in the restoration of a world from which all dross must be eliminated. That is precisely the point of the parable of the weeds that is told in Matthew 13 and that Christ himself then interprets:

Then, dismissing the crowds, he went into the house. His disciples approached him and said, "Explain to us the parable of the weeds in the field." He said in reply, "He who sows good seed is the Son of Man, the field is the world, the good seed the children of the kingdom. The weeds are the children of the evil one, and the enemy who sows them is the devil. The harvest is the end of the age, and the harvesters are angels. Just as weeds are collected and burned [up] with fire, so will it be at the end of the age. The Son of Man will send his angels, and they will collect out of his kingdom all who cause others to sin and all evildoers. They will throw them into the fiery furnace, where there will be wailing and grinding of teeth. Then the righteous will shine like the sun in the kingdom of their Father. Whoever has ears, ought to hear. (Matt 13:36-43)

This negative phase in the restoration guarantees the building of a new world with no trace of Satan or evil in it. All this will happen when "Heaven and earth will pass away" (Mark 13:31). For, Jesus says,

Amen, I say to you that you who have followed me, in the new age, when the Son of Man is seated on his throne of glory, will yourselves sit on twelve thrones, judging the twelve tribes of Israel. And everyone who has given up houses or brothers or sisters or father or mother or children or lands for the sake of my name will receive a hundred times more, and will inherit eternal life. (Matt 19:28-29)

The Twelve will be there with him, Christ promises:

In my Father's house there are many dwelling places. If there were not, would I have told you that I am going to prepare a place for you? And if I go and prepare a place for you, I will come back again and take you to myself, so that where I am you also may be. (John 14:2-3)

The whole Gospel, therefore, clearly manifests the certainty of a second coming that brings judgment, gathering, and renewal. The Acts of the Apostles reports what Peter said to the people of Jerusalem and thereby enables us to understand what we might call the early Church's theology of Advent. His sermons also show us what the main lines of our own theology of Advent should be.

Repent, therefore, and be converted, that your sins may be wiped away, and that the Lord may grant you times of refreshment and send you the Messiah already appointed for you, Jesus, whom heaven must receive until the times of universal restoration of which God spoke through the mouth of his holy prophets from of old. For Moses said:

"A prophet like me will the Lord, your God, raise up for you
    from among your own kinsmen;
to him you shall listen in all that he may say to you.
Everyone who does not listen to that prophet
    will be cut off from the people."

Moreover, all the prophets who spoke, from Samuel and those after-
wards, also announced these days. You are the children of the prophets
and of the covenant that God made with your ancestors when he said
to Abraham, "In your offspring all the families of the earth shall be
blessed." For you first, God raised up his servant and sent him to bless
you by turning each of you from your evil ways. (Acts 3:19-26)

We find here a concept identical with that in Matthew: Christ's
return is accompanied by judgment and the renewal of the world.
We should note the absence of any apocalyptic imagery and of any
preoccupation with the signs of the Lord's coming. The real issue is
the understanding of the present age, which was begun by Christ
and will reach its climax and end with his return. Repentance and
conversion hasten the time of definitive salvation and that restoration
of the world that Isaiah had foretold in his prophecy of new heavens
and a new earth (Isa 65:17; 66:22). But, though the parousia is certainly
kept in mind, it is not the principal focus of attention; the important
thing for the moment is to live properly in the present age, which
extends from the first coming of Christ to the establishment of the
everlasting kingdom.

St. Paul takes up the same theme when he addresses the philoso-
phers of Athens: "God has overlooked the times of ignorance, but
now he demands that all people everywhere repent because he has
established a day on which he will 'judge the world with justice'
through a man he has appointed, and he has provided confirmation
for all by raising him from the dead" (Acts 17:30-31).

He does not mention the renewal of the world, but he does show
how people should view the time that separates them from the unknown day of Christ's return. A day has been set for judgment; we
on earth, who are drawn by the risen Christ, must repent. That is
what the Thessalonians did, turning away from idols in order to serve
the living God and await his Son from heaven (1 Thess 1:9-10). We
know how these people impatiently awaited that great day and the
kinds of questions they asked about it (2 Thess 3:10-22). The Second
Letter of Peter shows that many were becoming discouraged and
bitter.

> Know this first of all, that in the last days scoffers will come [to] scoff, living according to their own desires and saying, "Where is the promise of his coming? From the time when our ancestors fell asleep, everything has remained as it was from the beginning of creation." They deliberately ignore the fact that the heavens existed of old and earth was formed out of water and through water by the word of God; through these the world that then existed was destroyed, deluged with water. The present heavens and earth have been reserved by the same word for fire, kept for the day of judgment and of destruction of the godless.
>
> But do not ignore this one fact, beloved, that with the Lord one day is like a thousand years and a thousand years like one day. The Lord does not delay his promise, as some regard "delay," but he is patient with you, not wishing that any should perish, but that all should come to repentance. (2 Pet 3:3-9)

Christians wait for the Lord. The words *"Marana tha"* (Lord, come!), which we find in St. Paul (1 Cor 16:22) and in the liturgical text in the *Didache* (10:6), show the desire of the community, expressed in prayer form, for the coming of the day of the Lord. We would mistake the emphasis in this expectation if we were to reduce it to an expectation of personal salvation. What is awaited is rather the salvation of all humankind and even of all creation.

> For creation awaits with eager expectation the revelation of the children of God; for creation was made subject to futility, not of its own accord but because of the one who subjected it, in hope that creation itself would be set free from slavery to corruption and share in the glorious freedom of the children of God. We know that all of creation is groaning in labor pains even until now; and not only that, but we ourselves, who have the firstfruits of the Spirit, we also groan within ourselves as we wait for adoption, the redemption of our bodies. (Rom 8:19-23)

All creation, then, exists in a perpetual Advent season as it waits to be delivered from corruption by an outpouring of God's glory. In Adam the world was fragmented by sin; the new Adam will restore the whole creation to unity.

Watchfulness: He Will Come Like a Thief

No one will be expecting the last day when it comes; it will be upon people before they become aware of it. In this respect the Flood is a good parallel. For those contemporary with the event, everything had been going on as before, as though nothing extraordinary were imminent: sin, false joy, the struggle for a livelihood and for mastery of others, the quest for importance, eroticism—in short, all that we see going on today in the lives of those who have no sense of permanent values. And it was all still going on when the Flood took them by surprise.

Christ's warning is clear: "So too, you also must be prepared, for at an hour you do not expect, the Son of Man will come" (Matt 24:44). Isaiah foresaw this coming. For him, it is not chiefly a day of catastrophe but the day when the Lord will come to gather the nations and to bring them into a kingdom of everlasting peace (Isa 2:1-5). The Church will take the same view and, in response to Isaiah's prophecy, will sing Psalm 122: "Let us go to the house of the LORD."

We can easily judge from the New Testament the reactions of the newborn Church as a whole and what it considered to be the meaning of its present life and of the world's historical existence.

St. Paul instructed his brothers and sisters, of course, on what their attitude ought to be. He has no teaching on the proximity of the last day. The only thing he has to say on this is what he received from the Lord, who describes his own coming as unexpected and sudden as the coming of a thief. The Letter to Titus offers a program of life for the time between Christ's first coming and his return.

> For the grace of God has appeared, saving all and training us to reject godless ways and worldly desires and to live temperately, justly, and devoutly in this age, as we await the blessed hope, the appearance of the glory of the great God and of our savior Jesus Christ. (Titus 2:11-13)

Paul calls for the proper use of created things; justice, that is, a life conformed to God's plan; devotion, that is, truthfulness in our attitude to God.

The Thessalonians were impatient and were thrown off the true course by an overly human interpretation of the parousia. The two letters to them likewise describe for us a very practical line to follow. Purity of life, charity, hard work (1 Thess 4:1-12, 13-22), prayer, and, again, hard work (2 Thess 3) should mark the Christian who lives in a pagan world. Such should be our life as we await our blessed hope, the glorious coming of our great God and Savior Jesus Christ.

Our ignorance of the moment of Christ's coming should be a spur to us. In correspondence with the Gospel of Mark (13:33-37; Mass, first Sunday [B]), Second Isaiah expresses our longing expectation, as he says to the Lord: "Oh, that you would rend the heavens and come down" (Isa 63:16b-17; 64:1, 3b-8; first Sunday [B]). After the Exile the people of God ardently desires its own complete and lasting restoration, but it knows that God alone can save a nation that has been destroyed and restore its unity. Psalm 80, which is sung in response to the reading from Isaiah, expresses the drama in lyric terms: "O God, bring us back; / let your face shine on us, and we shall be saved. / . . . O shepherd of Israel, hear us. . . . Rouse up your might and come to save us" (80:4, 2-3; responsorial psalm, first Sunday [B]).

Such is our situation in the Church between the two comings of Christ. But we are not abandoned and left to our own resources: "you are not lacking in any spiritual gift as you wait for the revelation of our Lord Jesus Christ" (1 Cor 1:3-9; Mass, first Sunday [B]).

In any event, our redemption is near at hand, and we must be vigilant. This means abandoning vices and attitudes irreconcilable with a genuine expectation of the Lord's coming. This is the warning given by a number of texts used in the Advent liturgy. Be watchful (Matt 24:37-44, first Sunday [A]; Mark 13:33-37, first Sunday [B]; Luke 21:25-28, 34-36, first Sunday [C]) and prepare the way for the Lord (Matt 3:1-6, second Sunday [A]; Mark 1:1-8, second Sunday [B]; Luke 3:1-6, second Sunday [C]): these are the themes most emphasized. We must live as children of the light who have put on Christ, for salvation is now nearer at hand than it was when we first received the faith (1 Thess 3:12–4:2, first Sunday [C]).

And yet all this does not eliminate optimism, for the end of time will also be a constructive event. The Lord who is coming is "our justice" (Jer 33:14-16, first Sunday [C]). We must ask him to lead us along the right way and to teach us, for he is the God who saves, and the ways of the Lord are love and truth (Ps 25, first Sunday [C]). May the Lord permit no earthly undertaking to hinder us as we set out in haste to meet his Son; may he grant us the heavenly wisdom that will prepare us to welcome him and to gain us admittance into his company (collect, second Sunday). May he grant his faithful the resolve to meet Christ with righteous deeds at his coming, and may he call them at the judgment to take possession of the heavenly kingdom (collect, first Sunday).

Waiting for What Is Already Here

In Israel, even in the time of John the Baptist, waiting meant hoping for what was already possessed. For there were signs that proved that the object of hope was not a poetic abstraction. The object of hope was rather a concrete situation that was already present, even though still awaited.

As we have already pointed out, this paradox expresses what is specific to Christian hope: we wait for what we already possess! The same paradox marks the liturgy of Advent, which stresses the presence, here and now, of what is expected at the end of time. The texts have to be read carefully in their contexts in order to eliminate any ambiguity. But then, Jesus himself, as we know, did not hesitate to speak of the kingdom as already present in our midst. Among the signs of this presence of a reality whose full manifestation we still await, the following are important: the cures, the preaching of the Good News to the poor, and the prefigurations of the messianic banquet.

The Blind See

The cures are proof that the reign of God is already present. Christ's answer to the messengers from John the Baptist is unambiguous: "Go and tell John what you have seen and heard: the blind regain their sight, the lame walk, lepers are cleansed, the deaf hear, the dead are raised, the poor have the good news proclaimed to them" (Luke 7:19-23, Wednesday, third week).

When St. Matthew relates the cures that Christ wrought, his intention evidently is to show that the messianic age has begun. He records Jesus' reply to John in the very same words as Luke (Matt 11:2-11, third Sunday [A]). Quite naturally, the first reading, chosen to correspond to the Gospel, is a prophecy of Isaiah that lists the signs of the Messiah's coming:

> Be strong, fear not!
> Here is your God,
>   he comes with vindication;
> with divine recompense
>   he comes to save you.
> Then will the eyes of the blind be opened,
>   the ears of the deaf be cleared;

then will the lame leap like a stag,
    then the tongue of the mute will sing. (Isa 35:1-19, third Sunday [A])

In the weekday readings of Advent, there are many accounts of the cures that are signs that the messianic age is here. St. Matthew goes out of his way to emphasize the coming of God's salvation. He has numerous reports of divine actions that show God taking the initiative in renewing his relationship with the world and with people. Jesus invites the afflicted to come to him and be consoled (Matt 11:28-30, Wednesday, second week). A reading from Isaiah reinforces this theology of the divine initiative in the work of our salvation: it is the Lord who gives strength to the fainting and vigor to the weak (Isa 40:25-31, Wednesday, second week). Jesus takes pity on the crowd and bids his disciples freely give what they have freely received (Matt 9:35–10:1, 5a, 6-8, Saturday, first week). Isaiah tells us we need only cry out to the Lord and he will have pity on us (Isa 30:19-21, 23-26, Saturday, first week). The Lord's attentive compassion is directed first and foremost to the little ones, whom he does not wish to see lost. At this moment he sees himself as the shepherd in charge of them and therefore leaves the other sheep behind to go in search of the one who has strayed (Matt 18:12-14, Tuesday, second week). He is the loving Shepherd who collects his lambs and carries them on his breast; he takes care of the sheep that are nursing their young (Isa 40:1-11, Tuesday, second week).

The Lord works many miracles. St. Matthew tells us that great crowds came to him bringing the lame, the blind, the maimed, the dumb, and many other kinds of sick people; they brought them to Jesus and he cured them (Matt 15:29-37, Wednesday, first week). He is indeed the Lord who the Apocalypse of Isaiah says will wipe the tears from every face (Isa 25:6-10a, Wednesday, first week). In particular, he cures two blind men who believe in him. Their cry of faith, "Son of David, have pity on us," touched him (Matt 9:27-31, Friday, first week). We recall that Isaiah saw in the curing of the blind a sign that the kingdom is at hand (Isa 29:17-24, Friday, first week).

But St. Matthew also notes, on several occasions, how unbelief blinds individuals: they will not listen either to John the Baptist or to the Son (Matt 17:10-13, Saturday, second week); John the Baptist has come, but they have not believed his message (Matt 21:28-32, Tuesday, third week).

St. Luke likewise recounts the miracles of Jesus. In Jesus the reign of God is truly present, for he has the power to forgive sins (Luke 5:17-26, Monday, second week).

The cures, then, are not only responses to faith; nor are they worked simply in order to arouse faith. They are also a sign that the kingdom is here.

In a reading chosen for the Office on Wednesday of the Second Week of Advent, St. Augustine speaks to us in his commentary on the psalms. The central theme of the passage is that God fulfills his promises to us through the mediation of his Son.

> [God] has promised men divinity, mortals immortality, sinners justification, the poor a rising to glory.
>
> But, brethren, because God's promises seemed impossible to men— equality with the angels in exchange for mortality, corruption, poverty, weakness, dust and ashes—God not only made a written contract with men, to win their belief but also established a mediator of his good faith, not a prince or angel or archangel, but his only Son. He wanted, through his Son, to show us and give us the way he would lead us to the goal he has promised.
>
> It was not enough for God to make his Son our guide to the way; he made him the way itself, that you might travel with him as leader, and by him as the way. . . .
>
> All this had therefore to be prophesied, foretold, and impressed on us as an event in the future, in order that we might wait for it in faith, not find it a sudden and dreadful reality.[9]

Thus it was through increasingly clear signs that the age to come was proclaimed and is now present.

The Good News Is Preached to the Poor

We have a sufficient grasp by now of what the word "poor" means in the Old Testament. Let us sum up its content briefly.

It is the presence or absence of this poverty that determined the course of Israel's history from its very beginnings as recorded in the first three chapters of Genesis. This poverty, as we have already seen, is not destitution, whether material or intellectual or social, but an attitude of humility and detachment in the presence of the Lord, along with the humble acknowledgment of one's sins. We must note, however, that the "poor" of the Beatitudes are not simply those "spiritually poor," while the material poverty from which the Israelites suffered during their Exile stimulated them to "spiritual poverty."[10] It was the "poverty" of the Israelites, with its various components, that moved the Lord to action: "I have witnessed the affliction [= poverty] of my people in Egypt and have heard their cry against their taskmasters" (Exod 3:7).

Their affliction becomes an occasion for the manifestation of God's goodness; he hears the prayers of those who cry out to him (Judg 3:9; 3:15; 4:3). When God protects the oppressed, this is not simply a companionable act on his part; what he is concerned with, above all, is the restoration of justice, for justice is a reflection of his being. Humans must be good as God is good—this is the real basis of the whole legislation on behalf of the poor. Biblical poverty cannot be reduced to material poverty; the Scriptures, after all, consider wealth to be a gift of God. Biblical poverty has a spiritual dimension; the real "poor one of Yahweh" is the one who serves God and his brothers and sisters, the one described for us in the Servant poem of Isaiah 42.

One of the signs Jesus gave to the disciples of John the Baptist was that "the poor have the good news proclaimed to them" (Luke 7:19-23, Wednesday, third week). Second Isaiah had spoken of this sign: "The spirit of the Lord GOD is upon me, / because the LORD has anointed me; / he has sent me to bring glad tidings to the poor" (Isa 61:1, 10-11, third Sunday [B]).

The natural response to this prophecy of Isaiah, which Christ was later to read and apply to himself in the synagogue at Nazareth (Luke 4:16-21), is the *Magnificat*, in which the Virgin shows herself to be the humble servant whose role is to give birth to the Messiah: "he has looked upon his handmaid's lowliness" (Luke 1:48).

Zephaniah likewise puts messianic salvation within the reach of the poor: "I will leave as a remnant in your midst / a people humble and lowly, / Who shall take refuge in the name of the LORD" (Zeph 3:12; see Tuesday, third week). For "This lowly one called; the LORD heard" (Ps 34:7; refrain for responsorial psalm, Tuesday, third week).

The preaching of the Good News to the poor is a sign that the Messiah is here. The right moment has come: there are people whose hearts humility has opened and who are ready to receive the message that salvation is now given to the nations. Such universalism is a further sign of the messianic age. The Lord cannot forget the poor but stays with them. Now the Lord comes, preceded by the proclamation of the Good News of his coming.

The Messianic Banquet

A further sign of the presence of the kingdom is the banquet. Here, as with the poor, we have a basic image of Scripture. A meal is a sign of the restoration of union with God and a sign too of the world's renewal. Eating at the Lord's table is a favorite theme of the Bible, and Christ will often use the image of a meal. The ancient liturgies realized how important a theme this was for the period of waiting. Our own liturgy has taken as an Advent reading the multiplication of the loaves, with its several levels of significance (Matt 15:29-37, Wednesday, first week). Isaiah speaks of the joy of being at the Lord's table (Isa 25:6-10a, same day). The book of Proverbs uses the same image to describe the joy of the wise person (Prov 5:1).

The two themes of banquet and the poor are very closely linked, since the banqueters will be all who are hungry; their lack of money does not matter (Isa 55:1). The banquet is essentially an image related to the parousia. Jesus describes it to his disciples as a meal to be shared by all who believe as did Abraham, Isaac, and Jacob (Matt 8:11). It is the meal at which we shall meet the Lord; therefore, we must be wearing a wedding garment (Matt 22:11-14). Revelation gives a poetic description of the parousaic supper: "Behold, I stand at the door and knock. If anyone hears my voice and opens the door, [then] I will enter his house and dine with him, and he with me" (Rev 3:20).

Waiting for the Incarnation

When St. Mark recounts the first multiplication of the loaves, he apparently wishes us to see the multiplied loaves as a sign of Jesus' word and Jesus' body (Mark 6:30-34). St. John speaks of Jesus as the real Bread (John 6:32).

The multiplication of the loaves is both an eschatological sign and a sign of the incarnation of the Word, who is Bread from heaven.

We shall not insist further on the "sacramental" character of the Christmas feast as an actualization of the incarnation. It is this actualization that prescribes the very nature of our waiting. If we are to reach the parousia, we must pass by way of efficacious signs, of which the incarnation is the first. We are capable of sharing in the final banquet at Christ's return because we journey toward him now in the light of his incarnation, which is prolonged through signs and which is the ground sustaining all the other signs of salvation. For now, "we recognize in him God made visible" (Preface I of the Nativity of the Lord).

Christians are now in contact with the mystery that is rendered present for them. As they wait each year for the incarnation, they acquire a deeper understanding of the signs of salvation. They discover anew the Church and its sacred signs; in the Body of Christ as signified in the Church and the sacraments, they discover anew humankind and the world, which are called to undergo the radical transformation that the incarnation effects in all things. To wait for the incarnation is deliberately to enter more deeply into death with Christ so that we may rise with him and take possession of the kingdom with him. Consequently, to wait for the incarnation is also to wait for Christ's return at the end of time.

To accept the law of incarnation is the humble attitude of the believer, the attitude of one who is poor. People can enter into glory only if they obey the humbling law of incarnation and learn to discover God through signs that are tailored to their limitations and thus could easily prevent them from seeing through to the riches they contain. For the Church to celebrate the incarnation, then, is to become aware once again of what she is: both divine and human. She is required to try to make the human in her ever more worthy of the divine. She is forced to examine her conscience, for though she is the instrument of Christ's presence on earth, she is not Christ and must strive at every moment to resemble him more and more. The celebration of the incarnation is also the occasion for the Church to see whether or not her signs correspond sufficiently to the law established by the incarnation, in which they have their roots. According to that law, her signs must serve the sanctification of humanity and the transformation of the world, as well as the glory of God.

Waiting, Even in Our Day?

All that has been said thus far by way of explanation may leave us still in doubt. Can the kind of ideas we have been developing awaken any chord in our contemporaries?

At first sight the answer might well seem to be no. And yet the minds of many today seem to show two tendencies: a type of despair but also an irresistible desire to build a new future.

Despite this desire, when we look, even as believers, at our present world, the success of Christianity seems dubious. Christians cannot, of course, believe that Christianity will simply fail. They are, however, tempted to minimize the achievements of the past, and such an attitude will, if their faith is not fed and if it does not send down deeper roots, close their mind to the theology we have been exposing in these pages.

At this point, then, it will be in place to attempt a brief analysis of the difficulties Christians of today find in "waiting for the Lord's coming."

Renewal of the "Soul" for a Purely Future World?

We may well ask whether the basic obstacle is not our progressive estrangement from the Scriptures and their outlook. The estrangement began at least as early as the tenth century. Philosophical systems, applied to the elucidation of Christian dogma, have divided soul from body, and the present world (which is always evil) from the future world (which does away with the present world). Some sense of the destiny proper to the whole of creation may have been preserved, but any notion of ongoing renewal has been limited to the soul, which seeks renewal with a view to a world that is wholly future.

This dichotomy is undoubtedly responsible, in good measure, for the reactions we see today. "Waiting" is at best thought of as the waiting of the soul for perfection—a soul that alone is to be saved and to grow in charity. There is little or no room in this kind of expectation for the human person in its entirety. A "spirituality" thus limited to the soul alone is disappearing, but to the extent that it survives, it has no room for the kind of hopes that move people today.

Once we admit that God intervenes in the world, that he has intervened to the point of entering the world himself, and that he continues to act in the world through his Spirit, we can no longer make the soul alone the focus of properly Christian expectation. No, the expectation embraces the whole human person. Moreover, the expectation cannot focus on a future world, in the sense that the present world must simply disappear and give way to another. The building of a new world has already begun, and the elements of the present world are contributing to it.

When we think of God intervening, we are too quick to conceive his action after the pattern of ours. How, for example, do we conceive the institution of the sacraments? For many Christians, the institution means that Christ simply created the saving sign in its entirety. There was no background, no religious context we need consider. The sign whose role is to change and renew us by bringing us into contact with God could not (we think) be shaped out of what already existed; there must be a new creation and a total contrast with all that had gone before.

This picture is quite false. It is one of the great merits of contemporary theology to have shown, on the basis of history, that Christ, in "instituting" a sacrament, gave new content to a preexisting form. Here we have a parallel to the manner in which we ought to understand our expectation of a new world. The renewal is not something that belongs to a future, different world; rather, it occurs within preexisting forms. Consequently, we can say that our expectation of a new world is not purely passive but that we must ourselves work for the transformation of the content of a world whose structures already exist.

Expectation of the renewal of the human person and of our world is both possible and encouraging to us. It will draw out all our energies and make us share in the common task of building a future whose firstfruits are already ours.

Vocation of Humans and Humankind

Such an expectation, if conceived as we have explained, is really an essential element in the vocation both of humans and of humankind. But here again we must grasp things correctly. The Christian expectation does not turn our attention from essential changes in ourselves and the world, as though we had to watch these passively and from a distance. On the contrary, as we obey God, we are responsible for such changes taking place. God intervenes in history; the first stimulus to renewal comes from God; our first activity must be to listen to God. But none of this makes us any less responsible for the future and the great restoration. We may not wait passively for it to come about but must work actively and intelligently to bring it to pass.

Our contribution, however, is a collective one. We cannot work in isolation or we will fail. It is as part of a community that we actively await our own and the world's restoration.

Interior Dualism and Desacralization

Such a view is, theoretically, able to rouse individuals and the world to enthusiasm for a future that has already begun. In the concrete, distortions inevitably occur. I regard two deviations in particular as serious and capable of checking all real progress. One is an interior dualism; the other is a desacralization that affects the Christian's own interior life.

Spiritual or interior dualism has always existed. The great spiritual writers have warned of the danger. St. Paul was convinced of its reality and found fault with himself on account of it: "For I do not do the good I want, but I do the evil I do not want" (Rom 7:19).

At the moment, however, I am not thinking of this dualism insofar as it affects us all because of humanity's inherent weakness. Weakness, after all, does not destroy the will to seek the good. I see this dualism at work rather in the attitude that would cut one's religious life off from one's ordinary life, as though the religious life were in a sealed compartment of its own and a person could think of religious problems only at certain special moments. In recent times people have become more aware of the unity there must be between what they like to call "spiritual life" and "the political order."

As far as I can see, this subtle but convenient separation of life into compartments is at work every time the Church or an individual Christian stagnates and is content to indulge in purely "spiritual" expectations. My purpose here is not to arraign anybody or to give a course in spirituality. My concern is simply to emphasize the problem; others can go into it in greater detail. I wish only to remind the reader that the attitude I have been describing makes Christian expectation impossible and makes it impossible too to enter into a liturgy whose purpose is to give vitality to that expectation. Fortunately, the thirst for authenticity is so strong today that the compartmentalization I have described is, if not impossible (the unconscious and human weakness are always at work!), at least increasingly infrequent. This is to the credit of today's Church.

The second deviation is an erroneous kind of interior desacralization. We tend to separate the sacred from the profane within us. (In so doing, we find ourselves back in the dualism just described.) Biblical figures know no separation between sacred and profane. For the Bible, the only thing truly sacred is God himself, and creatures cannot exist except to the extent that they are properly ordered to this one sacred reality. Human existence, therefore, would be meaningless if it were not directed to the sacred, even though human existence in itself is profane. There is a right kind of secularization: that which attributes to humanity and the world their true value; God also is truly sacred; only Christ's redemptive action and the sacraments that continue his work among us can sacralize our world, which is profane. Consequently, humanity and the world truly have meaning only when they are ordered to the sacred.

In other words, once humanity and creation become their own end, once they choose for themselves a goal other than the one that God and Christ assign them, we have a false secularization and an erroneous kind of desacralization. Unfortunately, these deviations do not remain in the order of ideas alone; they are a rejection of God and destroy his plan.

Faith, Action, and Expectation

As we can easily see, waiting or expectation is possible only where there is faith. "Faith" here is a wide-ranging virtue. We must have faith not only in God who is Master of history and rules the world and its progress but also in a Church that is the extension on earth of the glorified heavenly body of Christ and that is able to actualize Christ's presence and his mysteries so that they may contribute to the ultimate restoration of the world. Without this faith (which is also indispensable for the reception of the sacraments), the Advent liturgy becomes simply a seductive poetic representation of the path followed by God's people.

At this point we may take up our earlier train of thought and ask: If the believer is one who expects, what can and ought he expect? How is he to wait?

Believers today, like believers in Old and New Testament days, are not to expect that their life will be humanly happy because they await the last day. At the same time, it seems inaccurate to speak of a "spiritual" waiting. After all, as we said earlier, it is an entire person who is advancing, together with this world, toward the end of time, and there is no turning back. Now, while such expectation does not have human happiness as its primary result, neither does it exclude such a result. On the contrary, we may say that the awareness of the Lord's real presence in the midst of people in this world is a source of harmony and balance in all the activities of life, whether in the sphere of human love or in scientific research, artistic endeavor, and all else that brings a person happiness and well-being.

Consciousness of the presence of the Lord who guides the world and each individual toward the future he wills gives us a sense of optimism and a constancy that enables us to learn serenity through conflict and to pass unscathed through all situations, foreseen and unforeseen. No circumstances can dismay or lead astray one whose hope is directed by God himself.

We must be honest, however, and admit that these dispositions and such a harmony of mentality and reactions with those displayed by the Church in the Advent liturgy are not universally found among Christians. We might even be inclined to say that they will be found only in an elite (a cultural elite as well as a chosen body of faithful). That is a false impression. A deep faith is indeed required if we are to enter fully into what the Church proposes to us; on the other hand, the biblical themes, once given a modicum of explanation, have power to lay hold on those who are looking for an authentic Christianity.

We may also say that the liturgy, as we have been describing it, is congenial to the outlook of our contemporaries as they inquire into the meaning of the human person, the sacred, and the world. The Lord already dwells in humans and in the world he seeks to restore. Consequently, humans and the world are not simply passively undergoing a remaking but are taking an active part in their own renewal. They share the sacredness proper to everyone who is moving toward a future that is wholly focused on a unity that will restore, in a more perfect form, the unity that creation originally possessed.

The demands that such a vision makes are indeed great. It would be a mistake, however, to believe that a superhuman life of waiting is the only adequate response. Far from it! Once people lead a completely and concretely human life in a human world, but a life that also has for its center the already present reality of the future, they will be capable of giving an authentic response to the demands inherent in waiting and expectation. The human being who most perfectly embodies the expectation of the world to come is one who lives a humanly normal life in a fully normal way. Such persons, when they are believers, show in the whole of their lives a divine balance between prudence and boldness, peace and conflict, love and reserve.

We prepare, amid waiting, for the future world whenever we sacrifice our selfish interests and accept life as it is and events as they are, that is, as an unpredictable sum total of joys, sufferings and anxieties, brutal separations and painful confrontations. The active acceptance of all this is required of us on our mysterious journey through time to the end the Lord has foreseen. In suffering as in joy (we have little power over either), we are summoned to travel over high mountains, in realms far beyond our normal human condition and at altitudes where, left to ourselves, we could not breathe. Yet we are to journey as though that air were native to us.

Structure and Themes
of the Advent Liturgy

4. INTRODUCTION

Structure of the Sundays and the Weeks

As we have seen, the Church had a twofold expectation in the celebration of her Advent liturgy and had to make both of these clear to the faithful. She could not speak of the one without the other. When the time came, however, for the postconciliar reform of the liturgy, some of those involved wanted to make of Advent simply a time of preparation for Christmas, a time of waiting for the incarnation of the Word. But they forgot that the Church can never celebrate a liturgy without emphasizing the eschatological dimension of her hope. The real need, then, was for celebrations that would accustom the people to seeing (and not just in a theoretical way) both objects of the Church's expectation in their intimate relationship. This would not, of course, make it wrong to lay a greater emphasis on the expectation of the incarnation as the feast of Christmas draws near.

In order to develop more fully the authentic spirit of waiting, some liturgists urged a return to a season of six Sundays and thus to the earlier tradition. It was decided, however, to retain a four-Sunday season. But at the same time, the liturgy of the season was notably enriched. In the ancient tradition with its six Sundays, no special readings were provided for the weekdays; this continued to be the case in the later tradition with its four-week season. Now, the general principle that increased use should be made of Scripture in the liturgy has led to an extensive development of the already rich Advent season.

Thus, though Advent still has only four Sundays, there is now a three-year cycle of readings for these Sundays (Years A, B, and C). Consequently, from the viewpoint of the use of Scripture, we have twelve different celebrations for the Sundays of Advent. The liturgical reform did not stop there but has also provided readings for each day of the four weeks. The Sundays each have three readings; the weekdays each have two (the same each year). The readings have been so organized that each of the four Sundays emphasizes a different aspect of the mystery; the aspect proper to each Sunday receives several varying expressions in the course of the three-year cycle. The readings on the weekdays are usually related to the theology expressed in the preceding Sunday's liturgy.

Let us look a little more closely at the structure of the Sundays. The first two Sundays focus chiefly on the second coming of Christ; as we have already pointed out, they also express expectation of the incarnation, but the emphasis is not on this. If we wish to give a descriptive title to the three-year cycle proper to each of these first two Sundays, we can say that the first emphasizes the coming of the Lord and the attitude of vigilance that marks our expectation of it; a suitable title for this week of the cycle would be: "Vigilant waiting for the Lord who is coming." The second Sunday concentrates on the preparation for this coming, and the readings naturally refer to the warnings issued by John the Baptist. The title for the readings proper to the second Sunday would be: "The warning of John the Baptist: Prepare the way of the Lord."

The third Sunday has a special function. It has traditionally given expression to the joy Christians feel at the coming that is now imminent. In the reformed liturgy the third Sunday retains this purpose and tone. It concentrates not only on the future coming but on the signs of the actual presence of the messianic kingdom; in other words, it looks to Christ already present and to Christ who is coming. It is thus a kind of transitional Sunday between the first two, which express a general attitude of expectation, and the fourth and last Sunday, which concentrates clearly on expectation of the incarnation. The readings for the third Sunday might be titled: "The messianic age is here. Rejoice!"

There is no difficulty about the interpretation of the fourth Sunday; its celebration is clearly a preparation for "The incarnation of the Word."

A table will be given, a little further on, that contains the title of each Sunday, a list of the readings, and a few words to sum up the content of each reading; a similar table will be given of the weekday readings. To simplify our constant references to the readings, each will be given a number: 1 to 36 for the Sundays, 37 to 84 for the weekdays. We shall also provide a table of the biblical readings in the Liturgy of the Hours (nos. 85 to 111).

Liturgical Reading of Scripture

In this section of the book we intend to treat at least each of the Sundays as a well-defined entity. The procedure is justified, because the texts were chosen so as to form a whole, without, however, forcing them to make all three express the same theme.

In order to understand the liturgical theology expressed in celebrations such as those of the Sundays of Advent, we must, I think, approach them in three different ways. The first is to get a panoramic view of all the Sundays in the series and to uncover the continuity that gives this liturgical season its specific character.

The second approach, and the one that seeks a deeper penetration, requires more attention, for it has to do with the authentically liturgical reading of the Bible.

What do we mean when we speak of a "liturgical reading of the Bible"? To begin with, it cannot mean the abandonment of all scientific exegesis. A strict exegesis, such as is now practiced in universities and other centers and given to us in books by experts, is an indispensable basis for further study. But, given such a basis, the liturgical reading of Scripture still retains its special character.

Let us explain by taking a concrete example. Usually the general lines of the theology expressed in a celebration of the word are given by the gospel. Take the familiar passage in which Zacchaeus climbs a tree in order to catch sight of the Lord; Jesus sees him and visits his home (Luke 19:1-10). An exegetical commentary will study each point in the passage and try to situate it in its proper historical and social framework. Now, the gospel in itself has numerous theological aspects; to develop all of them would be to compose a commentary on the passage, not to do a liturgical reading of it. For, in sheer point of fact, when this particular passage is used on the day of the consecration of a church, the emphasis is on the Lord's coming into the home of Zacchaeus; that is why the passage was chosen, and all other aspects of the passage are secondary in this context.

When we read the same passage on the thirty-first Sunday of the year, what is the main point in it that makes it appropriate to this new context? Well, the first reading, which is from the Old Testament, is intended to correspond to the gospel passage and therefore can give an indication of why the latter was chosen. The Old Testament passage is from the book of Wisdom (11:22–12:2) and speaks of God's long patience as he actively seeks the conversion of individuals. This tells us that the main point in the gospel is not Christ's coming to the home of Zacchaeus but rather the process leading to faith. Zacchaeus wants to see Jesus and does everything he can to see him as he really is. Christ responds to Zacchaeus' desire, and the latter enters upon the path of conversion, as he shows by telling the Lord how he intends to live as one converted.

Sometimes, though not always, the second reading on the Sundays of the year will add details that confirm the interpretation already made of the gospel. That is the case here. Paul tells the Thessalonians that God is constantly calling us and endeavoring to make our faith alive and active (2 Thess 1:11–2:2).

Now, in all this we are not trying to compose a commentary on the gospel passage but simply determining how, in the liturgical context, we are to read the gospel; we are learning which aspect or teaching of the passage we are intended to concentrate on, while treating everything else as secondary. This second approach to the liturgical theology of a given celebration is not always easy, but it is essential.

There is a third approach, a third level of reading, as it were. Here it is a reading of the entire Liturgy of the Word as it presents itself to us. It may be that the chant that introduces the gospel will give us the essential point of the day's liturgy. The entrance antiphon, the collect, and sometimes the communion antiphon that picks up something from the gospel may also help us determine the essential point that the Liturgy of the Word as a whole intends to proclaim.

In the following pages we shall be using the threefold approach we have been describing. This does not mean that we will expressly use the three successive methods; for the most part we shall simply present the results reached through the application of the three types of reading.

The earlier chapters of the book have given a general theology of Advent. The last few pages have sketched an overall view of the Sundays of Advent. Now we turn to the themes proper to each of the four weeks.

Readings for the Sundays of Advent

Sundays	Prophet
	1 A The nations gather; Isa 2:1-5
1. Vigilant waiting for the Lord	2 B May God come down; Isa 63:16a-17; 64:1, 3b-8
	3 C A just shoot; Jer 33:14-16
	10 A The Spirit of the Lord is upon him; Isa 11:1-10
2. Warning of John the Baptist: Prepare the way of the Lord	11 B Fill in the valleys; Isa 40:1-5, 9-11
	12 C Every lofty mountain is laid low; Bar 5:1-9
	19 A Cures: Signs of the times; Isa 35:1-6a, 10
3. The Messianic	20 B The Good News to the poor; Isa 61:1-2, 10-11
	21 C Rejoice! God is in your midst; Zeph 3:14-18a
	28 A A virgin shall give birth; Isa 7:10-14
4. The incarnation of the Word	29 B Your house forever before me; 2 Sam 7:1-5, 8b-12, 14a, 16
	30 C She who is to give birth; Mic 5:2-5a

Apostle	Gospel
4 A The day is near; Rom 13:11-14	7 A Watch! Matt 24:37-44
5 B Day of the Lord; 1 Cor 1:3-9	8 B Watch! Mark 13:33-37
6 C Day of the Lord's coming; 1 Thess 3:12–4:2	9 C Watch! Luke 21:25-28, 34-36
13 A Promises fulfilled in Jesus; Rom 15:4-9	16 A Prepare the way; Matt 3:1-12
14 B New heavens and a new earth; 2 Pet 3:8-14	17 B Prepare the way; Mark 1:1-8
15 C Day of the Lord's coming; Phil 1:4-6, 8-11	18 C Prepare the way; Luke 3:1-6
22 A Patience until the Lord comes; Jas 5:7-10	25 A Cures as signs; Matt 11:2-11
23 B Joy at the Lord's coming; 1 Thess 5:16-24	26 B Christ in our midst; John 1:6-8, 19-28
24 C Rejoice! The Lord is here; Phil 4:4-7	27 C A mightier is coming; Luke 3:10-18
31 A Of David's line according to the flesh; Rom 1:1-7	34 A Message to Joseph; Matt 1:18-24
32 B The mystery revealed to all; Rom 16:25-27	35 B Annunciation to Mary; Luke 1:26-38
33 C Christ, coming, says, "Here I am"; Heb 10:5-10	36 C Message to Elizabeth; Luke 1:39-45

Readings for the Weekdays of Advent

1	Monday	37	Gathering of the nations in peace; Isa 2:1-5[1]	38	They will come from the east and the west; Matt 8:5-11
	Tuesday	39	The Spirit of the Lord is upon him; Isa 11:1-10	40	The Father revealed in the Son; Luke 10:21-24
	Wednesday	41	Joy at the table of the Lord; Isa 25:6-10a	42	Cures and multiplications of loaves; Matt 15:29-37
	Thursday	43	Let a just nation enter in; Isa 26:1-6	44	Doing the Father's will; Matt 7:21, 24-27
	Friday	45	The blind shall see; Isa 29:17-24	46	Cure of two blind men who have faith; Matt 9:27-31
	Saturday	47	The Lord hears our cry; Isa 30:19-21, 23-26	48	Jesus has pity on the crowd; Matt 9:35–10:1, 5a, 6-8
2	Monday	49	God comes to save us; Isa 35:1-10	50	The miracles of Jesus; Luke 5:17-26
	Tuesday	51	God comes to renew the world; Isa 40:1-11	52	God does not wish the little ones to be lost; Matt 18:12-14
	Wednesday	53	The Lord is the strength of the weary; Isa 40:25-31	54	Come to me, all who are weary; Matt 11:28-30
	Thursday	55	The redeemer, the Holy One of Israel; Isa 41:13-20	56	John the Baptist, greatest of the prophets; Matt 11:11-15
	Friday	57	Observing the commandments; Isa 48:17-19	58	They listen neither to John nor to the Son; Matt 11:16-19
	Saturday	59	Elias will return;[2] Sir 48:1-3, 9-11	60	Elias has come and not been recognized; Matt 17:10-13
3	Monday	61	A star rises out of Jacob; Num 24:2-7, 15-17a	62	Baptism of Jesus; Matt 21:23-27
	Tuesday	63	Messianic salvation and the poor; Zeph 3:1-2, 9-13	64	John came, and they did not believe him; Matt 21:28-32
	Wednesday	65	Let the heavens open; Isa 45:6b-8, 18, 21b-25	66	The kingdom is present; Luke 7:19-23
	Thursday	67	The Lord takes back the deserted wife; Isa 54:1-10	68	John prepares the way; Luke 7:24-30
	Friday	69	The temple, a true house of prayer; Isa 56:1-3a, 6-8	70	John is a lamp burning bright; John 5:33-36
	December 17	71	The scepter shall remain with Judah; Gen 49:2, 8-10	72	Genealogy of Jesus; Matt 1:1-17
	December 18	73	A righteous shoot; Jer 23:5-8	74	Jesus, son of David, born of Mary; Matt 1:18-24
	December 19	75	Birth of Samson foretold by an angel; Judg 13:2-7, 24-25a	76	Birth of John the Baptist foretold by an angel; Luke 1:5-25
	December 20	77	A virgin shall conceive; Isa 7:10-14	78	You will conceive and give birth to a son; Luke 1:26-28
	December 21	79	The beloved comes from the mountains; Song 2:8-14	80	The visitation; Luke 1:39-42
	December 22	81	Anna gives thanks for the birth of Samuel; 1 Sam 1:24-28	82	God has done great things for me; Luke 1:46-56
	December 23	83	Elias will come before the day of the Lord; Mal 3:1-4; 23-24	84	Birth of John the Baptist; Luke 1:57-66

Scripture Readings in the Liturgy of the Hours

First Week

85 *Sunday*: Isa 1:1-18
Exhortation to conversion so as to
offer sacrifice. Israel has not acknowledged its God.

86 *Monday*: Isa 1:21-27; 2:1-5
Israel is unfaithful. Sion is the center
of the eschatological kingdom.

87 *Tuesday*: Isa 2:6-22; 4:2-6
The Lord comes to judge. He will renew
the world at the end of time.

88 *Wednesday*: Isa 5:1-7
The vineyard of the Lord, who sings a
song of love for his people; they must
change and be converted.

89 *Thursday*: Isa 16:1-5; 17:4-8
A kingdom of mercy is proclaimed.
Sion is a refuge for the Moabites.

90 *Friday*: Isa 19:16-25
Future conversion of the Egyptians
and Assyrians.

91 *Saturday*: Isa 21:6-12
Fall of Babylon.

Second Week

92 *Sunday*: Isa 22:8b-23
Pride and punishment of Jerusalem
and Shebna.

93 *Monday*: Isa 24:1-18
The manifestation of the Lord on
his "day."

94 *Tuesday*: Isa 24:19–25:5
The earth quakes. Judgment and reign
of Yahweh. Song of the saved.

95 *Wednesday*: Isa 25:6–26:6
The banquet of the Lord; Moab declared
a rebel. Hymn of triumph.

96 *Thursday*: Isa 26:7-21
The judgments of the Lord.
The resurrection.

97 *Friday*: Isa 27:1-13
The Lord's vineyard. Restoration of
Israel. The deserted city.

98 *Saturday*: Isa 29:1-8
God's judgment on Jerusalem.

Third Week

99 *Sunday*: Isa 29:13-24
Religious formalism. The Lord threatens.
Salvation on the last day.

100 *Monday*: Isa 30:18-26
Conversion of the people. Promise of
future happiness.

101 *Tuesday*: Isa 30:27-33; 31:4-9
Coming of the Lord and punishment
of Assyria.

102 *Wednesday*: Isa 31:1-3; 32:1-8
The reign of peace.

103 *Thursday*: Isa 32:15–33:6
Restoration. Hope in the Lord.

104 *Friday*: Isa 33:7-24
Future salvation.

Fourth Week

105 *December 17*: Isa 45:1-13
The salvation of Israel.

106 *December 18*: Isa 46:1-13
The Lord rejects the idols of Babylon.

107 *December 19*: Isa 47:1, 3b-15
Lament over Babylon.

108 *December 20*: Isa 48:1-11
God is sole master of the coming age.

109 *December 21*: Isa 48:12-21; 49:9b-13
The new exodus.

110 *December 22*: Isa 49:14–50:1
The restoration of Sion.

111 *December 23*: Isa 51:1-11
Promise of salvation to the children
of Abraham.

5. FIRST WEEK OF ADVENT: WATCH AND PRAY

Vigilant Waiting for the Lord

The words "vigilant waiting" capture the mood of the First Sunday of Advent. Each year the gospel reading is a passage from the Synoptics that speaks of the last day and the need to be vigilant [7, 8, 9]. The prayers and chants chosen for this day all focus on this expectation of the Lord. The deeply meaningful and traditional entrance antiphon expresses the attitude of the entire Church on this day—a trusting, fervent prayer and a hopeful expectation that will not be disappointed: "To you, O Lord, I lift up my soul. / In you, O my God, I have trusted; / let me not be put to shame; / let not my enemies exult over me. / Let none who hope in you be put to shame" (cf. Ps 25 [24]:1-3).

This antiphon and the collect in the Liturgy of the Word show that foremost in the Church's mind is the expectation of the last day and the judgment that it will bring. The faithful must advance courageously to meet the Lord; they are called to enter into the kingdom of heaven at the judgment. Here we have the Church's intention clearly expressed, as well as the key for interpreting the readings of the liturgy.

(A) The Lord proclaims his return. Let us be vigilant.
The nations are gathering. The day is near.

The Lord's proclamation of his return for judgment, in the Gospel of St. Matthew [7], can undoubtedly give rise to a pessimism that may obscure for the listener the teaching in the other two readings. The suddenness of his coming is disturbing. And yet the perspectives opened up for us by the prophet Isaiah convey a deep sense of optimism and peace [1].

There is no real opposition between the two tonalities. The end of the world and the return of Christ are indeed sudden and calculated to arouse a certain fear. It is no less true, however, that the return presupposes a great success, namely, the gathering of the nations. Isaiah presents us with a vision of the created world being restored to unity, and this is an aspect of the judgment that is often overlooked. "[T]he mountain of the LORD's house / shall be established as the highest mountain / and raised above the hills. / All nations shall stream toward it; . . . / one nation shall not raise the sword against another" (Isa 2:2, 4). The responsorial psalm likewise makes the point that the last day is the day on which we shall enter the Lord's house: "I rejoiced when they said to me, / 'Let us go to the house of the LORD'" (Ps 122:1).

In this context Psalm 122 becomes first and foremost a psalm of expectation. We should advert to the broadening of perspective that such a vision of the last day effects. Individualism has been eliminated, for I shall be part of a universal gathering that embraces all the nations. A kind of moralism and an overemphasis on the particular judgment have to some extent made the Latin Church lose sight of the social aspect of the last day.

Isaiah urges us to walk in the light of the Lord. St. Paul, for his part, when warning us that the last day is close at hand, urges us to emerge from the darkness and to arm ourselves for the struggle on behalf of the light [4]. He makes his exhortation very concrete, reproaching the faithful for carousing and drunkenness, sexual excess and lust, quarreling and jealousy. The Liturgy of the Hours likewise exhorts us to be converted [85]. "An ox knows its owner, / and an ass, its master's manger," but Israel has not known its Lord. The important thing is not to offer sacrifices the Lord does not want but to be converted, to cease from evil, and to seek justice. Then the Lord will pardon us, even if our sins be like scarlet (Isa 1:1-18).

(B) We must be vigilant, since we are waiting for the
Lord Jesus to manifest himself. If he comes,
everything—the world and each of us—will be restored.

In the gospel passage read on this Sunday, St. Mark does not refer to the tragic circumstances that will mark the end of time, but he does urge us to be vigilant, since we do not know precisely when the Master will come [8]. On the other hand, our attitude toward his coming is not to be one of pure fear; we must also hope for that coming and petition for it with loud cries. The coming is the coming of a father; he is a potter, and we are all of us the work of his hands [2]. If we hope in him, live justly, and are mindful of him in all we do, he will come to meet us. The vision of the return is thus optimistic, even if it makes strict demands of us.

St. Paul repeats the optimistic note. God has enriched us with speech and knowledge, and the Christ who is coming will enable us to be steadfast to the end, so that he will have nothing to reproach us with on the last day [5]. This is the kind of realism that encourages us. We may be constantly searching and not allowed to settle down anywhere, but we are always under the protection of the Christ who is coming to meet us, and there is no place for anxiety.

(C) Be vigilant and ready to appear before the Son of Man.
A righteous branch will spring up on the last day,
a day for which we must always be ready in holiness.

Luke depicts the majestic coming of the Son of Man. He touches on the terror that the end of time will strike in peoples' hearts, but he evidently gives greater importance to the coming of the Son of Man in majesty on the clouds. His advice is that we look up and raise our heads, because our salvation is drawing near. The end of time is thus presented here as a necessary stage, but it points to the coming of redemption [9]. Justice will be established, Jerusalem will dwell in security, and the name given her will be "The LORD our justice" [3].

Here justice is once again seen as something primarily positive: it justifies people and builds them up rather than destroys them. St. Paul asks the Lord to establish us solidly in blameless holiness against the day when the Lord will come. He offers the same advice that he gives in his First Letter to the Corinthians [5], referring to the way we must conduct ourselves if we are to please God. He has elsewhere listed the attitudes a Christian must avoid as he keeps in mind the day of the Lord's coming [4].

Psalm 25, which provides the responsorial for this first Sunday (C), shows us how we should pray during this time of waiting: "O LORD, make me know your ways. / Teach me your paths. / Guide me in your truth, and teach me; / for you are the God of my salvation." We have a shepherd to lead us: "O shepherd of Israel, hear us, / . . . enthroned on the cherubim, shine forth. / . . . Rouse up your might and come to save us" (Ps 80, responsorial for first Sunday, B).

The whole orientation of the First Sunday of Advent is thus clearly eschatological. It provides an opportunity for us to ask ourselves what place the "last day" and the meeting of the whole people of God with its Lord has in our real lives. We are challenged, not to forget our personal meeting with the Lord and the need of making ready for it, but rather to broaden our vision so as to embrace the entire world and to set our sights on the rebuilding of that world against the day of the Lord's coming.

Such a broadening of perspective will also affect our sense of urgency with regard to conversion and a moral life. We will be able to see how our personal decisions—and our efforts to live as God would have us live—do not simply affect us as individuals but contribute to the reconstruction of creation as a whole. The object of our faith-inspired hope will likewise become far more vast, and we will forget the paltry expectations we cherished when we thought merely of our own narrow life.

In all this there is a theology to be found and lived by (since it is concrete in character and makes demands of us). A Christianity inspired by such a theology will be so open and all-embracing that it will force itself upon the attention of all, even those who do not yet believe but are searching. It is a theology that can also knock down the barriers that too often still separate the followers of the Christ who came to save the world and will come again at the end of time.

Characteristics of Our Messianic Age

The weekdays will express in greater detail the theology contained in the liturgy of the first Sunday and show us the characteristic traits of the messianic era that has begun and of our expectation of the last day.

The special signs of the hidden presence of God's reign are the cures of the blind [45, 46]; the Lord's compassion for the crowds [47, 48]; and the multiplication of the loaves, which symbolizes the joyous messianic banquet [41, 42]. We shall know the Lord who will reveal himself in the Son by the power of the Spirit [39, 40]. The last day will be a day on which unity is made perfect [37, 38]. In the interim period, which is that of our lives, we must do the Father's will and live righteously [43, 44].

The readings of the Old and New Testaments complement each other admirably during this first week. We must now go into the various themes a bit more fully; as we do, we shall meet numerous points that have now become more familiar to us.

Cure of the Blind Who Believe

There can be no doubt that the real point here for us is the spiritual blindness of which physical blindness is an eloquent symbol. But as we reflect on spiritual blindness, we are once again (as in the earlier pages of this book) confronted with the problem of faith. There are two ways of attacking the problem, and they seem contradictory.

On the one hand, the cure, the light, the "knowledge," gives rise to faith. Certain "lights" that the Lord gives us through people or events or some intellectual and spiritual development or some important experience have the power to open us to faith and make us more receptive to the gift given us. The gift is an invitation to be more attentive to persons and things, to circumstances and events, and to judge them with greater circumspection. The habit of judging more spiritually the events that impinge upon us and sometimes condition our whole lives henceforth can give our faith a scope and range we would not have suspected. The search for the meaning of an event or for the place of a human being, friend or enemy, in our life is a properly Christian activity and quite difficult to carry out. It is likely that a lukewarm faith originates in extensive negligence or pride in the way we evaluate the circumstances and people among whom we live our lives. Expectation of the last day should arouse us to renew our sensitivity to surroundings we too often think of as dangerous or, even more often, as a burden.

But the problem has its other side, because the gift of faith is what enlightens us. Because we believe, we understand more perfectly, and our vision of the environment in which we are placed acquires a special character that we can make intelligible to the nonbeliever only with great difficulty. The understanding of the Christian paradox is entirely dependent on this gift of light. It is a simple fact that we more often experience this to be true than otherwise. The gift of faith opens new perspectives to the believing mind.

But are we cured because we believe, or do we believe because we are cured? There is no set, definitive answer to this question, and we must therefore be very attentive. Faith in all its dimensions is thus brought to the fore during the season of Advent, which is intended to be a stimulus to the faith of the Church and to faith in the Church. We can understand how in some liturgies—for example, the Gallican—Advent, like Lent, was a period in which catechumens were prepared for baptism (on Epiphany). Advent is a time both of faith and of healing.

The Lord's Compassion

There is a kind of theology that worries about the "precise moment" when Christ "instituted" the sacrament of the forgiveness of sins. Unfortunately, those who practice such a theology are not sufficiently concerned about finding and teaching the countless passages of Scripture in which the Lord seeks out the sinner and, in response to the sinner's first cry to him, tries to convert and cure him. We have grown accustomed to a juridical conception of forgiveness and have set down conditions God must observe, although he himself set only one condition: we will be pardoned in the way that we ourselves pardon others.

Advent seems to be a good time to recall how God's mercy is not limited by my deficiencies, be they great or small, nor measured by my spiritual pulse, but extends to the whole world. It becomes intelligible only when we realize that he intends a new creation that is to be formed out of our old world, which must be renewed by accepting and cooperating in its own redemption. It is to the entire people that the Lord stoops when he hears its cry; it is to the entire people that he shows the way; and at the end he will bind up his people's hurts and heal their wounds [47]. God's mercy embraces both the world and me individually. It is true enough that the Lord heals the brokenhearted (Ps 147; responsorial for Saturday of first week), but we must not limit his mercy to our personal troubles. If he keeps them in mind—and he does—it is because our healing is part of the reconstruction of the world.

The gospel repeats this aspect of God's mercy [48]. Jesus is fulfilling the prophecy of Isaiah, to which we have already alluded: he has mercy on the crowds and sends out his disciples to work cures. These cures in turn will be a sign that the kingdom is already here. The basic point, I think, is this: God's mercy on the Church today, on the world today, on me at this very moment, is first and foremost a sign that the reign of God is here. His mercy is a deliverance, such as is petitioned in the collect for the First Saturday of Advent: "bestow on those who devoutly await [your Son] the grace of your compassion from on high, that we may attain the prize of true freedom." The prayer shows that God's mercy is exercised not so much to cure us as to liberate us and that the liberation is granted not for its own sake or to make us more balanced creatures but so that we may be able to love God. These few words from a simple prayer at the beginning of the first Saturday's liturgy surely provide a remarkable approach to penance and forgiveness.

Joy at the Table of the Lord

The emphasis on the multiplication of the loaves [42] and on the meal taken with the Lord at the end of time [41] is in full accord with the eschatological orientation established on the First Sunday of Advent. The collect for the Wednesday celebration likewise emphasizes the eschatological aspect: "so that at the coming of Christ your Son we may be found worthy of the banquet of eternal life and merit to receive heavenly nourishment from his hands."

We may leave aside the literary aspect of this prayer. (It is difficult to see how Jesus can hand us nourishment, since all signs will have lost their point once we are in the direct presence of Christ; it is also difficult to understand in what sense the Eucharist would continue to exist.) The important thing is the emphatic link between eating and eschatology. The salient aspect of this meal will be its joyousness. God will have taken away the veil of sorrow that covers the nations and will have wiped away the tears from all faces, Isaiah tells us. He also makes clear to us what it is that we are really hoping for: "Behold our God, to whom we looked to save us! / This is the LORD for whom we looked; / let us rejoice and be glad that he has saved us!" [41].

Psalm 23, "The LORD is my shepherd," had a privileged place in the rite of Christian initiation and has been perhaps the most popular of the psalms in our time. It serves as a very apt response to the above reading from Isaiah on the First Wednesday of Advent.

Cures of the sick, multiplication of the loaves [42], and eating with the Lord on the last day [41]—these are the signs of God's reign that is already here and is still coming.

From this viewpoint, the Church's Eucharist once again acquires dimensions unknown in the narrow presentations sometimes made of this sacrament, even today. The eucharistic celebration should awaken all these resonances in us. More than that, every Christian meal is evidently an anticipation of the messianic joy. Many monasteries, thank God, have advanced beyond the rediscovery of a rather superficial kind of "brotherhood" and have maintained the ancient tradition of the meal taken in silence and recollection and consciously linked with the joyous, eschatological eucharistic banquet. The Eucharist is the most familial of meals as far as reality and depth of expression are concerned.

Revelation of the Father in the Son through the Spirit

We spoke of faith when commenting on the cure of the blind. The Father reveals himself to us lowly creatures, provided we accept his Son [40]. When we thus accept him, the Spirit acts, and we know the Father in the Son. Then the secret of the kingdom is revealed to us, a secret having to do essentially with the Trinity.

The gospel of the First Tuesday of Advent is undoubtedly one of those best suited to help us enter more easily into the mystery of the Trinity. It speaks of God loving the world enough to send his Son as its Savior and of the Spirit tracing in us the image of the Son who reveals the Father. Each time the Father gazes upon us he finds in us his own Son, and each time we come in contact with the Son we discover the Father. That, basically, is what it means to enter the kingdom of God, and our entry has already begun. The collect of the Mass for this first Tuesday emphasizes this point: "consoled by the presence of your Son, whose coming we now await."

The Spirit of the Lord rests upon Christ with his gifts of wisdom, understanding, and counsel, and the same Spirit rests upon us. This same text of Isaiah [39] is used in the rite of confirmation at the moment when the laying on of hands symbolizes the coming of the Spirit upon us. We are thus committed to help bring about the definitive reign of God, wherein we shall live in the company of Father, Son, and Spirit, sharing their trinitarian life.

Unity Restored

Here we can observe once again that the focus of this first week is eschatological, for in these readings we are bidden to contemplate the unity that the world will possess when it is reconstructed.

This is another of the very meaningful themes of Advent. Unity is indeed a basic thrust of Christianity: unity between the elements of the world, unity between us and them, unity within ourselves, unity with other people, and, above all, unity with God. Unity is also an object of Christian hope. Yet how petty and narrow our view of the purposes of human life too often is! There is no doubt, of course, that our salvation is important, but are we justified in concentrating on it apart from its proper context? Is it really possible to conceive of a salvation that is separable from the restored unity of the world as a whole? Our hope, then, must be essentially missionary, and any concern for personal salvation must be incomplete and even illegitimate if it is not accompanied by concern for the salvation of other people in the world. In this regard, Advent proves once again to be a fine school of Christian formation and a basis for broadening the perspectives that guide such a formation.

We should note that in the gospel for the First Monday of Advent [38] Christ once again uses the image of the messianic banquet. And he sees even Gentiles seated at God's table in the kingdom! Here is indeed a single vision of the world and salvation, and one to which the Advent season should make us receptive.

The Will of the Father

These various considerations cannot remain a matter of merely passive contemplation; we must also do the Father's will. The collect for Thursday of this first week suggests a point with which we are not very familiar; it emphasizes the social aspect of salvation and our responsibility for it: "come to our help with mighty strength, that what our sins impede the grace of your mercy may hasten." We are hardly accustomed to think of salvation as being delayed by our faults!

The responsorial psalm for this same day echoes the reading from Isaiah [43] by using Psalm 118, "[H]is mercy endures forever!" It is upon this mercy, and not on people, that we must rely, for the Lord is able to bring the just into his kingdom and give them victory and salvation.

Entry into the kingdom has a prerequisite: we must do the Father's will. If we are to enter the kingdom, it is not enough to call upon the Lord's name; we must also live as he bids us live. If we hear this word and put it into practice, we act as prudent people who build their houses on a solid foundation [44]. Thus does Jesus speak to us in the gospel for this first Thursday. The activity that should fill the time of waiting is the doing of the Father's will.

Overview

The eucharistic liturgies throughout the first week, along with the readings from the Liturgy of the Hours, provide us with very important indications as to how we are to understand and live the first stage of Advent. Let us try to summarize and synthesize these indications in a few words.

The whole of this first week is focused on the end of time and the return of Christ on the last day. We must be vigilant [7, 8, 9]. But this vigilant waiting is not passive. The day is close at hand, and we must do the Father's will by living a life based on love of the Lord and on righteousness [4, 5, 6, 43, 44]. The readings in the Liturgy of the Hours lay a heavy emphasis on conversion [85, 88, 89, 90], especially in the splendid canticle of the vineyard [88]. Conversion is rightly shown to be essential and far more important than the offering of sacrifices [85]. The emphasis is meant to put us on guard against falling back (as we easily can) into a ritualism that would excuse us from living the true Christian life of love. Christians must do more than "practice"; they must truly be Christian.

Our Christian life of waiting is entirely concentrated on one object: the Lord's return to gather his people. The perspective that controls our lives, our searching, and our action is therefore broad indeed, for we disdain religious egocentrism and embrace the entire world. To reach the goal is beyond our unaided powers, and we can achieve it only through faith—a faith that is stimulated in us by the light God bestows upon us through people and events but also a faith that in turn enables us to judge events as God himself does [45, 46].

The light and the grace to advance on the paths that lead to Christ's return have been given us by a merciful God. His compassion embraces each of us and the world in its entirety, since it is the world as a whole that is to reach a state of righteousness and peace [47, 48]. In faith and by the limitless mercy of God, we are able to know the Father even now, for the Son reveals him to us through the Spirit [39, 40].

As we move toward the last day, fortified by the signs that proclaim the presence of the kingdom among us, we glimpse the era of justice

and peace [3, 43] that lies ahead. Sion is the center of this eschatological expectation [86]; we know that all of creation will be restored
to the unity that God originally intended. That is how God wins his
victory over evil [1, 37, 38, 87].

Here and now, while we are still on earth, we know that we already
have pledges of the reality to come. The cure of the blind—ourselves!—the multiplication of the loaves, and the Eucharist are signs
of the eschatological banquet that we already celebrate with joy as
an efficacious symbol of the gathering that will take place on the last
day [41, 42].

6. SECOND WEEK OF ADVENT: PREPARE THE WAY

The gospels chosen for the Second Sunday of Advent all have as their theme the preparation of the way of the Lord [16, 17, 18]. John's urgent warning has echoed throughout the world ever since he spoke it, and as it reaches us today it has a twofold reference: prepare for the Lord's coming at Christmas, but prepare also for his return on the last day. The collect of this Sunday can be understood as referring to both comings, but if we set it alongside the other prayers of the day and the readings, it is in fact more concerned with the Lord's return: "[M]ay no earthly undertaking hinder those who set out in haste to meet your Son, but may our learning of heavenly wisdom gain us admittance to his company."

If we look closely, we will see that the first part of this prayer looks to the parousia, while the second is concerned rather with Christ's coming in the flesh, where we can meet him and share his life through the sacraments.

The entrance antiphon, on the other hand, though it too can refer to either coming, readily applies to the incarnation of the Word that saves: "O people of Sion, behold, the Lord will come to save the nations, and the Lord will make the glory of his voice heard in the joy of your heart" (cf. Isa 30:19, 30).

(A) Prepare the way for the Lord.
The Spirit is upon him, and in him the promises are fulfilled.

The voice crying in the desert will echo until the end of time [16], since conversion will always be necessary, and the work of conversion will never be finished. It is not enough to belong to a Christian people, just as it was not enough to have Abraham for a father. We must produce the fruits in which conversion finds expression. This conversion leading to the forgiveness of sins is closely connected with baptism: both the baptism of John, which led to conversion, and the baptism of Christ, which is a baptism in fire and the Spirit, giving a divine rebirth and gathering together the people of God.

John uses uncompromising words to emphasize the need of conversion and of purifying baptism: "His winnowing fan is in his hand. He will clear his threshing floor and gather his wheat into his barn, but the chaff he will burn with unquenchable fire" [16].

The image is harsh, its meaning inescapable; it is difficult simply to ignore John's warning and close one's ears. Preparing the way for the Lord requires a constant effort at conversion: "Even now the ax lies at the root of the trees. Therefore every tree that does not bear good fruit will be cut down and thrown into the fire."

But what is involved in "being converted"? St. Paul suggests the starting point of every conversion: the patient courage to live in harmony with one another according to the spirit of Christ Jesus [13]. That was the point Paul emphasized in a Church that was still new and very young. He was speaking of a love that is open and in accordance with the spirit of Christ; we are to accept one another as we ourselves have been accepted by Christ. Starting with that, we can go on to achieve a second objective of our conversion: the possibility of giving glory to God, that is, of finding the essential motive for the creation of the world and of humanity. Christ, who came as a servant, guarantees the fulfillment of the promise made to the patriarchs: that, because God is merciful, even the Gentile nations, once converted, will be able to glorify God. Conversion means we are able to sing to the Lord: "*I will praise you among the Gentiles, and sing praises to your name*" [13].

Jesus is, then, according to Romans, the guarantor of our salvation, that is, of our ability to give glory to the Father. That is our hope, and we go forward sustained by the lessons of patience and words of encouragement found in the Scriptures. We hope for the salvation of all people, that is, that all will be made capable of glorifying God.

We can see here why the sacrament of penance is an act of worship. As an efficacious sign of conversion, it is thereby a hymn of praise to God for his mercy in sending his Son, who has accomplished the work of our salvation by making us capable of praising the glory of God. Conversion, then, is not only a cure and the regaining of a certain psychological balance; it gives, above all, the possibility of taking our place once again in the concert of praise that rises from creation to the glory of the Father.

He who makes possible the conversion of the world and of humans is the Messiah upon whom the Spirit of the Lord rests: "Justice shall be the band around his waist, and faithfulness a belt upon his hips" [10]. Singled out by the Spirit of the Lord for the bestowal of his gifts of wisdom and understanding, counsel and strength, knowledge and fear of the Lord, the Messiah will restore justice and unite the world. The passage is a poem on the "golden age"; we commented on it, from this point of view, in chapter 3. The responsorial psalm (Ps 72) expresses a wish for the Messiah: "May his name endure forever, / his name continue like the sun. / Every tribe shall be blest in him, / all nations shall call him blessed."

Despite external appearances, we are already living, through faith, in this golden age, which has already begun. But appearances are our problem! How can we see the golden age in a world that is adrift, a world in which virtue and vice are so mingled? We can only respond by pointing to the fact that the Good News is being preached to the poor, the blind see, and the dead rise—since the Church accomplishes all these miracles in the spiritual order. The outlook of faith and a hope grounded in faith—these alone can enable us to see the presence of the golden age in its beginnings. Advent is the season of Christian optimism.

(B) To prepare the way is to prepare
for a new world, a new earth.

The Good News of Jesus Christ, the Son of God, begins, in St. Mark's gospel, with the exhortation of John the Baptist: *"Prepare the way of the Lord, make straight his paths"* [17].

The Good News is thus the news of our conversion and the possibility of our meeting the Lord as he comes. John the Baptist was simply repeating the words of the prophet Isaiah: "Every valley shall be filled in, / every mountain and hill shall be made low; / the rugged land shall be made a plain, / the rough country, a broad valley. / Then the glory of the LORD shall be revealed, / and all people shall see it together; / for the mouth of the LORD has spoken" [11].

Every Christian, by his conversion, is a preacher of the Good News of the Lord who comes and gathers his sheep. It is Good News for us as it was for Jerusalem, because our sins are forgiven, and we have received double punishment at the Lord's hand for all our faults [11].

The Lord wishes that we all be converted, but we must also make the effort to be worthy preachers of a new earth. And even though the Lord does not consent to the loss of some but wills that all have the opportunity for conversion, he will come nonetheless like a thief. Such is the teaching of St. Peter, who follows in this the teaching of the gospels [14]. Peter is aware that a new heaven and a new earth are coming, but his concern is to remind us of what such a renewal requires of us: "what sort of persons ought you to be, conducting yourselves in holiness and devotion, waiting for and hastening the coming of the day of God. . . . Therefore, beloved, since you await these things, be eager to be found without spot or blemish before him, at peace."

(C) See the salvation of God, don the cloak of justice,
and wear the mitre of glory.

When we read the third set of texts for the second Sunday, it is hard not to feel that, while charming, they foster illusions and seek to lull us in distress by softening the pain of suffering. It would, of course, be blasphemous to agree that this impression is justified. Our real problem is that we have difficulty in believing what lies ahead for us: that all people shall see the salvation of God, once the crooked ways have been made straight [18].

Baruch's prophecy, however, goes beyond this rather general statement, and we may well find it amazing. He shows us the Church at the end of time clad in God's own splendor, wrapped in the cloak of justice that comes from him, and wearing on her head the mitre that displays the glory of the eternal name. Jerusalem is told to look and see her children being gathered, from east to west, by the word of the holy God. We should read this entire poem of Baruch, which describes the victory of Jerusalem and Israel. It is encouraging. In fact, it may even stir in us a kind of triumphalism. That is a temptation that the Church, as we know, has not always resisted. But to yield to it would be to show that we had not grasped the difficult road the people of God must travel in order to reach the day of Christ.

St. Paul, addressing the Philippians and now us, does not hide the problems and difficulties the Christian must face [15]. Yet he is not pessimistic but finds that the work has been well begun by God himself, who will bring it to completion. Each of us, however, must do our part and make continual progress in true understanding and in that clarity of mind that enables us "to approve what is excellent."

The last admonition of St. Paul is astonishingly relevant today. At a time when the world is being renewed, and when one civilization is coming to an end and another, it seems, is beginning, we are well aware that it is no simple matter to discern what is really important as we live our lives. And yet it is absolutely necessary that we advance upright and without stumbling toward the day of Christ. The problem of our age is to acquire a right vision of reality, so that we can hold on to the essential without imperiling it by an imprudent neglect of the secondary; this is a burning issue in the world today. To draw back from the problem is to condemn ourselves to mediocrity and even to death. We must take the risk, but we must make sure that in taking it we are guided by a higher vision of what is necessary. The crisis now facing institutions can be summed up as the task of choosing what is most important. Today's task is to refuse to get trapped in the past, while also refusing to jettison secondary things that are so interwoven with the essentials that they cannot be separated without infinite patience. Experience has already shown that impatience and getting bogged down in the past are alike the result of a lack of deep faith and of a blindness that refuses to see that everything in this world, even the most traditional institutions, has meaning only with reference to what will abide when the day of Christ has come [15].

John the Baptist, Greatest of Humans

The readings of the season have brought us into continual contact with the personality of Isaiah the prophet. Now, on the second Thursday, we hear Jesus speaking of John the Baptist as the greatest among humans [56]. The gospel for this day sings the praises of the Precursor. But Christ then goes a step further and speaks of the children of God's kingdom as superbeings: "the least in the Kingdom of heaven is greater than he [John]." And yet only the violent will be part of that kingdom!

Isaiah seeks to give us a foretaste of this kingdom of heaven by his description of the restoration of the world: "I will turn the desert into a marshland, / and the dry ground into springs of water. / . . . I will set in the wasteland the cypress, / together with the plane tree and the pine, / That all may see and know, / observe and understand, /

That the hand of the LORD has done this, / the Holy One of Israel has created it" [55].

Psalm 145 sings of these great deeds of the Lord in response to the reading of the prophecy of Isaiah: "All your works shall thank you, O LORD, / and all your faithful ones bless you. / They shall speak of the glory of your reign, / and declare your mighty deeds."

Elijah Has Come, but They Have Not Recognized Him

In the gospel for the second Thursday, Christ said, "if you are willing to accept it, he [John] is Elijah, the one who is to come" [56]. The gospel of the second Saturday picks up this theme. John had been imprisoned and has now been beheaded. The disciples inquire of Jesus concerning the coming of Elijah, who is to precede the Messiah. Jesus' answer is clear: Elijah has already come in the person of John the Baptist, but they failed to recognize him, just as they will fail to recognize in Jesus the suffering Messiah [60].

The book of Sirach the sage foretold the coming of Elijah at the end of time; in so doing, it was repeating what had already been written. Elijah's function would be "To turn back the hearts of fathers toward their sons, / and to re-establish the tribes of Jacob" [59]. In other words, he was to unify people.

The failure to recognize Elijah's coming is a permanent lesson for us, and a hard one. More frequently than we think, God comes to us through things and events, in order that he might restore the world. Recognizing and accepting these "prophecies" is no simple matter, since there are so many false prophecies around today. The criterion by which we will recognize them is, of course, their fruits.

The Strength of the Weary

Expectation is always long, even if life is short, because waiting is made up of suffering and contradictions. That is the experience of each of us, and that will be the world's experience until the moment of its definitive meeting with the Lord on the last day. It is difficult not to be sluggish; sluggishness seems quite legitimate, being part of human life, stuck to it like a vile garment. And yet faith can completely eliminate the glumness from our lives. Many of the Scripture texts read on the weekdays of this second week call our attention to the presence of God at our side as we pursue our difficult way under skies that are often overcast.

The Lord is coming to save us: "Be strong, fear not! / Here is your God. / . . . he comes to save you" [49]. The world will at last be made one with the unity God wants, and our efforts will prove not to have been in vain. Psalm 85, which supplies the response to the above reading of Isaiah on the second Monday, voices the joy a person experiences while waiting calmly in faith: "[T]he Lord will bestow his bounty, / and our earth shall yield its increase. / Justice will march before him, / and guide his steps on the way."

In addition, Jesus is not stingy with his wonders. The cures he effects are connected with the forgiveness of sins, for he has within himself the very power of God. The paralytic has his sins forgiven and walks, and everyone praises God: "We have seen incredible things today" [50]. This cry is not an exclamation proper only to the past; it can well be ours today, and in fact it should be ours. Is there any truly believing Catholic who has not seen, through faith-enlightened eyes, things really extraordinary: healings of the soul, unexpected transformations of people we thought lost, miracles of friendship in God, limitless charity for the wretched of the world, complete and lifelong commitments to God and one's neighbors? We do see extraordinary things that are signs of the kingdom already present and signs that we are advancing toward the great meeting with Christ. Such things are the joys the life of faith brings.

A despairing spirit of criticism is abroad in our day and has "seen through" all the enthusiasms. Everything has been tarnished: religious life, married life, any life of commitment. Criticism that is wholly negative has discredited everything pure. There are people whose greatest talent is to wipe their dirty hands on all the white cloths. In the process, a wellspring of strength has dried up. The past was indeed not perfect, but it showed tremendous energy and deserves to be praised for it. It is the easiest thing in the world to laugh at past and present, but in doing so we close eyes that might have seen extraordinary things. The proud have had their momentary triumph. But have they not often been soon confounded?

God, who comes to renew the world [51], does not want his little ones to be lost, and so he watches over them and leads them as a shepherd does his flock [52]. He is present to help the afflicted [54] and the weary [53]. True enough the words of Christ sometimes sound like idle poetry—"My yoke is easy, and my burden light"—but that is because only the ears of faith can understand them. Nonetheless, they are addressed to all of us—just as we are. At moments when we are tempted to give up, we should repeat these words of Christ over and over, like an obsessive melody. If we do, they will, through faith, effect in us what they signify. For even if depression is a psychophysical fact, it also originates in the fear of committing ourselves unreservedly to the life of faith. Making ourselves drunk on these words of Christ might be the best remedy for our depression and the strongest stimulus to stride forward with the Church as she advances toward her Lord.

They Listen Neither to John Nor to the Son

They did not see that Elijah had come in the person of John, nor did they recognize the Son when he came. "For John came neither eating nor drinking, and they said, 'He is possessed by a demon.' The Son of man came eating and drinking and they said, 'Look, he is a glutton and a drunkard, a friend of tax collectors and sinners'" [58].

It is easy to find specious reasons for rejecting God's messengers and refusing to face the questions they put to us. Entire generations of Christians have chosen this alternative, building a wall of pretexts lest they see and hear and understand. The present generation wants to avoid this kind of hypocrisy that shelters behind tradition as a way of avoiding all questions. Will it succeed? Yes, to the extent that in the questions it asks it is not simply looking for itself; to the extent that it does not decide on its own what the questions are to be, thus unwittingly ensuring that it will find only itself, but accepts the questions God wants to ask.

There is a kind of snobbery possible when it comes to problems (especially false problems!), and it is easy to fool ourselves in this matter. We think we are looking for objective solutions, but we are really standing before a mirror and indulging in a spiritual narcissism that is hard to cure because it springs from what is most blind and ineradicable in us: egotism and pride.

And yet the gospel of the second Friday tells us, for our joy, that God's wisdom is revealed precisely by what he does.

If we wish to hear and answer the questions God puts to us, we need but follow a modest yet difficult method: *obey his commandments*

[57]. Perhaps because of the narrow way in which the commandments are often presented to us, we mistakenly think of Isaiah's advice as mere moralism, as though the commandments were not meant to be the work of love and the way to build up and restore both humanity and its world. We often look at the commandments through the wrong end of the telescope and with a feeling that we are humiliating ourselves, theologically, by focusing our attention on them. Perhaps, however, concentration on the commandments will be the beginning of a lowly journey on which we will learn to judge wisely the things of this world and to hold firm to the things of heaven (see the prayer after Communion on the Second Friday of Advent).

Overview

The Second Week of Advent is still focused in good measure on the last days. All the communion antiphons, except for Monday's, should be interpreted as referring to the second coming of Christ, which has already begun for us through our reception of the Eucharist. It is to be expected that communion antiphons generally should relate in a special way to the parousia. Take, for example, the antiphon for Saturday of this second week: "Behold, I am coming soon and my recompense is with me, says the Lord, to bestow a reward according to the deeds of each." Or the Friday antiphon: "We await a savior, the Lord Jesus Christ, who will change our mortal bodies, to conform with his glorified body."

The collects of this week's Masses, on the contrary, are not thus clearly oriented to the second coming. Those of Monday and Tuesday clearly have the incarnation in view: "May our prayer of petition rise before you, we pray, O Lord, that, with purity unblemished, we, your servants, may come, as we desire, to celebrate the great mystery of the Incarnation of your Only Begotten Son" (Monday). The collects on the other days can be understood as referring to both comings. "Almighty God, who command us to prepare the way for Christ the Lord, grant in your kindness, we pray, that no infirmity may weary us as we long for the comforting presence of our heavenly physician" (Wednesday).

The readings, however, as we have already seen, focus on the expectation of the last day. The Scripture readings in the Liturgy of the Hours for the second week have likewise been chosen solely with the second coming in mind: manifestation of the Lord on the last day [93], quaking of the earth and reign of the Lord [94], banquet with the Lord and victory song [95], judgment of the Lord [96, 98], resurrection [96], and gathering at Jerusalem [97]. All these passages immediately turn our thoughts to Christ's return.

If we go back now to the readings at Mass during the second week, we find that they adopt the same perspective and are concerned to show us how we should wait for the return of Christ. We are to try to recognize and accept the comings of the Lord in the person of his messengers and to listen to them [59, 60, 58]. To accept these comings means concretely to fall in with the plan of reconstruction they offer us [57]. The Lord's will is our source of strength [50, 53, 54]; in his work of renewing the world, he passes over no one, not even the lowly [52].

Isaiah, a Model for Those Who Wait

The readings for Advent have brought us into frequent contact with Isaiah. It will be worth our while to reflect briefly on his personality.

The gospels say nothing directly about Isaiah as a person, but they do cite him, and we may glimpse his presence in the mind and even on the lips of Christ. He is the great prophet of the time of waiting; he is surprisingly close to us; he is one of us, a man of today. What makes him this is his longing for deliverance and his desire for the absolute, that is, for God. He belongs to us by the implacable logic of his life, which is a life of struggle and combat. He is of our time by his literary art, in which our century can see reflected its own preference for images that are bare yet powerful to the point of being harsh. He is one of the violent to whom Christ has promised the kingdom of God. No obstacle can halt this visionary gripped by the splendor of the future kingdom that a prince of peace and justice will inaugurate. In Isaiah we find the serene, unshakable power of a man who is possessed by the Spirit, a man who has no choice but to proclaim what the Lord tells him, even if the proclamation goes against his own grain.

This prophet is hardly known to us except through his actions, but these are so characteristic that through them we glimpse and love him as a person. How amazingly close to us is this figure from the eighth century BC! He seems to be part of our daily lives, though as one whose spiritual stature makes him tower over the rest of us.

Isaiah lived in a brilliant and prosperous age. Rarely had the kingdoms of Judah and Samaria felt so optimistic, for their political stability allowed them to dream ambitious dreams. People of religious conviction attributed this political good fortune to God; their very religion led them to expect that success would be unbroken. Then the bubble of happiness burst, as Isaiah came forward courageously to carry out his mission of showing the people the disaster that lay ahead, brought on by their own negligence.

Isaiah probably belonged to the aristocracy of Jerusalem. His mind was shaped by the writings of his predecessors, especially Amos and Hosea. Inspired by God as they were, Isaiah foresaw what his nation's history was to be. He looked beyond the present situation, with all its criminality and compromises, and saw the coming chastisement that would once again make the crooked ways straight.

Lodts writes of the prophets: "Thinking perhaps that they were calling for a return to the past, they in fact made a gigantic leap forward. These reactionaries were also revolutionaries."[1] Such a one was Isaiah, on whom the Lord laid his hand "in the year King Uzziah died," that is, around 740, and whose lips the Lord purified in the temple with an ember brought by a seraph (Isa 6:1-3). From that moment on, Isaiah was no longer his own man. This did not mean that he became a purely passive instrument in the hands of Yahweh; on the contrary, his every power was put at the service of his God, whose messenger he became. But in this case the messenger roused terror, for he told how Israel would be stripped naked and left barely alive.

Isaiah's early prophecies (one of which has given us the background for the ox and the ass at the crib of Jesus) showed what his thinking and his role were to be. He tells his people that while Yahweh wishes to be everything to his people, Israel ignores that God and proves itself far more stupid than the ox, which at least recognizes the cowman who cares for it. "Hear, O heavens, and listen, O earth; / for the LORD speaks: / Sons have I raised and reared, / but they have rebelled against me! / An ox knows its owner, / and an ass, its master's manger; / But Israel does not know, / my people has not understood" (Isa 1:2-3).

Then the prophet's curse is uttered:

Ah! Sinful nation, people laden with wickedness,
    evil offspring, corrupt children!
They have forsaken the LORD,
    spurned the Holy One of Israel,
    apostatized,
Why would you yet be struck,
    that you continue to rebel?
The whole head is sick,
    the whole heart faint.
From the sole of the foot to the head,
    there is no sound spot in it;
Just bruise and welt and oozing wound,
    not drained, or bandaged,
    or eased with salve.
Your country is waste,
    your cities burnt with fire;
Your land—before your eyes
    strangers devour it,
    a waste like the devastation of Sodom.
And daughter Zion is left
    like a hut in a vineyard,
Like a shed in a melon patch,
    like a city blockaded.
If the LORD of hosts had not
    left us a small remnant,
We would have become as Sodom,
    would have resembled Gomorrah. (Isa 1:4-9)

A Virgin Shall Bear a Child

But Isaiah did not confine himself to the role of preacher of morality. Instead, he became for all generations the great prophet of the parousia, of Yahweh's coming. As Amos had risen up to protest the lust for domination that had been stimulated by the flourishing economic situation of Judah and Samaria in the eighth century, so Isaiah predicted the disaster that the day of Yahweh would bring (Isa 2:1-17). The day of Yahweh was to be a day of judgment upon Israel. In Isaiah's view, as later in Paul's and John's, the coming of the Lord would mean the triumph of true justice.

Chapters 7 to 11 describe for us the prince who would rule in peace and justice. In chapter 7 there is an extremely important passage:

Again the LORD spoke to Ahaz: Ask for a sign from the LORD, your God; let it be deep as Sheol, or high as the sky! But Ahaz answered, "I will not ask! I will not tempt the LORD!" Then he said: Listen, house of David! Is it not enough that you weary human beings? Must you also weary my God? Therefore the Lord himself will give you a sign; the young woman, pregnant and about to bear a son, shall name him Emmanuel. Curds and honey he will eat so that he may learn to reject evil and choose good; for before the child learns to reject evil and choose good, the land of those two kings whom you dread shall be deserted.

The LORD shall bring upon you and your people and your father's house such days as have not come since Ephraim seceded from Judah (the king of Assyria). (Isa 7:10-17)

It is important that we familiarize ourselves with the twofold meaning of this text. For unless we grasp the ambiguous reality of which it speaks, we shall always be unable to understand the Scriptures, including certain passages of the gospel, and to experience the full impact of the liturgy. The gospel for the First Sunday of Advent, which deals with the two perspectives of Advent—the end of the world and the parousia—is an example of the same specifically biblical phenomenon in which one and the same event points to two different realities.

The kingdom of Judah must undergo devastation and ruin. The contemptuous infidelity of King Ahaz must be punished. Nevertheless, God's promise to David by the mouth of Nathan the prophet will not be cancelled out. The sign given to Ahaz and the house of David is the certain destruction to come upon Jerusalem and the royal dynasty. But Yahweh will remain true to his word, and "Emmanuel" will indeed bless Israel with his presence. In the meantime, however, the sign given to Ahaz will have long been fulfilled in the destruction of his house and kingdom.

The Golden Age

Moreover, the literary form of the oracle and the manner in which Isaiah speaks of the birth and early years of this child hint to us that the prophet is looking beyond the political situation of his time and seeing the child as one who will save the entire world. In later oracles Isaiah will describe the characteristics of this Messiah. Here he is content simply to note them incidentally, reserving their detailed description for later. Here is how he describes this just king:

> But a shoot shall sprout from the stump of Jesse,
> and from his roots a bud shall blossom.
> The spirit of the LORD shall rest upon him:
> a spirit of wisdom and understanding,
> A spirit of counsel and of strength,
> a spirit of knowledge and of fear of the LORD,
> and his delight shall be in fear of the LORD.
> Not by appearance shall he judge,
> nor by hearsay shall he decide,
> But he shall judge the poor with justice,
> and decide fairly for the land's afflicted.
> He shall strike the ruthless with the rod of his mouth,
> and with the breath of his lips he shall slay the wicked.
> Justice shall be the band around his waist,
> and faithfulness a belt upon his hips.
> Then the wolf shall be a guest of the lamb,
> and the leopard shall lie down with the young goat;
> The calf and the young lion shall browse together,
> with a little child to guide them.
> The cow and the bear shall graze,
> together their young shall lie down;
> the lion shall eat hay like the ox.
> The baby shall play by the viper's den,
> and the child lay his hand on the adder's lair.
> They shall not harm or destroy on all my holy mountain;
> for the earth shall be filled with knowledge of the LORD,
> as water covers the sea. (Isa 11:1-9)

In the past, the attribution of this passage to Isaiah was called into question, but no one today openly challenges its authenticity. The reader will, of course, have recognized it as the source of the traditional doctrine of the seven gifts of the Holy Spirit.

The prophecy describes the ideal judge, who is also a warrior, a priest, and a prophet. The restoration of justice and order turns a world of strife into a true earthly paradise, in which beasts we know as ferocious live side by side with the meeker animals. The prince of justice reconstitutes the unity that had been lost.

Here again, a twofold interpretation may be called for. Ezechias is about to take the throne, and the poem is written—if we are to believe certain critics—in praise of him. But how can a weak human being possess so many eminent qualities? Is Isaiah not seeing here, behind Ezechias, the figure of the Messiah? That, at least, is how the Church understands the passage; she assigns the reading to the Second Sunday of Advent (A).

We have already heard Isaiah, in the second chapter of his book, prophesying a parousia that would also be a judgment. In chapter 13 he describes the fall of Babylon when it was captured by Cyrus. Once again, we are invited to look beyond this historical event to the coming of Yahweh on his "day." The description of the cataclysms that will occur are repeated by Joel and again in Revelation.

> Indeed, the day of the LORD comes,
>   cruel, with wrath and burning anger;
> To lay waste the land
>   and destroy the sinners within it!
> The stars of the heavens and their constellations
>   will send forth no light;
> The sun will be dark at its rising,
>   and the moon will not give its light.
> Thus I will punish the world for its evil
>   and the wicked for their guilt.
> I will put an end to the pride of the arrogant,
>   the insolence of tyrants I will humble. (Isa 13:9-11)

At his coming Yahweh will crush the one who had willed to become God's equal (Isa 14). St. John, in the book of Revelation, will use similar images to describe the overthrow of the devil.

Beginning on Monday of the Second Week of Advent, the Church has us read lengthy passages from the "Apocalypse" of Isaiah (chaps. 24–27) in the Office of Readings. Modern critics propose that these chapters did not come from Isaiah; the poems, however, are certainly expressive of his outlook. They depict the day of Yahweh and the parousia; that is why the Church reads them during this season. The overall choice of readings from Isaiah is a further proof that the liturgy of Advent is concerned with the two comings of Christ, for the readings are sometimes from the passages on Emmanuel, sometimes from those that speak of the parousia.

At Mass on the Second Monday of Advent (A), we find Isaiah describing the coming of Yahweh: "The burning sands will become pools, / and the thirsty ground, springs of water" (35:7). We see here a reference to the curse that had come upon creation as the result of human sin (Gen). Yahweh is coming, however, and will restore everything to its proper form. At the same time, Isaiah foretells the healings that Jesus will use as a way of proclaiming God's reign: "Then will the eyes of the blind be opened, / the ears of the deaf be cleared; / then will the lame leap like a stag, / then the tongue of the mute will sing" (35:5-6). Jesus will allude to this passage when he sends the messengers back to John in prison [25].

We can summarize the whole of the prophet's work by relating it to two objectives. The first was to deal with a present historical situation, by struggling against it and by providing a remedy for it. That very remedy necessarily involved his second objective: the more distant messianic future and the restoration of the world to Yahweh's good grace. Isaiah comes before us as the messenger of a God whom he has seen face to face. As though hypnotized by this God, Isaiah speaks of him in every line he writes. Yet his very descriptions also bring home to us the fact that Yahweh is the Holy One, the one who is apart from us, and the one whom, therefore, we cannot fully understand. He is the one who refuses to let us know him. Or, more accurately, we can know him only through his works, which concentrate above all on holiness or justice. To establish justice, Yahweh intervenes constantly in the course of history. The prophet may give a literary form to his description of these interventions, but they are nonetheless really historical, both in fact and in the prophet's conception of them. At the same time, however, as we read Isaiah we are constantly looking beyond the historical interventions of God to the coming age of the Messiah.

How attractive a person Isaiah is: a man awed by the greatness of his God, a man convinced that God is constantly intervening in his creation through specific, historical, even contemporary actions, yet also a man who has his mind fixed on the greatest of all these interventions, the final realization of the divine redemptive plan in the Messiah.

The Messiah will be born of a woman and thus be part of the dynasty of David, as Matthew reminds us at the beginning of his gospel. But the Messiah's coming is not the end. Isaiah bids us look beyond him to the day of Yahweh, a day that is all-decisive and terrible, yet also a day of justice and peace when the world will find itself once again ordered and at one with its Maker.

Thus we find in Isaiah the two great perspectives of the Advent season and liturgy.

7. THIRD WEEK OF ADVENT: THE MESSIANIC AGE

The Third Sunday of Advent has traditionally been marked by the note of joy. As we shall see, the joy has two causes: the proximate coming of the Lord in the incarnation and his return at the end of time. The collect for this Sunday speaks of God's people, who "faithfully await the feast of the Lord's Nativity," while the collect for Wednesday of this week asks: "that the coming solemnity of your Son may bestow healing upon us in this present life and bring us the rewards of life eternal." In fact, the prayers on the whole are clearly inspired by joyful expectation of the Nativity. Moreover, this week thinks of the kingdom as already present [66].

> (A) God is coming to save us; his coming is at hand;
> the cures are signs of his presence.

The cures in the gospels are always presented as signs of the messianic age. This point is emphasized in both the first reading [19] and the gospel [25] for this third Sunday. The focus is on the presence now of the messianic age. Nothing could be simpler or more impressive than the answer Jesus gives to the messengers sent by John the Baptist; both John and his messengers are, of course, well aware of Isaiah's prophecy [19]. As we observed earlier, the capacity we now have for seeing, understanding, and living a new kind of life is a sign that God's reign has begun and that we now await its definitive establishment in us and the world.

St. James exhorts us to patience as we wait for the day not too far distant when God's kingdom will be fully established [22]. He compares the patience we must have to that of a farmer. Like him, we plant the seed and then must await the harvest. The exhortation is one by now familiar to us: Wait in patience and mutual love. Christian hope is compounded of patience and love, and St. James offers us as a model the sufferings and persevering patience of the prophets.

(B) In our midst is one we do not recognize.
Rejoice in the presence of him who bears the Spirit's mark.

After identifying himself in a negative way, John the Baptist directs his hearers' attention to one who is among his people but unrecognized by them: "[T]here is one among you whom you do not recognize, the one who is coming after me, whose sandal strap I am not worthy to untie" [26]. Observe that John denies that he is Elijah, and yet Christ says that John was indeed Elijah but no one recognized him [56]. The presence of the Messiah makes conversion necessary to enter the kingdom that is now here.

Isaiah foretells the coming of the Messiah and gives us an attractive picture of this man whom the Spirit has consecrated [20]. The one on whom the Spirit rests will preach the Good News to the poor and heal the brokenhearted. He will establish justice in the presence of all the nations. We have already had occasion to emphasize these characteristic traits of the Messiah. The new element on this third Sunday, the element that gives the day its special tone, is the joy that fills him who has been sent to proclaim salvation: "I rejoice heartily in the LORD, / in my God is the joy of my soul; / for he has clothed me with a robe of salvation / and wrapped me in a mantle of justice" [20].

This poem of Isaiah evidently parallels the *Magnificat* of the Blessed Virgin. The Church therefore uses the latter as a responsorial psalm after the reading from Isaiah: "My soul proclaims the greatness of the Lord; / my spirit rejoices in God my Savior."

St. Paul, in his First Letter to the Thessalonians, gives advice on how we are to await the Lord's coming. Three things, he says, are essential: joy, constant prayer, and thanksgiving in all circumstances. These are what should basically characterize the life of the Christian. But there is another virtue that is extremely important: not to quench the Spirit. This means not to grow content, even with our joy or prayer or thanksgiving, but to be flexible enough to accept the questions raised by another whom the Spirit has moved. In all things, however, we must exercise discernment.

There is a thought that will prove very strengthening to us as we wait. It is that the God who calls us is faithful and will do all that he has promised.

(C) One mightier than John the Baptist is coming.
Rejoice, for he is here!
Now is the time of brotherhood and justice.

As soon as they realized that the messianic age was at hand, all—crowds, tax collectors, soldiers—had to ask themselves: "What should we do?" [27]. The same question arises at times in our own minds: "What should we do?" Unfortunately, the question, as we ask it, refers too exclusively to practices that we hope will be sure ways of reaching eternal life. John's answer is simple. No matter who asks the question of him, he answers: "Be just in the work you do. Live as you should, being righteous and conscious of the needs of others." That is, in fact, the only valid answer. The Christian should always be a person of joy, with serenity evident to all. A Christian cannot be disturbed but must in all circumstances pray and thank God, while also addressing petitions to him. That, for the believer, is the source of the peace "that surpasses all understanding" [24].

John tells us that the Messiah's coming is imminent; he is at hand. And in a joyful poem Zephaniah assures us: "[T]he King of Israel, the LORD, is in your midst. / . . . The LORD, your God, is in your midst, / a mighty savior" [21].

The Kingdom Is Here

The blind see, the lame walk, the lepers are cleansed, the deaf regain their hearing, the dead rise, and the Good News is preached to the poor [66]. Always the same signs of the same presence. We must be always interpreting them and seeing how they apply today, in our lives. They are disturbing signs, because they confront us with a demanding choice, but they are also reassuring, because they are a sign of victory. Isaiah is very positive on this last point: "[F]or I am God; there is no other! / By myself I swear, / uttering my just decree, / and my unalterable word: / To me every knee shall bend; / by me every tongue shall swear. . . . / In the LORD shall be the vindication and the glory / of all the descendants of Israel" [65].

In chapter 31 Isaiah describes the final victory in another fashion, by recalling the Lord's triumphs over his enemies. The passage is read in Office on Wednesday of this third week [102].

The Office also contains a text of St. Irenaeus of Lyons, who comments on the coming of Christ and the possibility of our seeing God:

> By his own powers man cannot see God, yet God will be seen by men because he wills it. He will be seen by those he chooses, at the time he chooses, and in the way he chooses, for God can do all things. He was seen of old through the Spirit in prophecy; he is seen through the Son by our adoption as his children, and he will be seen in the kingdom of heaven in his own being as the Father. The Spirit prepares man to receive the Son of God, the Son leads him to the Father, and the Father, freeing him from change and decay, bestows the eternal life that comes to everyone from seeing God.
>
> As those who see light are in the light sharing its brilliance, so those who see God are in God sharing his glory, and that glory gives them life. To see God is to share in life.[1]

A Star Shall Arise

The proclamation of Jesus the Messiah becomes ever clearer. In the book of Numbers, which is read on the Third Monday of Advent, the pagan prophet Balaam says: "I see him, though not now; / I behold him, though not near: / A star shall advance from Jacob, / and a staff shall rise from Israel" [61].

In the gospel of the same day, Jesus has no desire to hide the source of his authority, but because the chief priests are unwilling to admit the authority by which John baptized, neither will Jesus tell them by what authority he himself teaches: "Neither shall I tell you by what authority I do these things" [62].

The entrance antiphon on this day proclaims the coming of the Messiah in the words of Jeremiah and Isaiah: "Hear the word of the Lord, O nations; declare it to the distant lands: Behold, our Savior will come; you need no longer fear" (see Jer 31:10; Isa 35:4).

But we must look for and discover this Lord who has already come. It is of this that the collect at Mass on this Monday speaks: "casting light on the darkness of our hearts, visit us with the grace of your Son."

John prepares the way for the Lord. That is why he was sent. "Then what did you go out to see? A prophet? Yes, I tell you, and more than a prophet. This is the one about whom Scripture says, *Behold, I am sending my messenger ahead of you, he will prepare your way before you*" [68].

The Office for Thursday of the third week, in order to highlight John's prophetic function, emphasizes the role of Christ himself. For this purpose it uses a text of Vatican II on revelation:

> After God had spoken many times and in various ways through the prophets, "in these last days he has spoken to us by a Son" (Heb 1:1-2). For he sent his Son, the eternal Word who enlightens all humankind, to live among them and to tell them about the inner life of God. Hence, Jesus Christ, sent as "a man being men and women," "speaks the words of God" (Jn 3:34), and accomplishes the saving work which the Father gave him to do (see Jn 5:36; 17:4). As a result, he himself—to see whom is to see the Father (see Jn 14:9)—completed and perfected revelation and confirmed it with divine guarantees. Everything to do with his presence and his manifestation of himself was involved in achieving this: his words and works, signs and miracles, but above all his death and glorious resurrection from the dead, and finally his sending of the Spirit of truth. He revealed that God was with us, to deliver us from the darkness of sin and death, and to raise us up to eternal life.[2]

This revelation is given because the Lord loves his people and is calling them back to himself like a wife who had been abandoned. This is what Isaiah tells us in the reading for the Mass of the third Thursday. God in his anger had hidden his face for a moment, but his eternal love won out and he took pity on humanity. His love will be unchanging, and his covenant of peace shall never be shaken [67].

John, a Lamp Burning Bright

With increasing clarity Jesus asserts that he is the Messiah who has come among us. "John was a burning and shining lamp, and for a while you were content to rejoice in his light. But I have testimony greater than John's. The works that the Father gave me to accomplish, these works that I perform testify on my behalf that the Father has sent me" [70].

He is the Christ who brings salvation and gathers us into unity. The reading from Isaiah at Mass on the third Friday emphasizes this fact once more: "[F]or my salvation is about to come, / my justice, about to be revealed." The universal scope of the salvation that the Messiah brings becomes increasingly clear in the prophets. Even foreigners will come "to my holy mountain," and the Lord will make them happy in his "house of prayer." His house shall be called "a house of prayer for all peoples" [69].

Here the gathering of all people and their meeting with the Lord are thought of as taking place in a "house of prayer." And indeed the desire to meet the Lord is to some extent identical with prayer. St. Augustine develops this theme in commenting on Psalm 37:13-14, and the passage has been taken into the Office for the Third Friday of Advent. Here is a short extract from it:

> For the desire of your heart is itself your prayer. And if the desire is constant, so is your prayer. The Apostle Paul had a purpose in saying: *Pray without ceasing.* Are we then ceaselessly to bend our knees, to lie prostrate, or to lift up our hands? Is this what is meant in saying: *Pray without ceasing*? Even if we admit that we pray in this fashion, I do not believe that we can do so all the time.
>
> Yet there is another, interior kind of prayer without ceasing, namely, the desire of the heart. . . . Therefore, if you wish to pray without ceasing, do not cease to desire.[3]

Expectation, then, means desire based on faith and is a form of prayer. John came, but they did not believe him [64]. Now the salvation brought by the Messiah has been preached to the poor [63], but we must actually accept that salvation. If we are to accept it, we must desire it, and to desire it is to pray for it. Such is the attitude to which we have been exhorted on several occasions during this season.

Overview

The readings in the Office for this week always concentrate on the Lord's return at the end and on future salvation [99–104]. The readings at Mass, however, emphasize rather the presence among us of the messianic age and the kingdom. We are at a critical point in the time before Christmas, and the liturgy is beginning to focus more on the fact of Christ's coming in the flesh.

We are bidden, in the Office, to meditate on a subject by now quite familiar, and we might easily think of ourselves as marking time while we do it. Salvation on the last day [99], the pressing need of conversion and the future happiness we can now glimpse [100], the coming of the Lord to punish the Assyrians, a prefiguring of the Messiah's triumph over evil [101], the establishment of the reign of justice [102], a restoration of the world that should be the subject of our hope in the Lord [103] and turn our thoughts to our future salvation [104]—such are the themes proposed to us in the Office of Readings. True, they are not new, but there is certainly room for us to enter more deeply into them.

The Scripture readings at Mass are more concerned with the prediction of the Messiah and with his presence among us; meanwhile, the person of John the Baptist and his mission as Precursor are also emphasized. For this reason it will be good to reflect a bit on his personality.

John the Baptist, a Man of Expectation

If we limit the close relationship between John the Baptist and Isaiah to a mere matter of literary borrowing, we show that we have not understood either John or Isaiah. As a matter of fact, it is difficult to separate these two men; between them there is a continuity of thought, message, and role. Isaiah is present to us in John the Baptist, just as John is present in him whose way he prepares and who will say of him: "Amen, I say to you, among those born of women there has been none greater than John the Baptist" [25].

We know Isaiah only through his writings. For John, on the contrary, we have the gospel to inform us of his origins, his words, and his attitudes. St. Luke reports in detail the announcement of the birth of the Baptist (Luke 1:5-25). The miraculous entry on the scene of a person who will represent a very important milestone in the execution of the divine plan is quite common in the Old Testament tradition. All living beings were to be wiped out by the Flood, but Noah and his family were saved in the ark. Isaac was born of Sarah when she was too old to have children. David, a young boy without experience in battle, laid Goliath low. Moses, the future leader of the Israelites, was found in a basket (the word in Hebrew also means "ark") and saved from death. In all these occurrences God was making it clear that he was taking the initiative in the salvation of his people and choosing for himself the instruments he would use as he saw fit.

The announcement of John's birth is a solemn one that occurs within the framework of the temple liturgy. Everything about the child, including his name, which means "Yahweh is gracious," is part of God's careful preparation of the instrument he has chosen. John's birth will not go unnoticed but will be a source of joy for many (Luke

1:14). He will be one consecrated to the Lord and therefore, as prescribed in the book of Numbers (6:1-21), will drink neither wine nor strong drink. This Nazirite vow points ahead to John's calling to be an ascetic and one in whom the Holy Spirit has dwelt since he was in his mother's womb.

In addition to being an ascetic, John is to be a leader of his people (Luke 1:18) and will go before the Messiah, a role that Malachi (3:23) assigns to Elijah. At John's circumcision, the fact that God is setting him apart is made clear in a new way: he is given a name that no one among his kinsfolk has borne (Luke 1:61); despite custom, God wishes him to be named John. The Lord has chosen this child; the Lord is controlling events and leading his people.

"Blessed Be the Lord God of Israel"

John's birth is the occasion for a splendid poem that is both a song of thanksgiving and a description of the child's future role. The Church recites this poem daily at the end of Morning Praise, expressing through it her praise of God for the salvation he has given her and her gratitude for John who continues to show her "the path of peace."

> Blessed be the Lord, the God of Israel,
> > for he has visited and brought redemption to his people.
> He has raised up a horn for our salvation
> > within the house of David his servant,
> even as he promised by the mouth of his holy prophets from of old:
> > salvation from our enemies and from the hand of all who hate us,
> to show mercy to our fathers
> > and to be mindful of his holy covenant
> and of the oath he swore to Abraham our father,
> > and to grant us that,
> rescued from the hand of enemies,
> > without fear we might worship him
> in holiness and righteousness
> > before him all our days.
> And you, child, will be called prophet of the Most High,
> > for you will go before the Lord to prepare his ways,
> to give his people knowledge of salvation
> > through the forgiveness of their sins,
> because of the tender mercy of our God,
> > by which the daybreak from on high will visit us

to shine on those who sit in darkness and death's shadow,
    to guide our feet into the path of peace. (Luke 1:68-79; NABRE)

John the Baptist is a sign that God is again intervening in his people's history. The Lord is visiting them, saving them, and bringing about the covenant he had promised. The Precursor's role is clearly defined: it is to prepare the way for the Lord (see Isa 40:3) and to bring his people "knowledge of salvation."

The exclusive subject of Israel's speculation and contemplation was precisely the knowledge of salvation and of God's marvelous plan for his people. Such knowledge it was that prompted the thanksgiving, blessing, and proclamation of God's benefits that we find in Zechariah's canticle. "Blessed be the Lord, the God of Israel" was in fact the traditional formula Israel used in expressing its gratitude and wonder at God's plan. Abraham's servant uses the words when he thanks Yahweh (Gen 24:26). Jethro, father-in-law of Moses, uses them in his response to the amazing story of what Yahweh had done in rescuing Israel from the hands of the Egyptians (Exod 18:10).

The salvation that John will make known consists in the forgiveness of sins and is the work of God's tender mercy (Luke 1:77-78). John's role will be to announce a baptism in the Spirit that will effect the forgiveness of sins. But this baptism will not be purely negative in its effects; it will also bring enlightenment. For the tender mercy of God will send us a Messiah who, according to two passages of Isaiah (9:1; 42:7) to which Christ alludes (John 8:12), will "shine on those who sit in darkness and death's shadow" (Luke 1:79).

John's mission will be to go before the Lord to prepare straight paths for him. He is aware of this and speaks of himself, in Isaiah's words, as "the voice of one crying out in the desert, / 'Make straight the way of the Lord'" (John 1:23). He will act in an even more positive way by making known the one who is already there but unrecognized (John 1:26) and pointing him out when he comes: "Behold, the Lamb of God, who takes away the sin of the world" (John 1:29).

John wishes to, and does, live up to what had been foretold of him, namely, that he would bear witness to the Messiah's presence. The way in which he speaks of the Messiah shows what the latter meant to him: the Messiah is "the Lamb of God." John knew, of course, the fourteenth chapter of Leviticus, which describes the immolation of a lamb in expiation for legal impurity. When he read it, he thought of the Servant of Yahweh, whom Isaiah had described in chapter 53 as carrying the guilt of all Israel. In pointing Christ out to his disciples, John already has a vision of him as the true Passover Lamb whose death will be far more effective than that of the Passover Lamb in Exodus (12:1) and will bring salvation to the whole world.

The greatness of John the Baptist is due to his humility and self-effacement. He is bathed in the radiant light of the Messiah, whom he is so anxious not to hide from others: "He must increase; I must decrease" (John 3:30).

"All Flesh Shall See the Salvation of God"

John's role and his determination to be self-effacing have made him a vital figure down the centuries. We cannot speak of him without speaking of Christ, but the Church has also reversed that relationship and never recalls Christ's coming without also recalling his Precursor. The Precursor is linked not only to Christ's coming but to his work as well, for John announces that work as being the redemption of the world and the rebuilding of the world through the years until the parousia. Each year the Church reminds us of John's testimony and of his attitude toward the message he preaches.

In consequence, John is present at every point in the Advent liturgy. As a matter of fact, the Church should constantly have his example before her eyes, since it is her mission, and that of each of us, to prepare the way for the Lord and to proclaim the Good News. Fulfillment of this mission, however, requires a conversion. If one is really to be the instrument of Christ, one must be divested of self. Without such an asceticism on our part, Christ can be in the midst of the world and go unrecognized (see John 1:26). Like John, the Church and her members have an obligation not to stand between humanity and the light but rather to bear witness to the light (John 1:7).

The Bride, who is the Church, must yield place to the Bridegroom; she is a witness and must let attention be focused on him to whom she bears witness. It is difficult to be present in the world, present to the point even of suffering martyrdom, and yet not to focus attention on some "institution" instead of on Christ himself. "He must increase; I must decrease." It is difficult to proclaim the Good News and not this or that spirituality or religious order or special form of Catholic Action or parochial interest. It is difficult to act like John and show our disciples where they can find the "Lamb of God" and not keep them for ourselves as though we were their light.

This lesson is always valid and always necessary, as is the lesson of John's desert asceticism and of a loving inwardness for the sake of being a better witness. The eloquent silence of the desert is the foundation for any genuinely effective proclamation of the Good News.

In his commentary on St. Luke's gospel, Origen writes, "For myself, I think that the mystery of John is still being fulfilled in the world, even today."[4] The Church is continuing the work of the Precursor, showing Christ to us and directing us to the coming of the Lord.

During Advent, the great figure of the Baptist is a living reality for us in our century as we advance toward the Day of Christ. Christ himself, referring to Malachi 3:1, speaks of John as a "messenger" [25], and John speaks of himself in the same way [26]. St. Luke describes John as a preacher who calls for an unqualified conversion and a renewal: "Every valley shall be filled / and every mountain and hill shall be made low. / The winding roads shall be made straight, / and the rough ways made smooth, / and all flesh shall see the salvation of God" (Luke 3:5-6). The words are from a poem of Isaiah (40:4-5) that Luke uses in order to describe John's work. John is calling for a renewal, a shake-up, a conversion that consists chiefly in the effort to practice love of neighbor.

> The crowds asked John the Baptist, "What should we do?" He said to them in reply, "Whoever has two cloaks should share with the person who has none. And whoever has food should do likewise." Even tax collectors came to be baptized and they said to him, "Teacher, what should we do?" He answered them, "Stop collecting more than what is prescribed." Soldiers also asked him, "And what is it that we should do?" He told them, "Do not practice extortion, do not falsely accuse anyone, and be satisfied with your wages." [27]

Luke sums up the whole of John's activity in a short sentence: "he preached good news to the people" [27]. John's role, then, was to prepare the way for the Lord and to preach the Good News. He exhorts us to do the same.

The task is no simpler today than it was in John's time, and it is incumbent on each of us. John was martyred, in the last analysis, because he was frank and honest in his denunciation of sin. Christians today often compromise, under the pretext of being more open to the world; in the end, they are in danger of becoming like Herodias and strangling the voice. What a contrast! An age that is all for authenticity also tries to drown out the voice of anyone who makes demands on it! This is not the only paradox in human life, of course, but it is one of which we must be aware.

John the Baptist announced the Lamb of God. He was the first to give this name to Christ, anticipating the book of Revelation, which invites us to the marriage feast of the victorious Lamb after he has shed his blood for the redemption of the world. This is why we cannot participate in the eucharistic banquet, which is the wedding feast of the Lamb on earth, without at the same time proclaiming the death and resurrection of the Lord and the demands made upon us who have been baptized into that death and resurrection. This is the inexorable logic of Christian life; John lived by this logic and bore witness to it with his blood.

We must quote here the beautiful preface recently introduced into the liturgy for the feast of the martyrdom of St. John the Baptist; it is a fine summation of his life and his role:

> His birth brought great rejoicing; even in the womb he leapt for joy at the coming of human salvation. He alone of all the prophets pointed out the Lamb of redemption. And to make holy the flowing waters, he baptized the very author of Baptism and was privileged to bear him supreme witness by the shedding of his blood.

8. FOURTH WEEK OF ADVENT: THE ANNUNCIATION OF THE MESSIAH'S COMING

The liturgy of Advent now turns its full attention to the coming birth of the Lord. The antiphons concentrate on it: for example, the entrance antiphon for the fourth Sunday, "Drop down dew from above, you heavens, and let the clouds rain down the Just One; let the earth be opened and bring forth a Savior" (Isa 45:8); and the communion antiphon for the same day, "Behold, a Virgin shall conceive and bear a son; and his name will be called Emmanuel" (Isa 7:14). The prayers too increase our awareness of the coming that is at hand: for example, the collect for the fourth Sunday: "the Incarnation of Christ your Son was made known by the message of an Angel."

We are making a definite transition, therefore, to the other major theme of the Advent liturgy: expectation of the incarnation of the Word.

(A) The annunciation to Joseph. A virgin shall conceive the
Son of God, Jesus Christ, who is of David's line.

St. Matthew's gospel describes the dramatic situation that St. Joseph finds himself in when he learns of his fiancée's state [34]. The narrative indicates three points that are extremely important for the history of salvation: the incarnation of the Word as a member of David's line; the intervention of the Spirit; the role of the one to be born, whose name "Jesus" means "The Lord saves," since it is he who will save the world from its sins. All this the angel announces, and Joseph's response is an act of faith.

The story may strike us as very unsophisticated. As a matter of fact, nothing changed as a result in the life of the times; life went on as it always had, the sun shone as before, people worked or played, did good or evil—nothing changed. Nor was there apparently any change in the outward lives of Joseph and Mary. This fact should put

127

us on guard against thinking of the events of salvation as theatrical in character. They are not. They respect and do not disturb the course of events, and for that very reason we sometimes minimize their importance. Here we are, for example, at the very turning point of world history, for history will be changed and take on an entirely new meaning. Yet nothing of this appears on the surface. Joseph goes on as before while he waits; he is caught up in the drama, but he is at peace ever since he accepted God's will in faith.

This is the sign the Lord gives: "Therefore the Lord himself will give you this sign; the virgin shall conceive, and bear a son, and shall name him Emmanuel" [28]. The responsorial psalm chosen for this reading brings out the divine rank of him who is to be born:

> The LORD's is the earth and its fullness,
> the world, and those who dwell in it.
> It is he who set it on the seas;
> on the rivers he made it firm. (Ps 24:1-2)

The psalm goes on to specify what is required of those who wish to draw near to this king:

> The clean of hands and pure of heart,
> whose soul is not set on vain things. (Ps 24:4)

St. Paul has no greater news to give the Romans than this. In fact, it is precisely to proclaim this Good News that he has been set apart as an apostle. It is the Good News concerning the Son of God, "descended from David according to the flesh, but established as Son of God in power according to the Spirit of holiness through resurrection from the dead, Jesus Christ our Lord" [31]. Paul is here pointing to the close link between the incarnation and the paschal mystery. It is this link that makes possible the actualization of the mystery of Christ's birth in the liturgy.

In the eucharistic prayer he suggests for the day of a bishop's consecration, St. Hippolytus of Rome* speaks in a way that is strange

---

* Throughout the work, Nocent assumes that the author of the source for Eucharistic Prayer II was Hippolytus. However, this now seems unlikely. See Paul F. Bradshaw, Maxwell E. Johnson, L. Edward Phillips, *The Apostolic Tradition: A Commentary*, Hermeneia (Minneapolis: Fortress Press, 2002), 1–6.

to us but one that brings out the importance of the incarnation. He says of Jesus: "[H]e was incarnate and manifested as your Son."[1] The Son is, of course, eternally the Son. Hippolytus has in mind, however, the fact on which John the Evangelist lays so much stress: the Son's essential role is to do the Father's will. Hippolytus thinks, therefore, that the Son truly merits his name of Son when he obeys the Father and does his will by giving his life for the redemption of the world. To do the Father's will in this fashion, the Son had to become human.

This idea of Hippolytus, which at first glance seems opposed to faith (since the Son is eternal), as a matter of fact throws light on the role of the incarnation in the history of salvation. We can never over-emphasize the reality of Christ's humanity and of his birth from a virgin in accordance with the prophecy [28].

(B) The annunciation to Mary.
The throne of David will last forever.
God is now revealing the mystery hidden through the ages.

To this account of the annunciation to Mary, which has so often been the subject of literary treatment and pictorial representation, our response should be one inspired by faith alone, as Mary's was at the time. The account, like all great things, is simple; we have trouble conceiving the event and get ourselves twisted up when we try to explain it. There is God's choice, the intervention of the Spirit, Mary's faith-inspired acceptance, and the conception of God's Son by a woman [35]. In straightforward fashion the angel says that the promise made to David by the prophet Nathan is being fulfilled. The first reading records this promise: "I will make you famous like the great ones of the earth. . . . Your house and your kingdom shall endure forever before me; your throne shall stand firm forever" [29].

Psalm 89 was a natural choice to provide a response to such a reading: "With my chosen one I have made a covenant; / I have sworn to David my servant: / I will establish your descendants forever, / and set up your throne through all ages" (Ps 89:4-5).

The mystery that has been hidden through the ages is now revealed. St. Paul cannot hide from the Romans his wonder at the execution of God's plan of reconstruction that was announced at the very moment of the Fall in the promise made to Eve and that was being implemented in silence down the centuries. "Mystery" here is not what we habitually take it to be: that which we can neither see nor understand. For Paul, it is something revealed to all, for the salvation of all. "[M]y gospel . . . according to the revelation of the mystery kept secret for long ages but now manifested through the prophetic writings and, according to the command of the eternal God, made known to all nations to bring about the obedience of faith." He concludes with a shout of enthusiasm: "to the only wise God, through Jesus Christ be glory forever and ever. Amen" [32].

(C) The annunciation to Elizabeth.
From Judah shall come forth one who shall rule Israel.
He comes to do God's will.

John the Baptist leaps for joy in his mother's womb as he meets the Lord, who is concealed in the Virgin's womb. Elizabeth's words to Mary are a profession of faith: "Blessed are you among women, and blessed is the fruit of your womb. And how does this happen to me, that the mother of my Lord should come to me?" [36].

The first two readings, which tell what the child will be, stand in contrast and yet are in profound harmony. The first, from the prophet Micah, speaks of the Messiah as one who shall shepherd his flock by the strength of the Lord. In his person, "he shall be peace" [30]. After a time of seeming abandonment, the Lord will send the Savior.

The responsorial psalm sings of this mighty Shepherd: "O shepherd of Israel, hear us, / . . . enthroned on the cherubim, shine forth. / . . . Rouse up your might and come to save us" (Ps 80:2-3).

The Letter to the Hebrews, for its part, already has its eye on the paschal mystery and the obedience unto death of the Messiah who comes among us. The coming of Christ in the flesh does away with all the other sacrifices, which the Father had not wanted. Jesus offers himself in expiation for sins. His sacrifice is first and foremost a spiritual sacrifice, which consists in doing the Father's will; his giving of himself to the point of bloodshed and death is a sign of that inner sacrifice. The author of the letter takes us fully into the paschal mystery when he adds: "By this 'will' [of the incarnate Word], we have been consecrated through the offering of the body of Jesus Christ once for all" [33].

Jesus, Son of David

Nothing could be more impressive than the genealogy of Jesus and its magnificent ending: "Jacob [was] the father of Joseph, the husband of Mary. Of her was born Jesus who is called the Christ" [72]. This entrance of God into the world as one of us is the event that towers over the whole of human history. In point of fact, however, it does not control our personal lives. Our faith is so weak that our attitudes do not befit the dignity proper to people in the ages after the Son entered the world. The collect for December 17 seems to be the prayer of one moved by the mystery: "O God, Creator and Redeemer of human nature, who willed that your Word should take flesh in an ever-virgin womb, look with favor on our prayers, that your Only Begotten Son, having taken to himself our humanity, may be pleased to grant us a share in his divinity." Thus, the scepter will not pass from Judah; God will keep his promise [71].

The gospel for December 18 concentrates once again on the birth of the Savior as a man. His birth is from a virgin, and his mission will be to "save," as his name, "Jesus," indicates. Thus the prophecy of Isaiah concerning the birth of Emmanuel will be fulfilled. He who is to come is both son of David and Son of God [74]. He will bring right and justice into the world [73].

The Birth of John the Baptist

The event is an important one and is spoken of twice in the readings of the final week of Advent. On December 19 the gospel recounts the announcement of John's birth to his father. It is an announcement resembling that made to Mary, but it is received in a very different way, leading to the punishment of Zechariah for his lack of faith. The power of God who alone chooses, and chooses as he wishes, is very much accentuated in this account. The Old Testament saw the impossible birth of Isaac, the handing over to Jacob of the rights proper to the firstborn son, and the saving of Moses from the waters. The New Testament now sees the birth of John and will soon see that of Christ. God uses the means, and the people, he chooses [76].

The first reading, from the book of Judges, offers the announcement of Samson's birth as a parallel, for an angel told his barren mother that the boy would be conceived and born. He would be a man consecrated to God from his conception until his death [75]. When the

Lord is determined to save, nothing can stop him—that is the message of Psalm 71, which supplies the response for this day. "Be my rock, my constant refuge, / a mighty stronghold to save me, / for you are my rock, my stronghold" (Ps 71:3).

At John's birth, Zechariah recovers his speech: " 'What, then, will this child be?' For surely the hand of the Lord was with him" [84]. John's birth precedes that of the Savior. That is why a parallel for the gospel of December 23 has been sought in Malachi, who speaks of Elijah the prophet being sent "Before the day of the LORD comes, / the great and terrible day" [83]. We will recall how Jesus pointed to John as the Elijah who was to come.

A Virgin Shall Conceive

The Church has already voiced this idea several times during these days, always with the same sense of wonder and the same faith. Now, on December 20, with Christmas so near, she recalls it once more [77]. Yesterday, on December 19, we heard of the birth of John; today's gospel is of the announcement of Jesus' birth [78]. On December 21 the liturgy will feature the account of the visitation [80] and a reading from the Song of Songs in which we see the beloved, Jesus, coming across the hills [79].

The facts recounted are familiar to us, but there is an air of enthusiasm and triumph about the liturgies of this week. The antiphons and responses are becoming increasingly joyful. "Exult, you just, in the Lord! Sing to him a new song" is the refrain used with Psalm 33 on December 21. And the entrance antiphon for December 22 shouts out: "O gates, lift high your heads; grow higher, ancient doors. Let him enter, the king of glory!" (Ps 24:7).

"He Who Is Mighty Has Done Great Things for Me"

To the successful execution of God's plan that had been hidden since the beginning of history, the Virgin's response, like that of Anna at the birth of Samuel [81], is a cry of astonished praise of God [82]. It was impossible to let Advent pass without recording her glorious hymn, and in fact the Church presents it to us in the gospel for December 22.

We have seen Isaiah as a model for those who wait and John as a man of expectation and proclamation. We must turn now to the Blessed Virgin.

Our Lady, the Woman Who Waits

The Masses of this season do not fail to present Mary to us for remembrance and praise. It is, however, the Liturgy of the Hours above all that contains many texts in praise of the Virgin.

First of all, there is daily an antiphon at Terce, Sext, and None that refers to the Blessed Virgin. "This is the good news the prophets foretold: The Savior will be born of the Virgin Mary" (Terce). "The angel Gabriel said to Mary in greeting: Hail, full of grace, the Lord is with you; blessed are you among women" (Sext). "Mary said: My soul is deeply troubled; what can this greeting mean? Am I to give birth to my King and yet remain a virgin for ever?" (None).

At Vespers on the First Sunday of Advent the antiphon for the *Magnificat* is taken from the gospel of the annunciation: "Do not be afraid, Mary, you have found favor with God; you will conceive and give birth to a Son, alleluia." At Vespers on Monday of the first week the antiphon is: "The angel of the Lord brought God's message to Mary, and she conceived by the power of the Holy Spirit, alleluia." For Thursday Vespers, it is: "Blessed are you among women, and blessed is the fruit of your womb." At Vespers for the Second Sunday of Advent: "Blessed are you, O Virgin Mary, for your great faith; all that the Lord promised you will come to pass through you, alleluia."

At Lauds for Wednesdays, the reading is from chapter 7 of Isaiah: "The virgin shall be with child, and bear a son, and shall name him Immanuel. He shall be living on curds and honey by the time he learns to reject the bad and choose the good." There is no point in continuing a list that would quickly become boring. The short list we have given here indicates the presence of the Virgin in the Advent Office, whether the emphasis is on the first coming of her Son or on his return at the end of time.

We will remember that the feast of the Immaculate Conception is celebrated during Advent. It fits in quite readily with the theme of Christ's birth, but it would be a mistake to think of that as the only theme of the feast. This celebration, like the others of the season, contains Old Testament perspectives as well as New; we are made aware that we are moving toward the end of time. "The events recorded of the people of God in the Old Testament lead up to Mary, and those of the New and Eternal Testament start from her. In this twofold aspect, she proclaims, prefigures, and realizes, in a wholly unique manner, all the sanctity to be attained ultimately by the Church, when it shall have reached its perfection."[2] The virgin "without spot or wrinkle" (Eph 5:27) who is to be presented to Christ at the end of time is the Church. Mary, consequently, is the promise already fulfilled and the pledge already given to us of what all of us together are to become.

What Origen said of John the Baptist can also be said of Mary: "The Mystery of Mary is still being fulfilled in the world, even today." During the Advent season the Church helps us see our Lady, the Mother of God, who is constantly present among us.

Respect is surely due to a devotion that has benefited many people, past and present. Yet it must be said, I think, with all due qualifications, that, despite the biblical and liturgical renewals, the Marian devotion of too many is characterized by an outmoded sentimentality and by excesses in language, attitude, and even devotion itself.

The Church undoubtedly has the right and even the duty to welcome new forms of piety. Undoubtedly too, her concern for the spiritual needs at each stage of history leads her to develop certain types of devotion as a way of meeting a lack. We must assert uncompromisingly that it is unjust and imprudent to advise people against a devotion on the pretext that it is not scripturally or liturgically inspired and without having first provided the faithful with a more solid spiritual food.

That having been said, it does not seem out of place to contrast the great attention given to the "month of May" with the almost total neglect of the Marian season of Advent. We must respect the efforts made during "Mary's month," but we cannot allow a tradition as old as the veneration of Mary during Advent to be overshadowed or even completely unknown. Many Christians are so unaware of the presence of God's Mother during Advent that they celebrate the Immaculate Conception as though it were an isolated feast, closely connected with Lourdes but unrelated to the rest of the Advent liturgy!

There is a lot of scope here for pastoral effort. The point is not to do away with a devotion that the Church has encouraged but rather to establish a hierarchy of values and to become conscious that a liturgical celebration such as that of Advent has a rightful priority over other forms of Marian devotion, however much more developed they may be.

For any mother, the birth of her child is a festive day she will never forget. But the time before birth, during which she is developing a special intimacy with her child, is also a privileged period. For Mary, Christmas is the supreme feast day of her motherhood, but the season of Advent that prepares for it is also a precious time. (For comment on the readings proper to the feast of the Immaculate Conception on December 8, see volume 2).

Overview

While the scriptural readings in the Masses of the final week concentrate on the incarnation, those in the Office continue our meditation on the prophecies of salvation, victory, and punishment [92–98]. The patristic readings afford a wealth of teaching on the period through which we are now living in the liturgy. On December 17, a passage from a letter of Pope St. Leo the Great presents Christ's birth as sacrament of our reconciliation.

> For unless the new man, by being made *in the likeness of sinful humanity*, had taken on himself the nature of our first parents, unless he had stooped to be one in substance with his mother while sharing the Father's substance and, being alone free from sin, united our nature to his, the whole human race would still be held captive under the dominion of Satan. The Conqueror's victory would have profited us nothing if the battle had been fought outside our human condition.[3]

The letter adds that we share in this "sacrament of our reconciliation" only if we are born of God.

On December 19, the Office has a text of St. Irenaeus that sums up the economy of salvation. He emphasizes our inability to save ourselves and, on the basis of the incarnation, asserts that the God who is with us brings about our salvation:

> For this reason *the Lord himself gave* as the sign of our salvation, the one who was born of *the Virgin, Emmanuel*. It was *the Lord himself who saved them*, for of themselves they had no power to be saved. For this reason

Paul speaks of the weakness of man, and says: *I know that no good dwells in my flesh*. He means that the blessing of our salvation comes not from us but from God. Again, he says: *I am a wretched man; who will free me from this body doomed to die?* Then he speaks of a liberator, thanks to Jesus Christ our Lord.[4]

The purpose of this Fourth Week of Advent is to prepare us for the final moments before the birth of Christ. For we know that we are celebrating not a fiction but an authentic presence in our own time.

The "O" Antiphons

Using a particular form that was very important in the Middle Ages, the Liturgy of the Hours speaks of the coming of Christ in a poetic form of which many people are unaware. We refer to the series of antiphons for the *Magnificat* that begins on December 17; each antiphon starts with an exclamation: "O Wisdom!" "O sacred Lord!" etc. These antiphons, seven in number, seem to have originated at Rome. In Germany and at Liege and Paris, two similar antiphons were added to the traditional seven; at times we find as many as twelve antiphons. The form must have been felt to be a very appropriate one. Later on, antiphons for the Doctors of the Church or for the feast of the ascension were cast in the same format.

The singing of the "O" antiphons during Advent was a very solemn affair in cathedrals and monasteries. In some places the solemnity has been preserved; the Liturgy of the Hours has kept at least the antiphons themselves. In them, as elsewhere, we are reminded of the two comings that give Advent its basic theme.

First Antiphon, December 17

O Wisdom, O holy Word of God [Sir 24:3], you govern all creation with your strong yet tender care [Wis 8:1]. Come and show your people the way to salvation [Isa 40:3-5].

The antiphon is addressed to the Son. We may recall here the Prologue to the Fourth Gospel: "In the beginning was the Word, / and the Word was with God, / and the Word was God." He is the Word who comes from the Father's mouth and creates the universe. Here we call upon him, and the invocation shows the two dimensions of our expectation: we need his coming so that he may teach us the way of salvation, and we need it so that we may be able to travel this road that will lead us to the end of time.

In the last analysis, "Come" is our only valid prayer; it sums up all of our need of God. It is our ceaseless cry ever since the expulsion from paradise. We remember that we chose evil; how, therefore, are we now to know the "way to salvation," or the "way of justice," as Scripture often phrases it? In the Old Testament, justice and judgment go together. "Justice" there is not an abstract ideal but something personal and concrete: it is the state of innocence proper to a person who is faithful to this indescribable ideal.[1] Isaiah, from whom the third part of the antiphon is taken, is the prophet who perhaps saw most clearly the role of the Messiah in relation to justice. "The essential role of the Davidic Messiah is, for Isaiah, the establishment of justice."[2] He comes to David's kingdom to uphold it with justice and with righteousness (see Isa 9:6).

"Justice" here is still conceived in somewhat material terms, that is, as a social justice that does away with favoritism, corruption among judges, and so forth. The concept of justice is gradually deepened, however, since the vision of Isaiah cannot become a reality except in an atmosphere of guiltlessness in which each person does the Lord's will. It is impossible, however, for the world to reach this state of peace and moral purity unless Yahweh himself intervenes. Therefore, he will destroy the sinner (Isa 5:3-15) and then bring a new world into being; Sion will be cleansed of its filth, and the bloodstains shall be washed from Jerusalem (Isa 4:3-5).

God's intervention in judgment is thus far from being merely condemnatory; both in intention and in fact, it leads to a reconstruction. Here we are confronted once again with the two dimensions of the parousia. Christ is to come, and we call upon him to lead us in this way of justice or salvation, that is, the way that leads to the complete renewal of the world on the day of judgment.

Second Antiphon, December 18

O sacred Lord of ancient Israel [Exod 6:2, 3, 12], who showed yourself to Moses in the burning bush [Exod 3:2], who gave him the holy law on Sinai mountain: come, stretch out your mighty hand to set us free [Exod 6:6].

The Lord made himself known to Moses by telling him his name. For a Semite, to tell another your name is to give that person power over you. It is clear, of course, that the God of Israel cannot hand himself over to the power of humans like a pagan god whose devotees invoke him with the idea that they can coerce him by magical practices and will therefore be heard. But the name "Yahweh" will always remind Israel of the great deeds God has done for her deliverance.[3]

This antiphon puts us in the context of the paschal mystery, since the coming of the Son is directly related to his redemptive mission.

The last part of the antiphon contains a profound thought to which we rarely attend. The words "come . . . to set us free" express, of course, the purpose of the incarnation and are a short statement of the theology of the incarnation that was current at the end of the sixth century. The rest of the words, however, namely, "stretch out your mighty hand," say something more, at least if we translate the Latin words literally: "come to redeem us with outstretched arm." The phrase "with outstretched arm" is scriptural and occurs, for example, in Exodus 6:6. The Hebrew root *zr*ᶜ means "to sow, to pour out or spread, to make fruitful." From this root two different nouns derive. One, *zera*ᶜ, means "time for sowing, vital seed, posterity, stock, stump, shoot"; in Isaiah it has a precise messianic significance. The other word, *zeroa*ᶜ, means "arm, power, virility, violence, support, help." The phrase "with outstretched arm" is thus complex and rich in meaning.

He who is to come is the "shoot . . . from the stump of Jesse" (Isa 11:1); he is the Messiah; he is also the one who comes in order to restore life to his people; he is power, support, and help. We must, of course, avoid pushing these juxtapositions too far, but it is at least worth noting that several times in his work *Against the Heresies* (*Adversus haereses*) St. Irenaeus uses the expression: "He stretched out his hand when he suffered [his Passion]."[4] This phrasing is rarely found elsewhere, but it does occur in the eucharistic prayer in the Apostolic Tradition[†] (third or fourth century): "[He] stretched out [his] hands when he was suffering, that he might release from suffering those who believed in you."[5]

Here, then, we call on Christ, and we expect him to continue his work of redemption in our world until the end of time.

Third Antiphon, December 19

O Flower of Jesse's stem, you have been raised up as a sign for all peoples [Isa 11:10; Rom 15:12]; kings stand silent in your presence [Isa 5:15]; the

---

[†] See note on p. 128.

nations bow down in worship before you. Come, let nothing keep you from coming to our aid [Hab 2:3; Heb 10:37].

This antiphon draws its main inspiration from chapter 11 of Isaiah. The prophet there sees the Messiah coming "as a signal for the peoples" (NABRE). We are reminded of Jesus' words and St. John's comment: "'And when I am lifted up from the earth, I will draw everyone to myself.' He said this indicating the kind of death he would die" (John 12:32-33). This death will be a victory that will silence the proud of this world. Even the Gentile nations will call upon the Savior: "On that day, / The root of Jesse, / set up as a signal for the peoples— / Him the nations will seek out; / his dwelling shall be glorious" (Isa 11:10).

Fourth Antiphon, December 20

O Key of David, O royal Power of Israel controlling at your will the gate of heaven [Isa 22:22; Rev 3:7]: come, break down the prison walls of death for those who dwell in darkness and the shadow of death; and lead your captive people into freedom [Isa 42:7; Ps 107:14; Luke 1:79].

It is the Messiah's prerogative to open or shut the gate into the kingdom. We call out to him. Let him come to rescue us, because the dark shadow of death will lie upon us until the kingdom of Satan is forever destroyed.

Fifth Antiphon, December 21

O Radiant Dawn [Zech 6:12], splendor of eternal light [Heb 1:3], sun of justice [Mal 4:2]: come, shine on those who dwell in darkness and the shadow of death [Luke 1:78-79; Isa 9:2].

The picture is that of Christ returning at the end of time, when his radiant light will once and for all dispel the darkness that still lies on hearts and souls. The end of the antiphon recalls the end of Zechariah's *Benedictus* (Luke 1:78-79).

Sixth Antiphon, December 22

O King of all the nations, the only joy of every human heart [Hag 2:8]; O Keystone [Isa 28:16] of the mighty arch of man [Eph 2:14], come and save the creature you fashioned from the dust [Gen 2:7].

The antiphon speaks of the Son as having already effected the gathering ("of the mighty arch of man" would read, in a literal translation, "who make the two one," an allusion to Eph 2:14). The Church begs him to come and save humanity, whom God has fashioned in his own image but whose features sin has distorted. We await the return of Christ, who is the Keystone, or, in a somewhat different image, the Cornerstone upon which the Church, as the definitive ingathering of humankind, is built.

Seventh Antiphon, December 23

> O Emmanuel [Isa 7:14, 8:8], king and lawgiver [Isa 33:22], desire of the nations [Gen 49:10], Savior of all people, come and set us free, Lord our God.

The theme here is the same as in the preceding antiphon. Our real lawgiver is Christ, who has liberated us from the yoke of the law. Jews and Gentiles together await him as King and Savior.

These antiphons express the theology of Advent and are the season's brightest jewels. The incarnation of the Son, salvation, the pursuit of our redemption until the end of time—these are the constant themes of Advent theology. From them we can see that the celebration of Advent, like that of Christmas, has its true center in the paschal mystery, wherein the death and resurrection of Christ accomplishes our salvation.

9. ADVENT IN THE LITURGIES OF THE PAST

This short inquiry into the celebration of Advent in the past is motivated neither by simple curiosity nor by an interest in things ancient for their own sake. A theological study could certainly be made of the material we present, and it would very likely bring to light largely unsuspected elements in the Advent celebration. But such a study would not fit with the purpose of this book. We shall restrict ourselves to brief indications, almost in the form of notes.

1. Advent in the Early Roman Liturgy

The Readings

During one week of December, the Roman Church kept a fast on Wednesday, Friday, and Saturday. These three Ember Days were not, however, the seed out of which the whole season developed. On the contrary, the Ember Days were integrated into the season.

Before the Würzburg epistolary, there is no text that alludes to any preparation for Christmas at Rome. The Würzburg Lectionary contains an epistolary and an evangeliary, but they date from different periods and are not necessarily in harmony. The list of epistles is regarded as dating from 602.[1]

The Advent Epistolary in the Würzburg Lectionary

First Sunday	Rom 13:11-14
Second Sunday	Jer 23:5-8
Third Sunday	Rom 15:4-13
Fourth Sunday	1 Cor 4:1-5
Fifth Sunday	Phil 4:4-7
Sixth Sunday	*Vacat*

Ember Day Readings

Wednesday	Isa 2:1-5
	Isa 7:10-15
Friday	Isa 11:1-5
Saturday	Isa 19:20-22
	Isa 35:1-7
	Isa 40:9-11
	Isa 42:1-9
	Isa 45:1-8
	2 Thess 2:1-8

It will be clear from the above list that the two themes of waiting for Christ's return and of waiting for his first coming are (probably unintentionally) intermingled.

The Würzburg Evangeliary

	Earlier Form	*Later Form*
First Sunday	John 6:5-14	Matt 21:1-9
Second Sunday	Matt 21:1-9	Luke 21:25-33
Third Sunday	Luke 21:25-33	Matt 11:2-10
Fourth Sunday	Matt 11:2-10	John 1:19-28
Fifth Sunday	John 1:19-28	

The "earlier form" here is a hypothetical reconstruction. John 6:5-14 was supposedly read on the first Sunday; if so, then the four Sundays of the "later form" must all be pushed back one, so that there would have been five Sundays, not four.[2]

The reader will observe that this lectionary makes no provision for weekday readings.

The selection of John 6:5-14 as a gospel reading is very meaningful, since the multiplication of the loaves is a double prophecy. It points both to the messianic banquet at the end of time and to the Eucharist, in which Christ is already present among us. As we shall see in a moment, a preface in one of the early sacramentaries speaks of "the birth of the eternal bread."

The Murbach Lectionary

This lectionary was composed in Murbach, France, toward the end of the eighth century. It later on acquired authority at Rome, and the Missal of Pius V made extensive use of it.[3]

In the following table, the asterisk indicates readings taken over into the lectionary of 1570 (Pius V), while the plus sign indicates readings taken from the Würzburg Lectionary.

First Sunday	Jer 23:5ff. +	John 6:5ff. +
First Wednesday	2 Thess 1:3-10b	Luke 10:3-13
First Friday		Mark 13:33-37
Second Sunday	Rom 13:11-14a * +	Matt 21:1ff. +
Second Wednesday	Jas 5:7-10	Matt 3:1-6
Second Friday		Luke 3:7-18
Third Sunday	Rom 15:4-13 * +	Luke 21:25ff. * +
Third Wednesday	Mal 3:1-18; 4:6a	Matt 11:11-14
Third Friday		Matt 1:1-16
Fourth Sunday	1 Cor 4:1-5 * +	Matt 11:2-10 * +
Fourth Wednesday	Isa 2:2-5 * + Isa 7:10-15 * +	Luke 1:26b-38 * +
Fourth Friday	Isa 11:1-5 * +	Luke 1:39ff. *
Fourth Saturday	Isa 19:20b-22 * + Isa 35:17a * + Isa 40:9b-11b * + Isa 45:1-8 * + 2 Thess 2:1-8 * + Dan 3:47-51 * +	Luke 3:1-6 *
Fifth Sunday	Phil 4:4-7 +	John 1:19b-28 * +

The Murbach Lectionary is much enriched by the addition of readings for the weekdays. There are five Sundays; readings are provided for Wednesdays and Fridays and for Ember Saturday. Only a gospel reading is noted for the first three Fridays.

The Lectionary of the 1570 Missal

St. Pius V decided to reform the liturgy in its entirety. As a matter of fact, the rubrics in the Missal promulgated in 1570 for the whole Church were those of the Missal of the Roman Curia from the preceding century (except for a few changes, most of which were no better than what they replaced). The readings were taken from the Murbach Lectionary, but the special readings for Wednesdays and Fridays were eliminated except for Ember Week. The gospel for Ember Saturday is repeated the next day (fourth Sunday). Historically, the Mass of Ember

Saturday had been celebrated during the night between Saturday and Sunday, and there was no Sunday liturgy.

The 1570 lectionary was thus poorer than its predecessors. Compare it with the lectionary issued after the Second Vatican Council, and see how rich a treasure of scriptural readings we now have for Advent. The season now constitutes an inexhaustible source of Christian spirituality.

Advent in the Missal of 1570

First Sunday	Rom 13:11-14	Luke 21:33-35
Second Sunday	Rom 15:4-13	Matt 11:2-20
Third Sunday	Phil 4:4-7	John 1:19-28
Third Wednesday	Isa 2:2-5 Isa 7:10-15	Luke 1:26-38
Third Friday	Isa 11:1-5	Luke 1:39-47
Third Saturday	Isa 19:20-22 Isa 35:1-7 Isa 40:9-11 Isa 45:1-8 Dan 3:47-51 2 Thess 2:1-8	Luke 3:1-6
Fourth Sunday	1 Cor 4:1-5	Luke 3:1-6

The Prayers

The sacramentaries contained prayer formulas for the various celebrations. The Verona Sacramentary is a collection of *libelli*, or booklets of formulas, to be used on various feasts and occasions. At one time their composition was attributed to St. Leo the Great, and the whole book was therefore called the Leonine Sacramentary. In fact, however, the prayers came from various sources. In the collection there are prayers for the Ember Week Masses in December.[4]

Among them we find these beautiful words: "so that we may not only enjoy the fruitfulness of the earth but may also receive with purified hearts, the birth of the eternal bread."[5]

Another sacramentary that is of far greater importance for Advent is the Gelasian Sacramentary. According to some scholars, this was composed at Rome and later copied in France, where local Mass formularies were also inserted. Other scholars, however, believe that the sacramentary was composed elsewhere than at Rome.[6] The manuscript dates from 750 and contains the first formularies we have for the Advent season. The texts have become disordered, however; we give here, using the numbers in Mohlberg's edition, the order of texts as proposed by A. Chavasse.[7]

	Collect			Secret	Preface	Prayer after Communion
	1	2	3			
First Sunday	1120	1121	1125	1122	1123	1124
Second Sunday	1126	1127	1128	1129	—	1130
Third Sunday	1136	1131	1132	1133	—	1134
Fourth Sunday	1140	1135	1137	1138	—	1139
Fifth Sunday	1141	1142	1143	1144	—	1145

A number of these prayers have been taken over into our present missal: first Sunday, collect, 1139; second Sunday, collect, 1153. From the beginning of Advent to December 16: first Monday, collect, 1128; first Wednesday, collect, 1154 and 1140; second Friday, collect, 1136; third Friday, collect, 1126. From December 17 to December 24: December 17, prayer over the offerings, 1175, and prayer after communion, 1134; December 20, prayer after communion, 1352; December 21, collect, 1145; December 23, prayer after communion, 996.

We shall indicate here a few interesting prayers that have not been taken into the new missal. "Lord, stir up your power and come, and in your mercy do as you promised your Church you would, until the end of time."[8] Alongside this beautiful eschatological prayer we may set a prayer after communion that exhorts us to move beyond earthly things toward the everlasting kingdom: "We have been filled with spiritual nourishment. We beg you, almighty God, that you would teach us, through our sharing in this mystery, to disdain earthly things and love those of heaven. Free us from the bonds of deadly desire and bring us into the kingdom of everlasting freedom."[9] Note here the very close connection between reception of the Eucharist and entrance into the kingdom.

A preface offers an interesting theology of the time of waiting and of Christ's birth. "Answer our prayers and show your Church the mercy in which she believes. Manifest to your people the marvelous sacrament of your Only Begotten Son so that the nations of the earth may receive what you promised in the gospel of your word, and your adopted children may possess that to which the Truth bore witness."[10]

2. Advent in the Ancient Liturgy of Milan

We know what the readings for Advent were in the Ambrosian liturgy of the Middle Ages.

Readings in the Ambrosian Mass in the Middle Ages

First Sunday	2 Thess 2:1-14	Matt 24:1-42
Second Sunday	Rom 15:1-13	Luke 3:1-18
Third Sunday	Rom 11:25-36	Matt 11:2-15
Fourth Sunday	Heb 10:35-39	Matt 21:1-9
Fifth Sunday	Gal 4:22–5:1	John 1:15-28
Sixth Sunday	*Bergamo*: Phil 4:4-9 *Biasca*: 1 Cor 1:4-9	Luke 1:39-45

A couple of points are specific to this liturgy: the reading of Hebrews 10:35-39; on the first Sunday the reading refers not only to the coming of the Lord but to what will precede it, namely, the Antichrist, apostasies, and the signs that proclaim the coming of the Lord at the end of time. The Milanese Advent had six Sundays; it also placed a great deal of emphasis on the Blessed Virgin, Isaiah, and John the Baptist. The chief liturgical books from which we derive our knowledge of this liturgy are the Sacramentary of Bergamo and the Sacramentary of Biasca.[11]

The Milanese liturgy provides us with some fine prayers. Here are three examples.

In the Sacramentary of Bergamo, the first Sunday takes us straight into the paschal mystery and thus gives Advent a very characteristic tone: "God, in your Son you made us a new creature for yourself. Look graciously on the work of your merciful hands, and by the coming of your Son cleanse us from all the corruption of our old selves."[12]

Two prefaces deserve to be generally known. On the second Sunday the preface speaks of the two comings of Christ.

> Through Christ our Lord, whose incarnation saved the world and whose Passion brought redemption to every person. Let him who

redeemed us from the darkness of hell lead us, we pray, to our eternal reward. Let him who redeemed us at his first coming justify us at his second.[13]

The sixth and final Sunday of Advent concentrates entirely on the Blessed Virgin. Its preface reads as follows:

From her womb came the fruit that nourished us with the bread of angels. What Eve destroyed by her sin, Mary restored for our salvation. The deeds of the serpent and the Virgin were opposed: from him came the poison of division, from her the mystery of the Savior; through him the creature fell, through her the Creator rose. Since then human nature has no longer been captive but has been restored to liberty and has received from Christ, the Author of life, what it had lost through Adam, its father.[14]

3. Advent in Merovingian Gaul

Several lectionaries give us insight into the rich Advent liturgy of Merovingian Gaul, although we can speak of it only briefly here. The table below is taken from Pierre Salmon's book on the Luxeuil Lectionary.[15]

The reader who takes the time to read the Scripture passages listed in the table will note, especially in the Bobbio Missal, both the emphasis on the paschal aspect of Advent and the theology of the last days and the return of Christ.

The prayers in the liturgy of Merovingian Gaul are of some interest, but we must again limit ourselves to a few examples. The Angouleme Sacramentary has some quite original prayers.[16] For instance: "Almighty God, purify our consciences by your daily visitation so that when your Son, our Lord, comes, he may find in us a dwelling prepared for him."[17] Or the following, which is somewhat baptismal in character: "Let our souls, we beg you, O God, be inflamed by your Spirit so that we may be filled with the divine gift and be brightly shining lamps when your Son comes."[18]

We should recall that in Merovingian Gaul, Advent was thought of as "St. Martin's Lent." The Bobbio Missal contains a special Mass for St. Martin.[19]

4. Advent in Spain

The surviving manuscripts are quite numerous. We have them from Toledo, though in mutilated or fragmentary condition.[20] The Silos Lectionary,[21] the Leon Lectionary of 1065–71,[22] and the San Millan de la Cogolla Lectionary of 1073[23] fill out the picture. It seems that Advent came into existence in two stages, with the passages from Isaiah being chosen in their order within the book, and the passages from the gospels being made to harmonize with Isaiah.

Note below the structure of the readings for the third Sunday. The reading from Ezekiel proclaims the coming of the Lord. The gospel reading tells of Jesus' entry into Jerusalem, when he is acclaimed as the one who comes in the name of the Lord. St. Paul relates it all to the Christian's life: When Christ is manifested, our own glory shall be revealed, but if that is to happen, we must live in a certain way now.

The Spanish liturgy was especially rich in prayers, rich enough to merit a whole book on the subject. We find them in the *Liber mozarabicus sacramentorum*; most of these prayers date from the years 400 to 450.[24] The prayers frequently juxtapose the two comings of Christ. There is, for example, this prayer before the Our Father on the First Sunday of Advent: "O Word of the Father, you who became flesh and dwelt among us, grant that we who believe you have already come and hope you will come again may be freed from all stain of sin."[25]

Then there is the collect for the Mass of the third Sunday. It recalls the cures as the signs that the kingdom is here:

> Let the hearts of your faithful be fortified by your coming, I pray, Lord Jesus Christ, and the knees of the weak be strengthened by your name. May your visitation heal the wounds of the sick, your rule make strong the feet of the lame, and your mercy untie the bonds of sin. Grant that those who accept you at your first coming may joyfully greet you when you come again for judgment, and lead them to the delights of paradise where they may live forever in gladness.[26]

First Stage
(No indication of readings from the letters.)

First Sunday	Isa 11:1-5; 4:2-3	Matt 3:1-11
Second Sunday	Isa 28:16-17; 29:17-24	Mark 1:1-8
Third Sunday	Isa 35:1-2	Luke 3:1-8

Second Stage

First Sunday	Isa 2:1-5; 4:2-3	Rom 11:25-30	Matt 3:1-11
Second Sunday	Isa 28:16-17; 29:17-24	1 Cor 4:1-5	Matt 11:2-15
Third Sunday	Ezek 36:6-11	Col 3:4-11	Matt 21:1-9
Fourth Sunday	Mal 3:1-4	1 Thess 5:14-23	Mark 1:1-8
Fifth Sunday	Isa 35:1-2	Phil 5:14-23	Luke 3:1-18

Sunday	W	S	S¹	V	B	P
First	Rom 15:9-13 Matt 20:29–21:3	Isa 7:1-10		Rom 1:1	Mal 3:1-6 Jas 5:7-12, 19, 20 Matt 11:2-5	John 1:35-51
Second		Isa 35:1-10		Rom (8:3)	Rom 8:3-6 Matt 3:1-12	Matt 24:15
Third		Isa 62:10-12; 45:8	Rom 11:30-36	Rom 11:25	Rom 15:8-13 Matt 24:27-44	Matt 11:2
Fourth		Isa 54:1-5	1 Thess 3:9-13	Rom 15:4		Luke 3:2
Fifth		Isa 49:1-10	1 Thess 3:9-13	Phil 4:4		Matt 3:1
Sixth		Isa 11:1-10	Col 1:23-29			Matt 21:1
Seventh, Vigil		Phil 4:4-9			Phil 4:4-7 Luke 12:35-37	

W = Wolfenbüttel Palimpsest, ca. 500. It seems to indicate readings for the First Sunday of Advent, but some take them as meant for the feast of the circumcision. Edited in Alban Dold, *Das älteste Liturgiebuch der lateinischen Kirche* (Texte und Arbeiten 26–28; Beuron, 1936). See Vogel, *op. cit.*, 290.

S = Merovingian Lectionary, ca. 700; originally from northern Italy. Partial edition in Germain Morin, "Un lectionnaire mérovingien de Sélestat, avec fragments du texte occidental des Actes," *Revue bénédictine* 25 (1908): 161–66; *idem* in *Etudes, Textes, Découvertes* 1 (Maredsous, 1913), 440–56. See Vogel, *op. cit.*, 292.

S¹ = Fragment of a lectionary from Sélestat, indicating the readings from the Third Sunday of Advent on. Edited in G. Morin, *art. cit.*, 166. See Vogel, *loc. cit.*

V = Vatican manuscript giving the "Bobbio List" or "Bobbio Epistolary," which indicates the pericopes from Paul; from northern Italy. See Vogel, *loc. cit.*

B = The eighth-century Bobbio Missal, preserved at Paris. Edited by E. J. Lowe and J. W. Legg, *The Bobbio Missal* 1: *Facsimile*; 2: *Text* (Henry Bradshaw Society 53 and 58; London, 1917–20). See Vogel, *op. cit.*, 293.

P = Marginal notations in the seventh-century evangeliary of Saint-Dénis. Edited by P. Salmon, "Le texte biblique de l'Evangéliaire de Saint-Dénis," *Miscellanea Mercati* 1 (Rome, 1946), 103–6. See Vogel, *op. cit.*, 295. The texts in the Luxeuil Lectionary start only with the Vigil of Christmas.

The
Christmas
Mystery

Biblico-Liturgical Reflections on Christmas

10. CHRISTMAS: A CHARMING MEMORY?

Is the Incarnation a Myth?

Our aim here is not apologetics, and we have no intention of using the methods proper to apologetics.* Our aim is rather to enter into the concerns of some among us today—perhaps some of the best among us—who are still looking for Christ and wish to meet him in a personal way. In present-day doctrinal teaching and catechetics, we do not hear much about the person of Christ. Everyone is interested in religious anthropology and religious sociology; eloquence lags when it comes to presenting Christ himself.† Even the young are objecting to this failure and are beginning to feel the emptiness of a Christian religion that no longer gives Christ first place.

At the same time, however, contemporary critical study, especially in the area of comparative religion, is suggesting new difficulties and creating problems for faith. One of humanity's oldest desires, after all, is that God should come to earth. In the classical religions it is often not easy to decide whether the appearance of a god on earth is an object of real belief or simply a consoling myth that may give people hope amid the distress of their earthly lives.

It may perhaps be said that Christianity, more than other religions, has developed a devotion of God-as-a-child and accepted all the artistic, romantic, and affective repercussions of such a devotion. But we must immediately add that this devotion of the manger was a late development in the Church and that Christmas originally laid

---

* Nocent displays a distaste for apologetics, a field that regained strength in the early twenty-first century.

† By the early twenty-first century, these studies—together with studies of world religions and atheism—have broken off from Christianity, making the centrality of Christ all the more important for Christians.

no such heavy emphasis on the infant condition of Jesus. On the contrary, the coming of the Word as flesh was closely connected with the paschal mystery. In fact, this connection is characteristic of the specifically Christian idea of God's incarnation. Incarnation means not only that God is with us but also that we are redeemed and with God. Fallen humanity is redeemed and shares the very life of God.

In the truly traditional thinking of the Church, there is nothing poetic about the incarnation. In fact, the emphasis is, if anything, on a rather brutal fact: The Word came to do God's will, even to the point of dying on a cross. Another element in the specifically Christian view of the incarnation is that God became human, not so that he might be with us, but so that we might be with him. In other words, the incarnation is the starting point of our divinization. But even this "divinization" is not an end in itself. It comes about so that, having become in a sense "divine," we may be capable of effectively working with Christ to rebuild the world for the glory of the Father. We are thus not passive bystanders at the incarnation. The incarnation radically transforms the history of the world and the personal history of each of us. Because of it, each of us must measure up to God's plan and play our proper role in it.

Now, for many, all this sounds rather unreal. But the problem that people have with it today is not the problem of Christ's one person in two natures that preoccupied the Christians of the fourth century; what people question today is rather the usefulness of such a coming of God among us.

The bewilderment that the divine method of ensuring salvation causes in the minds of many is due, I think, to the fact that the incarnation is looked upon too much as an isolated fact. It is not seen in continuity with the whole history of salvation and as the beginning of the final and supreme stage, the new and eternal covenant. We think of Christ's birth (and many other events recorded in the Bible) as an isolated "story," an event that belongs to folklore or as being mysterious. We forget that Christ's birth, and every biblical event, is linked to past, present, and future. The incarnation is seen in a new light as soon as we connect it with the paschal mystery and the covenant.

The incarnation as conceived by a Christian is quite different from the incarnations of the gods in pagan myth. Even so, it is something accepted on faith. Faith, of course, can and should be an enlightened faith. These days, indeed, we are more aware of the need of doing justice to the reality of the incarnation by avoiding too limited a view of it, without at the same time denying that God could legitimately use human sensibilities, art, and affectivity in order to draw humankind at various periods of its history into the living mystery of the Word made flesh.

The point, however, that we must emphasize here, and later on, is that the feast of Christmas originates in a celebration of radiant splendor. I am referring to the celebration of the sun's victory over the cold and storms of winter,[‡] a victory won at the very moment when Christians would be celebrating the birth of the Word made flesh. In its origin, then, the celebration of the incarnation was a paschal celebration of the Lord's triumph.

It is here that we can see the depth at which the Church's faith in the incarnation operated. This faith is of such a kind that some of the early writers exaggerated its importance and expressed themselves clumsily. For example, in the eucharistic prayer that St. Hippolytus of Rome, in his *Apostolic Tradition*,[§] suggests for the use of a newly consecrated bishop, he has a strange but very meaningful expression: the Word became flesh and "[was] manifested as your Son" (*filius tibi ostensus est*).[1] We might think that this language is not quite in keeping with Christian faith, since the Son is eternally the Son. But, in Hippolytus's view, the birth of the Word made flesh is so important because it allows the Son to prove that he is truly the Son. Why? Because what makes a son a son is that he does his father's will. If the Word was to do the Father's will, he had to become a human being.

What we really have here is the theology of the Fourth Gospel, with its sensitivity to Christ's mission as consisting in the doing of his Father's will. St. Hippolytus was well acquainted with the writings of St. Irenaeus of Lyons, who had been a disciple of Papias, who in turn had known St. John. The important thing for us about Hippolytus's viewpoint and manner of expressing himself is that it shows us how closely the early Church connected Christ's birth and his paschal mystery.

[‡] See note on p. 54.
[§] See note on p. 128.

But there are similarities, are there not, between Christ's birth and death and those of the gods in pagan myth? In saying this, however, we are forgetting certain things that are absolutely unique about the Christian faith. The incarnation is indeed the first step toward Christ's sacrifice and death, but we misunderstand that death if we think of it in isolation and as being an end in itself. The Scriptures are constantly emphasizing the uselessness of external sacrifices in themselves and insisting on the importance of the spiritual offering, that is, of self-giving. This holds for Christ as well. The entire value of his death derives from its being the sign of an interior submission to the Father's will. In his dying, the physical death is the outward sign of a spiritual sacrifice. The spiritual sacrifice, in turn, derives its whole worth from the fact that it is the sacrifice of an incarnate God, whose death becomes the sign and embodiment of an offering worthy of the Father.

Christ's death is, therefore, a sign. If it were merely a death, we could not be saved by it, since God has no more use for human sacrifices than he has for animal sacrifices. At the same time, however, Christ's death is necessary, especially and precisely because it is the sign of the incarnate God's submission to his Father's will and an act of love directed to the Father's glory.

It must also be said that if this death had not taken place, we would not have been saved. Why? Because there would be no way for us to verify and come into contact with the interior reality of self-offering on Christ's part. That self-offering finds its expression precisely in his death. Moreover, the sign by which we are united to each other would be lacking, a sign which is now sacramentally signified and made available to us in the ever-repeated Supper we call the Mass. In all of this the incarnation has supreme consequences that no myth ever envisaged.

Let us repeat: In saying what we have said, we have not been engaging in apologetics. Our whole appeal is to the faith of the person who meditates on the mystery of the incarnation.

The Celebration of Christmas—A Recollection of Folklore?

If people today, so anxious to be authentic, are to surmount the obstacles to a genuine celebration of Christmas, we must briefly summarize the history of this feast. Knowing its history, we will be in a better position to understand its theology and appreciate its realism.

As is generally known, December 25 was the day on which pagans celebrated the feast of the *Natalis solis invicti*, "the birth"—or rebirth—"of the unconquered sun." The "Chronographer of AD 354," the anonymous compiler of an almanac for Roman Christians, mentions this pagan feast on December 25 in one of his lists. Was it the Church's intention to counteract the influence of this solemn festival of the solar cult that had been supplanting the hitherto popular mystery religions such as the cult of Dionysos during the third century?

There can be no doubt that the worship of the sun had won an important place in contemporary life. St. Leo and St. Augustine were both concerned about the practice of this cult, toward which Christians at times showed excessive sympathy. Not surprisingly, then, we find in a Christian treatise, *De solstitiis et aequinoctibus* (On Solstices and Equinoxes), dating from the end of the third century, that Christ is presented to us as the true and always victorious Sun, while his birth is regarded as the only true birth of the only unconquered Sun.[2]

There is, then, a relation between the *Natalis solis invicti* and Christmas, but the relation has been explained in various ways. Some scholars, relying on the sermons of the fourth-century fathers, have thought that conjectures on the date of Christ's birth led to the choice of December 25 as the day of celebration.[3] But the arguments showing the fathers inquiring into the date of Christ's birth are valueless. What caused December 25 to be chosen for the celebration seems rather to have been the influence of the festival of the *Natalis solis invicti*.[¶] Among Christians, *natalis* had long meant "the anniversary of death," but through contact with pagans, the word also came to have for Christians the sense of "birthday."[4] This seems to show that there was a real relation between the pagan and the Christian feast.

Some see in the establishment of Christmas a counterfeast. Popular enthusiasm for the celebration of the pagan feast was to be diverted to a feast that was clearly Christian in character, an opposition feast that was in no way contaminated by the pagan feast.

It may also be admitted, however, that the Church simply decided to christianize the pagan feast of the winter solstice. There was little

---

[¶] Again, this theory is no longer widely held. See p. 54.

difficulty in doing so. Light and darkness were themes dear to St. John, as they were to the entire biblical and Christian tradition. It was a simple matter to make use of them in this new context and to focus on them the attention of the faithful, who were already used to them from reading Scripture and hearing sermons. Moreover, people in this period liked to assign dates in the annual cycle to the events of salvation; the equinoxes played a role in the determination of such dates.[5] Quite possibly, then, the Church simply took over and christianized the pagan feast of the *Natalis solis invicti.*

Is it possible to say just when this infusion of Christian doctrine into pagan forms took place? The anonymous Chronographer of 354 provides both a civil and a religious calendar. In his civil calendar he mentions, under December 25, *N(atale) invicti*. Then, at the head of the list of the bishops of Rome, whose date of death he gives, he notes, as occurring on December 25, the birth of Christ at Bethlehem in Judah.[6] This list seems to have been compiled in 336, so that the celebration of Christmas at Rome goes back at least to before that year.[7]

The fact that Christ's birth is mentioned in a list of dates for commemorating the anniversaries of the martyrs (dates always fixed and invariable) emphasizes the historical dimension of Christmas. Christmas relates to an event; the birth of the Lord, his appearance among us in the flesh, is a precise, concrete datum; it took place at a definite moment. While Easter is a movable feast, the birthday of the Lord is celebrated on a fixed day in the annual cycle. This fact suggests certain reflections to which we must now turn.

Christmas: Anniversary or Mystery?

St. Augustine seems to have been so struck by the fact that Christmas is celebrated on a fixed day that he regards it simply as an anniversary or *memoria*. It is, though, a very special *memoria*, for the Creator himself picked this day for his coming: "Born of the Father, he determines the courses of all the ages; born of his Mother, he consecrates a particular day: today."[8]

But, when all is said and done, Christmas is only an anniversary or *memoria* for Augustine. From our viewpoint today, we might be tempted to think of it, not as indeed a mere folkloric recollection, but as a recollection of a great moment, a great turning point in the history of the world and our own personal history. Thus, it would be the kind of recollection around which we build up a folklore.

If St. Augustine thinks of Christmas as a simple memorial, the reason is that he also knows of celebrations that are *sacramenta*. He speaks of these *sacramenta* in two letters. Around 400, Januarius, a layman, had asked him a series of questions about liturgy, and he gave his answer in the two letters. One of these (Letter 54) is fairly short; the other (Letter 55) turns into a treatise that gives us insight into Augustine's mind and contains his theology of the liturgy.

In Letter 54 he says that the Lord endowed his new society with a small number of *sacramenta* that are easy to carry out and whose meaning is marvelous indeed.[9] Augustine is here using the word *sacramentum* in a very broad sense. What is included among these *sacramenta* that are few in number and characterized by great simplicity? In his view, all the signs that are bearers of salvation, however varied they may be (and they include more than our seven sacraments), are *sacramenta*. Baptism and the Eucharist are *sacramenta*, but so is the celebration of Easter. It is not just the seven sacraments that make present again the mysteries of salvation. Every liturgical celebration makes present the mystery celebrated. This is teaching that will be repeated in Vatican II's Constitution on the Sacred Liturgy.[10]

But how can such efficacy be attributed to every liturgical celebration? St. Augustine explains in Letter 55: "A celebration is a 'sacrament' when the commemoration of a past event presents itself to us as the sign of a reality that must be received in a holy manner."[11]

Easter is a "sacrament" because we do not simply call to mind what Christ did for us (his death and resurrection). Rather, the celebration makes present to us, under a veil of signs, the sacred reality of that death and resurrection, and we must really receive it as the pledge of our own passage from death to life. The celebration is thus based on a sacred sign, but, through and by means of the sign, the celebration takes us into the reality signified. Every sign representative of Christ's—and our—passage from death to life is a sacred sign, and any celebration using this type of sign is a "sacrament."[12]

St. Augustine draws the conclusion that Christmas can only be a simple memorial, not a sacrament. The celebration of Easter is sacramental because it is a sign of Christ's death and resurrection; these events of our redemption find expression in the Easter solemnities, in baptismal initiation, and in the eucharistic liturgy. The feast of

Christmas, however, contains no such signs and is therefore simply an imaginative re-creation, a memorial or anniversary. On that feast we simply recall the fact of Christ's birth.[13]

Is Christmas, then, what Anton Baumstark liked to call an "Idea Feast"?[14] (Baumstark was motivated by a desire to give centrality and absolute primacy to the paschal mystery and its representation in the liturgical celebration.) It is true enough that Christmas did give expression to a basic truth about the two natures of Christ, which had been the subject of so much controversy. Some of the Christmas antiphons restated in poetic form the definition proclaimed by the Council of Chalcedon in 451, and the liturgy was an occasion for teaching the faithful how to think of the divine Person and two complete natures, human and divine, of Jesus.

Perhaps St. Augustine believed that December 25 was actually the date of Christ's birth; perhaps this impressed him so much that he could think of the feast only as a *Natale*, even though a very special one, since it was that of the Lord. But, as we have seen, it is impossible to connect the choice of December 25 with the historical date of Christ's birth or even with an inconsistent tradition about the date.

The choice of December 25, which was the time of the winter solstice, did establish a link between the biblical symbolism of light and darkness and Christ as the victorious, invincible Sun that dispels the darkness. Augustine was well aware of the pagan feast of the *Natale solis invicti*, for he mentions it in one of his sermons: "Let us celebrate this day, brothers, not because of the visible sun, but because of him who made this day."[15] It is surprising that Augustine was not struck by the connection between the winter solstice and the lightness-darkness symbolism, especially since, in writing to Januarius, he discoursed at length on the connection between the date of Easter and the lunar cycle. Augustine's attention was focused on the one mystery of our passage with Christ from death to life, and he was not sensitive to the elements of this mystery that were to be found in the feast of Christmas. Had he been sensitive to them, he would have seen that Christmas too, by his definition, was a "sacrament."

Christmas, a Mystery of Salvation

Pope St. Leo the Great will maintain the position St. Augustine did not reach. We will hear him using phrases in his sermons that Augustine would not have tended to use: *sacramentum Natalis Christi,* "sacrament of the day of Christ's birth," or *Nativitatis dominicae sacramentum*, "sacrament of the Lord's birth." He writes that the words of the gospels and prophets teach us "to think of the Lord's birth, wherein the Word became flesh, not as a past event which we recall, but as a present reality upon which we gaze."[16]

This is not to be taken as mere literary embellishment. In the preceding sermon St. Leo makes his thought even clearer: God became human "so that, by turning to that ineffable divine act of merciful abasement whereby the Creator of humanity deigned to become a human being, we might be found in the nature of him whom we adore in our own."[17]

In this celebration of Christmas, then, Christ takes an active part, since through the "divine act of merciful abasement" we will acquire "the nature of him whom we adore in our own." In other words, in this celebration the grace implied by the re-presentation is actively at work. That is why St. Leo can say, just before the words quoted above, that "today . . . the sacrament of the Lord's birth shines more brilliantly before our eyes."[18]

The Church of our day certainly intends to celebrate Christmas as a mystery that is present in her liturgy. This outlook likewise justifies the celebration of Advent as a time of waiting not only for Christ's return on the last day but also for his first coming at his incarnation. We shall see this theology at work in the prayers of Christmas time when we examine these later on.

Since, however, Christmas, like Easter, renders present the mystery of our passage from death to life with Christ, are the two feasts identical? Is Christmas simply a useless duplicate? St. Leo, after all, speaks of Christmas in the same terms he could have used in speaking of Easter: "the day chosen for the sacrament of the restoration of the human race in grace."[19]

St. Leo is not exaggerating, and Christmas is indeed a sacrament of salvation, but it is not therefore strictly a celebration of the paschal mystery as such. There is only one sacrament of salvation, but it is celebrated according to its various aspects. What Christmas renders present is the starting point of our salvation; it is ordered toward our redemption, which it already contains.[20]

The introduction of the crèche and all the Christmas folklore has been a good thing, and neither can nor should be simply rejected. We must admit, however, that the injection of these elements, especially at a time when both the liturgy and the knowledge of Scripture were in decline, has turned Christmas, for many, into the feast of tender piety; Mass during the Night is the most important thing to these Christians, and the feast has no further influence on their lives. The mistake is to have focused the celebration too much on the birth at Bethlehem and to have turned the object of the feast into a moving story.

Rome was the place where this feast, with its clearly paschal theology of the Sun's victory, was created. How ironic, then, that Rome should also be the home, even today, of the folklore that has almost completely obscured the deeper meaning of the celebration! And yet, all that would be needed in order to bring out once again the full meaning of the feast would be to connect with the crèches (often quite beautiful from an artistic viewpoint) a representation of the victorious sun.** "His birth at Bethlehem is rather the occasion than the object of the feast. The object is the total mystery of Redemption, the already announced Paschal Mystery."[21]

The Incarnation: Today? For Me?

Through the liturgical sign the incarnation of the eternal Word is therefore present, today and for me. But what can such a "presence" mean for me? What purpose does it serve? Does not Christmas seem to be an example of the wearisome redundancy to which theology succumbs when it tries to prove too much or when it exerts itself to make us feel at every moment a total dependence on God? Isn't it enough to celebrate Easter as present? Must we also turn the beginnings of the redemptive mystery into something present? We are not denying the incarnation, of course, but isn't it just a springboard? Why dwell on it? In what way can this feast be a source of inspiration and energy for people today? In fact, isn't Christmas really a kind of forced celebration, comparable to so many celebrations and commemorations we must endure in civic life? What can we gain from it? Or, if that be too utilitarian a viewpoint, what point of contact does Christmas have with the contemporary world that gets its back up at the thought of tender religious feelings?

** Again, concerning the origins of the date of Christmas, see p. 54.

I do not regard such questions as unprofitable, for they touch the very foundations of our Christianity. Admittedly, a person can become holy without knowing why the Church thought it good to actualize not only the paschal mystery but its beginnings as well. But we cannot on that account refuse to try to get clear the importance of actualizing the incarnation.

We will have occasion in the course of this book to see how the liturgy seeks to relate to our everyday lives the present graces of the incarnation. But even before seeing what the liturgy's view is, we shall not be wasting our time if we seek an overall view of the values inherent in the actualization of the incarnation.

Today, as in the past, the incarnate God is a cause of wonderment; he has also radically changed the course of history. And yet, in terms of the impact made on the world, the most eye-catching thing has been not the paschal mystery of Christ but the birth of the Word according to the flesh. The myth of a divine human being is to be found everywhere in the dreams of humanity, but when has the union of two complete natures in one divine person been studied with the same sense of wonder as by those who have set themselves to scrutinize the mystery of Christ's person?

This fact, however, does not yet tell us why the union of two complete natures in Christ at his incarnation should be of primordial importance for us. In this context, we must recall that redemption would have been impossible if Christ had not become fully a human being and thus head of the human race and a counterweight to Adam while at the same time being fully God. His action of self-offering would have lacked the perfection of love.

Today we are perhaps struck even more by the fact that Christ's incarnation was necessary for the understanding of all the sacraments, especially the celebration of the Last Supper and now the Mass.

How could there be a real contact with God if the incarnation had not occurred? If we can now know and touch God, it is because the Word became incarnate. Our relationship is with this incarnate Christ whose glorified body is now really present in the eucharistic celebration, although without being subject to the limitations of space and time. The eucharistic presence that is so essential to the Church's life is unintelligible without the presence of the glorified body of the risen Christ. The incarnation thus involves our humanity; it is our humanity that is divinized. How then can the incarnation fail to concern us? It is not a matter of indifference to us whether or not we celebrate the intimate union of two natures in Christ on the day when the Word was born according to the flesh.

We may indeed be indifferent, of course, if we have not grasped in a progressively deeper way the heights to which our nature has been raised by the incarnation and if we do not enter ever more fully into the mystery of the new life that comes to us through rebirth in water and the Spirit. These two births go together: the human birth of the Word as Prophet, Messiah, King, and Priest, and our rebirth, through water and Spirit, as adoptive children, when we too become prophets, priests, and kings, sharing the one priesthood of Christ in the measure proper to baptism.

The fact that the Word has become incarnate should, then, unsettle all my present attitudes. The human nature I have inherited is not human nature as it was before the incarnation. Far from being in any way diminished by the incarnation, human nature has gained a dignity that faith alone can properly appreciate but that is by any accounting extraordinary. It is not only human nature "in itself," as it were, that acquires this divine dimension from the incarnation but all its activities as well, especially its worship.

Because of the incarnation of the Word, we can boast of offering a worship that no other religion has ever been able to offer. The reason is that, according to Catholicism, Christ himself celebrates our liturgy and draws us into his self-giving to his Father. And if readers think these various considerations to be only pious reflections, they should realize that they lack essential elements of the faith and that their religion is very impoverished.

These important themes will be developed in the pages that follow. We had to present them succinctly here as justification for the creation of the feast of Christmas in the fourth century. We offer them also as evidence of the irreplaceable, always contemporary value of a celebration that, we hope, will gradually acquire once again its real and essential paschal meaning.

11. GOD AND HUMAN, KING AND SERVANT

In the Office of Readings on December 24, the invitatory, which will be repeated as the entrance antiphon of the Vigil Mass, reads thus: "Today you will know the Lord is coming, and in the morning you will see his glory."

In two passages of the book of Exodus, we find similar phrasing used to announce a miraculous deed that is a sign of God's extraordinary good will. "At evening you will know that it was the LORD who brought you out of the land of Egypt; and in the morning you will see the glory of the LORD" (Exod 16:6-7). And again: "In the evening twilight you will eat meat, and in the morning you will have your fill of bread" (Exod 16:12). It seems quite clear that these passages, like the liturgy, refer to two moments within a single act. God is miraculously present to serve humanity, and the "today" and "tomorrow" refer to two moments of this one presence.

John the Evangelist was using words in the most realistic possible way when he wrote in his Prologue: "we saw his glory" (John 1:14).

For Israel, to see the Lord's "glory" was the most miraculous of all events, for God's glory is the manifestation of his presence. The column of cloud and the column of fire were both manifestations of the divine presence (Exod 13:22), while the "glory" of God will also be said to be enclosed in a cloud. In this respect, the majestic theophany recorded in Exodus 19:16-25, with its storm and trumpet blasts and heavy cloud, gives a good idea of what Israel had in mind when it spoke of God's "glory" being manifested. God's "glory" is that awesome majesty no mortal eyes can see. But the prophet Ezekiel depicts that glory in human form in his vision of the "Chariot of Yahweh":

> Above the firmament over their heads was the likeness of a throne that looked like sapphire; and upon this likeness of a throne was seated, up above, a figure that looked like a human being. And I saw something like polished metal, like the appearance of fire enclosed on all sides, from what looked like the waist up; and from what looked like the waist down, I saw something like the appearance of fire and brilliant light

surrounding him. Just like the appearance of the rainbow in the clouds on a rainy day so was the appearance of brilliance that surrounded him. Such was the appearance of the likeness of the glory of the LORD. And when I saw it, I fell on my face. (Ezek 1:26-28)

God's glory is also his might, the power he brings to bear upon his enemies: "In your great majesty you overthrew your adversaries" (Exod 15:7). When the psalms sing of the Lord's glory, they will have their eye especially on the day of his definitive coming.

"That Which We Have Touched with Our Hands"

This glory no one can see: "You cannot see my face, for no one can see me and live" (Exod 33:20), and yet St. John says that we have indeed seen it. Why? Because "the Word became flesh / and made his dwelling among us" (John 1:14). The incarnation has thus overturned the old order of things. John wishes to show that God no longer limits himself, as under the old covenant, to an invisible presence in a place where he manifests himself (as in Gen 12:7 and especially in the theophanies at Mount Sinai, the "mountain of God"). To this end, he speaks in his first letter of his own experience:

> What was from the beginning,
>   what we have heard,
>   what we have seen with our eyes,
>   what we have looked upon
>   and touched with our hands
>   concerns the Word of life—
> for the life was made visible;
>   we have seen it and testify to it
>   and proclaim to you the eternal life
>   that was with the Father and was made visible to us—
> what we have seen and heard
>   we proclaim now to you. (1 John 1:1-3)

After reporting the miracle at the wedding in Cana, John says of Jesus: "Jesus did this as the beginning of his signs in Cana in Galilee, and so revealed his glory, and his disciples began to believe in him" (John 2:11). Later on, just as he is about to raise Lazarus, Jesus himself says to Martha, "Did I not tell you that if you believe you will see the glory of God?" (John 11:40). The glory of Jesus is seen in his mighty signs; it leads to faith when one has seen it, but faith is needed in order to see it. The Gospel of John frequently speaks of this double relationship.

This glory that the apostle John has contemplated and the whole world could have seen is also a judgment on this world. "'[N]ow the ruler of this world will be driven out. And when I am lifted up from the earth, I will draw everyone to myself.' He said this indicating the kind of death he would die" (John 12:31-33). When Christ is raised up on the cross, he is also raised up to heaven; he rises from the dead and receives his reward at the Father's right hand. His death, his resurrection, and his triumph form a single mystery, a point so well made in John 12: "The hour has come for the Son of Man to be glorified. Amen, amen, I say to you, unless a grain of wheat falls to the ground and dies, it remains just a grain of wheat; but if it dies, it produces much fruit" (John 12:23-24).

The glory of God that we have seen is also Christ's triumph when he returns on the last day. "In the morning you shall see the glory of the Lord." Morning is the time of radiant light, and the light here is the light of Christ's return on the last day to judge the living and the dead. Between now and then:

> His dominion is vast
>   and forever peaceful,
> Upon David's throne, and over his kingdom,
>   which he confirms and sustains
> By judgment and justice. (Isa 9:6)

From the Vigil on, then, Christmas evidently celebrates a threefold mystery: the coming of Christ to earth, the mystery of his death and resurrection (the redemptive act for which he comes), and his return for judgment. The collect of the Christmas Vigil Mass pulls this theology together: "O God, who gladden us year by year as we wait in hope for our redemption, grant that, just as we joyfully welcome your Only Begotten Son as our Redeemer, we may also merit to face him confidently when he comes again as our Judge."

The glory of God that St. John saw and the Word of life that he touched is the Lord who has come, who comes today, and who will come again. He is the King of peace, but a King who dies in order to save us, then triumphs and takes his seat at the Father's right hand, whence he shall come again to judge the living and the dead.

Of the invitatory for Matins and the entrance antiphon, derived from Exodus 17:7, St. Bernard writes:

> These words belong to a specific place and time in Scripture, but Mother Church has not unfittingly applied them to the Vigil of the Lord's Nativity. . . . When she modifies or applies a text taken from the divine Scriptures, her accommodation is weightier with meaning than the text was in its original context, as the truth is weightier with meaning than the prefiguration of it, the light than the shadow, the mistress than the handmaid.
>
> In my view, the text clearly speaks to us of two days. The first is the present life, which is short and gloomy. . . . The second will be the day that lasts forever amid the splendors of the saints. . . . Our [true] knowledge is to know that the Lord will indeed come, though we know not when. . . .
>
> Today, the coming of the only begotten Son lights in us the lamp of true knowledge, that is, the knowledge that the Lord will come again.[1]

We ourselves are fully involved in this mystery that is both one and threefold. The Lord comes, and we must welcome him, that is, we must go out of ourselves so as to suffer and die with him for our own redemption. Then we enter with him into glory and be henceforth united to the "King of glory." Then, forever and completely, "we shall see the Lord"; humanity, expelled from paradise, shall see God once more.

"We See Our God Made Visible"

When the Church celebrates the feast of Christmas, she cannot but connect it with the paschal mystery in its entirety. But she dwells upon one aspect of the total mystery: the incarnate God.

The God whom John saw and touched is the same God the Church claims to know now. She proclaims it to the Christian assembly: "We see our God made visible." Chapter 40 of Isaiah had foretold this: "Then the glory of the LORD shall be revealed, / and all flesh shall see it together" (Isa 40:5).

During the night of Christmas, the Church presents her Christ to us: he is the eternal Word, the Lord among his people, but he is also a Lord who has become flesh and dwelt among us. In the entrance antiphon of the Mass during the Night, she makes use of one particular psalm to express her faith-tradition: "The LORD said to me: You are my Son. It is I who have begotten you this day" (Ps 2:7).

When we read this psalm in the Bible and connect it with Psalm 45:8, Isaiah 9:6, Jeremiah 23:5, and Micah 5:2, we may well wonder what is the real meaning of the messianic prophecy to be found there. Is the text really speaking of a Messiah who is God? The exegetes have defended divergent interpretations. Around 1900 some claimed that the Messiah of whom the prophets spoke was indeed God. But even these exegetes distinguished between the thinking of the prophet himself and the thinking of his contemporaries. The latter, at least, did not think of the Messiah as being strictly divine.

> The prophecy concerning the Messiah has proved to be completely true, and this, like so many other prophecies, in a far more perfect way than the contemporaries of the prophet would have thought possible. They did not know the mystery of the Holy Trinity, and so when they distinguished between the future Messiah and Yahweh himself, they did not think of the Messiah as possessing the divine nature.[2]

Modern exegetes agree with the contemporaries of the prophets. They interpret Psalm 2:7 as referring, not to the eternal generation of the Word and thus his divinity, but to a purely adoptive sonship. If we set the verse of the psalm in its historical context, we see that it alludes to a promise of God in the Second Book of Samuel (7:14) that he will adopt as a son each king in the Davidic line, thus assuring David's dynasty of an eternal duration.

These quite different interpretations of the prophetic texts are due to the way in which prophecy as such is approached. If a prophecy is regarded as an exact report of what is going to happen, the interpreter will tend to take the Old Testament text exactly as it stands and pay no attention to the historical context of the prophecy. But is this approach legitimate? Is prophecy reducible to that sort of thing, so that it lacks any historical and psychological dimension? Can we imagine people perceiving such an immense religious revolution for humanity and yet not having at least an initial experience of a way so utterly new for them? Israel awaits both a Messiah and a meeting with its God, but does it connect in any way the "'day of Yahweh" that it awaits and the Messiah who is to restore Israel?[3]

It should be clear to us, then, that when the Church reads anew the prophets and the psalms in her liturgy, she elicits from them their full meaning and truth. To think that anthropomorphism in the Bible represents contamination by idolatrous paganism would be simplistic and even wrong. It was through such concrete descriptions of himself that God gradually made himself known. St. Irenaeus of Lyons said that through the Old Testament theophanies, the Word was gradually habituating himself to living among humanity. The anthropomorphisms of Scripture were slowly preparing humanity to receive a God who would also be human and able to experience hunger and thirst, physical and moral suffering, and even death.

A Concrete Theology

The incarnate God theme could not fail to receive a vibrant theological form in the liturgy. Rarely, in fact, do we find a theology more concrete in its expression; it is based on contrasts that the liturgy, like the fathers and commentators, delights in emphasizing.

The hymn *A solis ortus cardine*, attributed to Sedulius, which used to be sung at Christmas Lauds, developed its thought by means of such contrasts: "The blessed maker of the world assumed a servant's form. . . . He deigned to have hay for a bed, and did not refuse the shelter of a manger. He does not suffer even a bird to hunger, and yet He was fed with a little milk."[4] Some of the responsories in the older Office also reflected this realistic theology, as the following examples show.[5]

The fourth responsory for Christmas: "What a great mystery, what a wonderful sign, that animals should see the Lord, new-born, lying in a manger!" The eighth responsory at Matins on the Sunday within the octave of Christmas: "O King of heaven, to whom such homage is given! He who contains the universe dwells in a stable. He is laid in a manger and reigns in heaven." The sixth responsory at Matins on January 1: "He lay in the manger and shone in heaven." And the seventh responsory on the same day: "For you carried in your womb the One whom the heavens cannot contain."

St. Paul, when attempting to give the Athenians the essentials of Christianity, said to them: "[The Creator ordered seasons and regions] so that people might seek God, even perhaps grope for him and find him, though indeed he is not far from any one of us. For 'In him we live and move and have our being,' as even some of your poets have said, 'For we too are his offspring'" (Acts 17:27-28). And in the Letter to the Colossians he writes:

> He is the image of the invisible God,
>> the firstborn of all creation.
> For in him were created all things in heaven and on earth. . . .
> For in him all the fullness was pleased to dwell. (Col 1:15-16, 19)

The Word made flesh is the masterpiece and crown of creation.

It is with this God that we are now in contact: we see him and we touch him. The second reading for the Mass during the Day on Christmas says that "In times past, God spoke in partial and various ways to our ancestors through the prophets; in these last days he has spoken to us through the Son" (Heb 1:1-2). In the Old Testament theophanies God spoke to the leaders of his people; in the New Testament he gives people the privilege of seeing him as well as hearing him: "[Philip,] Whoever has seen me has seen the Father" (John 14:9). The older liturgy of Christmas used to give very concise expression to this wonderful shift from the hearing of God's word to the presence of the Word among us, for in the third lesson for Matins in the older Breviary, she read Isaiah 52:1 in a Latin that departed slightly from the original and had God saying, "I spoke to you of old, and lo! here I am!"

Christ as incarnate God and revealer of God—such is an essential to the vision early Christianity had. The knowledge of God (in the biblical sense of the phrase) was the supreme grace in the eyes of the early Christians.

The Wonderful Deeds of God

The last statement may seem rather strange to a "Christian" mentality that is unfortunately still widespread, despite the return, now well under way, to Scripture and tradition. Our redemption has been given an important place in our religious life, and rightly so, but at times it tends to exclude concern about knowing the God who sends the Savior to us, and this is inexcusable. What it means in practice is a "spiritual life" that is focused not on God primarily but on our own salvation.

To know God and the one whom God sent, Jesus Christ, is more than an intellectual activity comparable to the study of philosophy. Knowledge of God in the Old Testament and in Christianity goes far beyond metaphysics. In fact, the point is not so much to know what God is in himself as to know his "wonderful deeds," the extraordinary, amazing things he has done for us, or the divine plan of our salvation as God has implemented it through the centuries. These "wonderful deeds of God" are the basis and object of the "eucharists," or prayers of blessing, that we find scattered through the Old Testament.[6] The Christian is even more aware of what God has done to gather his people and make them one again. It is now the whole of this divine activity that the Christian sees through Christ, the revealer of God.

When the prayer in the *Didache* thanks God for "the knowledge you have given us through Jesus your Servant," it is referring to the whole of God's activity: the "wonderful deeds of God" in the Old Testament and the incarnation, death, and resurrection of the Son in the New Testament. For it is through God's "wonderful deeds" that have become tangible in Christ that we humans are able to "know God."[7]

St. Clement of Rome, in his Letter to the Corinthians, takes up the same theme: "through his beloved Son, Jesus Christ, who has called us from darkness to light, from ignorance to the knowledge of the glory of his name."[8] We should note, in the light of our earlier reflections, how St. Clement continues to use Old Testament terminology: the "knowledge" of "the glory of his name."

At the moment of martyrdom, St. Polycarp addresses God in a great prayer that is very like the ancient anaphoras (eucharistic prayers) and again harks back to the *Didache*: "O Lord, omnipotent God and Father of your blessed child Christ Jesus, through whom we have received our knowledge of you."[9] Finally, the Anaphora of Sarapion voices the same theology: "We praise you, who are known by the only-begotten Son and by him announced and explained and manifested to the saints."[10] These texts—and there are many others like them—give evidence of vital Christology in which the central theme is the Word made flesh as revealer of the Father.

For God to give such "knowledge" of himself means that he wishes to share his own life. Such an offer requires a response from us. "The grace of God has appeared, saving all and training us to reject godless ways and worldly desires" (Titus 2:11-12). Thus begins the second reading at Mass during the Night on Christmas. Similarly, St. Paul reminds the Galatians of what they are committed to by the knowledge they now have of God: "At a time when you did not know God, you became slaves to things that by nature are not gods; but now that you have come to know God, or rather to be known by God, how can you turn back again to the weak and destitute elemental powers? Do you want to be slaves to them all over again?" (Gal 4:8-9).

A Liturgical Catechesis

The liturgy provides a very careful catechesis on the two natures of Christ that we celebrate at Christmas. An antiphon at Lauds on the Solemnity of Mary, Mother of God (January 1), besides being beautifully harmonious, graceful, and lucidly clear, offers a perfect theological statement of the mystery of the incarnation. Research has dated the Latin text as composed at Rome at the end of the sixth or during the seventh century. It is, in fact, a translation of a troparion that was introduced into the Byzantine liturgy by a poet of the fifth century and is still sung in that liturgy on December 26. The poet in turn was inspired by a sermon that St. Gregory Nazianzen had preached at Constantinople on January 6, 379, and his composition is a succinct résumé of that sermon.[11] It reads: "Marvelous is the mystery proclaimed today: man's nature is made new as God becomes man; he remains what he was and becomes what he was not. Yet each nature stays distinct and for ever undivided."

There is an echo here of the ancient controversies concerning Christ and of the reactions these evoked. The author of the text knew what the Council of Chalcedon had said:

> one and the same Christ, son, Lord, only-begotten; acknowledged in two natures unconfusedly, unchangeably, indivisibly, inseparably; the difference of the natures being in no way removed because of the union, but rather the property of each nature being preserved, and [both] concurring into one person and one hypostasis.[12]

The feast of Christmas (Epiphany in the East) served, like many other liturgical feasts, to rectify the faith of the community and to preserve it from deviations. The *Gloria* of the Mass, originally a Greek hymn for the Office of Matins, entered the Roman liturgy as a song before Mass during the Night on Christmas. It contained, however, some Arian interpolations that showed the Son as inferior to the Father. St. Cyril of Jerusalem gave his catechumens the true explanation of the mystery of the two natures in Christ:

The incarnation was not merely a rumor or something people imagined; it took place in very truth. The Word did not pass through the Virgin as through a channel but was really made flesh out of her body; he really ate as we eat, and drank as we drink. For if his assumption of human nature had been only a pretense, so would our salvation be only a pretense. Christ was twofold: a human as far as humans could see, but also God, though hidden from the eye. As a man, he ate as we do and had the same fleshly experiences as we do, but as God he fed five thousand men with five loaves. As a man he really died, but as God he called a man four days dead back to life. As a man he really slept in the boat; as God he walked on the water.[13]

And St. Leo, in one of his Christmas sermons, likewise gives an accurate exposé of the Church's Christology:

One and the same Son of God existed in both natures, taking what belongs to us without losing what was his own, and thus as a human being renewing human beings, while remaining unchanged in himself. For the divine nature that he has in common with the Father suffered no loss of omnipotence, nor did the nature of a servant dishonor the nature of God, since the supreme and eternal essence that stooped to save the human race raised us up to share its own glory but did not cease to be what it was. Therefore, when the only Son of God professes himself to be less than the Father, yet also asserts his equality with the Father, he proves that both natures are real in him: the inequality shows the human nature, the equality the divine.[14]

In a like manner the Christmas liturgy presents us with the God made human in whom "all the fullness was pleased to dwell" (Col 1:19) and of whose "fullness we have all received" (John 1:16).

King and Servant

Nothing is more charged with meaning in the Old Testament than the words "king" and "glory." We have already met the theme "glory of Yahweh": the kingly glory, wrapped in clouds, which no one can look upon and live. The prophet Isaiah recorded his vision of it:

In the year King Uzziah died, I saw the Lord seated on a high and lofty throne, with the train of his garment filling the temple. Seraphim were stationed above; each of them had six wings: with two they covered their faces, with two they covered their feet, and with two they hovered. One cried out to the other:

> "Holy, holy, holy is the LORD of hosts!
>   All the earth is filled with his glory!"

At the sound of that cry, the frame of the door shook and the house was filled with smoke.
    Then I said, "Woe is me, I am doomed! For I am a man of unclean lips, living among a people of unclean lips, and my eyes have seen the King, the LORD of hosts!" (Isa 6:1-5)

The cloud that here veils Yahweh's glory is the smoke that fills the temple. Anyone dwelling among a people with impure lips cannot see the King in his glory.

Christmas introduces to us an incarnate God, a visible God who is also a King. The Christmas crèche and the application to it of Isaiah's inspired imagery that includes ass and ox were unthinkable in the early Christian period. Yet if such imagery had begun to develop then as it did later in the time of St. Francis of Assisi, it would not have become a kind of opaque screen that keeps many Christians at an unconscious or unacknowledged infantile level and causes them to develop a religious sensibility out of touch with real, concrete life. On the contrary, in the early Christian centuries, the representations of the stages of Christ's earthly life were not fragmentary, episodic, and isolated from one another, and far from constituting a barrier, they led to the knowledge of God by helping to touch the Word of life and thus to know the Father better. In and by means of the imagery of the crèche, the early Christians would immediately have seen God the King.

"He Will Be Called Wonderful"

The Roman liturgy of Christmas sings, in the first antiphon for Vespers, of "the King who is our peace; the whole world longs to see him." The first antiphon in the Office of Readings, an antiphon also used as entrance antiphon at the Mass during the Night, shows the Messiah who is King: "The LORD said to me: You are my Son. It is I who have begotten you this day" (Ps 2:7). Finally, all the liturgies use this passage from Isaiah: "For a child is born to us, a son is given us; / upon his shoulder dominion rests. / They name him Wonder-Counselor, God-Hero, / Father-Forever, Prince of Peace" (Isa 9:5).

This passage was chosen more for its description of the child's kingship than for its mention of his birth; it was chosen for a liturgy to celebrate what was regarded as a feast of glory. The Vulgate changed the text a bit, and in the older liturgy the passage read: "He will be called wonderful, counselor, God, mighty, Father of the world to come, Prince of peace."

The passage has been the object of many commentaries, and the Roman liturgy has used it at several points. Formerly, it was the first lesson at Christmas Matins and appeared again in the Christmas Mass at Dawn and as the fifth antiphon at Lauds. In the new liturgy, it is used at Mass during the Night and as the third antiphon at Lauds.

The Vulgate translation, which the liturgy used to follow, gives the child six titles or attributes, but it nonetheless respects the spirit of the original. The fathers took the word "wonderful" as a reference to Christ's birth from the Virgin, a miracle no one had anticipated. The text of the Septuagint was at one time reflected in the translation of the passage; the Septuagint has "Angel of the Great Counsel" rather than "Wonder-Counselor." Not all commentators interpreted this in the same way. Most concentrated on the idea of "angel" or "messenger," looking on Christ as the envoy sent to announce the divine plan of salvation and coming in order to make known the mystery hitherto hidden.

Along with Isaiah 9, the Letter to the Hebrews was also read in most liturgies for Christmas. The Roman liturgy now reads Hebrews 1:1-6 at the Christmas Mass during the Day and Hebrews 1:1-2 as a short reading at Lauds.

The Son of God has been made "heir of all things" (Heb 1:2). To him God has said: "Your throne, O God, stands forever and ever; / and a righteous scepter is the scepter of your kingdom" (Heb 1:8). Thus Christ is a King, and a King who distinguishes between good and evil. He is Master of the universe, which he created from the beginning. The Letter to the Hebrews cites at this point a number of psalms (2:7; 103:4; 45:7, 8; 102:25-27) as witnesses that the Son of God is indeed King of the universe.

"We Have Beheld His Glory"

The Christmas liturgy also gives an important place to the Prologue of the Fourth Gospel. If we dwell on this passage, it is not to focus on the Word as Creator of the world and eternally living with the Father but to emphasize the final verse of the pericope (short form) as used on Christmas at the Mass during the Day: "We saw his glory." This is the standpoint from which St. John likes to view the incarnation, and it is the standpoint the Church takes in the liturgy. The most important thing the incarnation reveals to the world is the glory of the Word's Godhead. In other words, the incarnation gives us access to the eternal kingship of Christ. This is not a viewpoint customary among us today, for we are more sensible of the self-abasement of the Son in becoming human than of the possibility given of reaching to the divine royalty of the Lord through his humanity.

Our new Roman liturgy has reconsidered especially the Scripture readings, and its choice makes it clear that the Christmas Child is indeed a King. The entrance antiphon, from Isaiah 9, which is used at the Mass during the Day, points in this direction, as we indicated earlier. In addition, there is a group of psalms for Christmas that have traditionally been used in all the liturgies (especially Pss 2, 19, 45, 89, 93, 98, 110, 130, 135), and the choice of these again shows the Church's emphasis on the royal and glorious side of Christmas. The new liturgy continues to use some of these psalms.

Various noninspired compositions of the Church likewise stress the royal character of the Christmas feast. The traditional Vespers hymn, *Christe, redemptor omnium,* describes the royal privileges of Christ: "Jesus, Redeemer of all, you were begotten by the mighty Father, before light was created, as his equal in glory. Do you, the Father's light and radiance and unfailing hope of all, accept the prayers of your servants the world over."[15]

The antiphon for the *Magnificat* at First Vespers announces the coming of the King of kings: "When the sun rises in the morning sky, you will see the King of kings coming forth from the Father like a radiant bridegroom from the bridal chamber." The collect at Mass during the Night, for its part, sees all in terms of light, the light that is God's royal splendor: "O God, who have made this most sacred night radiant with the splendor of the true light, grant, we pray, that we, who have known the mysteries of his light on earth, may also delight in his gladness in heaven."

The responsory in the Office of Readings follows the same theological line of emphasis on the kingship of Christ: "Today, for our sake, the King of heaven chose to be born of his virgin mother," while the third antiphon at Morning Prayer sings, "A little child is born for us today; little and yet called the mighty God, alleluia."

Evidently, then, it is indeed a King that the liturgy presents to us, and even when it shows us Christ in his human condition, it does so in order to bring us to him as King. This King is also a Servant. This is an idea with which, perhaps, we are more at ease, an idea to which our century is more responsive. It too, of course, is a New Testament concept, for St. Paul's focus is always on this God who took "the form of a slave" (Phil 2:7).

The antiphons that recall the lowly manger stand side by side with those that sing the King's glory. We already find the same juxtaposition in Luke's account: " 'you will find an infant wrapped in swaddling clothes and lying in a manger.' And suddenly there was a multitude of the heavenly host with the angel, praising God and saying: / 'Glory to God in the highest' " (Luke 2:12-13). The gospels for the Christmas Masses during the Night and at Dawn tell how Christ came in lowliness, and they stand in contrast to the second reading and gospel of the Mass during the Day, where we contemplate the kingship of the newborn Child.

Thus, at the moment when God is manifesting himself ("when the kindness and generous love / of God our savior appeared"; Titus 3:4), all that anyone sees is a little child! But every time that the liturgy reminds us of the lowly condition of the newborn Christ, it relates this, at least implicitly, to the divine will that through Christ's lowliness we should receive adoptive sonship.

The third of the Christmas Masses especially emphasizes the paradox of the King who is a Servant. The entrance antiphon strikes the tone: "A child is born for us"; we have already noted the messianic and royal resonances of this text from Isaiah.

"A Child Is Born for Us"

We can go a step further in our examination of this text, which reads in Latin: *Puer natus est nobis*. *Puer*, "child," also means "servant," and this meaning emerges here all the more clearly inasmuch as the *nobis*, "for us," has overtones of the paschal mystery that lies ahead. A "servant" is born for us and for our sake; he comes to carry out a mission that concerns not only his Father but us as well. He is the favored Servant, the Son with whom the Father is well pleased. "Through your Servant Jesus" was a formula the early Christians loved, and we find them using it in many of their prayers.

The word "servant" quite naturally brings to our minds the four Servant Songs in Isaiah (42:1-9; 49:1-6; 50:4-11; 52:13–53:12), and it is right that it should do so, since the New Testament recognizes in the Servant the person of Jesus Christ. The Greek word *pais*, which likewise means both "child" and "servant," enables the Scriptures and the liturgy to express the full meaning of Jesus. He is the Son whom the Father sends; he is also the Servant who comes to do the Father's will. When St. Matthew tells us of Jesus hearing the Father's voice at his baptism, the words recorded are: "This is my beloved Son, with whom I am well pleased" (3:17). Jesus is the favored Servant, but he is also the Son whom the Father sends. As early as the Acts of the Apostles, we find the expression "servant Jesus," which was such a favorite of the early Christian generations: "The God of Abraham, [the God] of Isaac, and [the God] of Jacob, the God of our ancestors, has glorified his servant Jesus" (3:13). Later on, when the eunuch, the official of Queen Candace of Ethiopia, reads Isaiah 53:7-8, the apostle Philip tells him that the lamb led to slaughter is Jesus (Acts 8:26-39).

The Suffering Servant, a theme dear to Isaiah and a personage in whom the New Testament and the Church see Christ reflected, was God's answer to the infidelity and disobedience of Adam, who was to have been the first of God's servants. He was God's favorite, his beloved, and God had created him after his own image. But because of his infidelity, he lost his identity as servant and became a slave. The Letter to the Galatians alludes to Adam and his fall in the second reading at Mass on the Solemnity of Mary, the Mother of God: "When the fullness of time had come, God sent his Son, born of a woman, born under the law, to ransom those under the law, so that we might receive adoption" (Gal 4:4-5).

Commenting on this passage from Galatians, Cerfaux writes:

> He is so much with us that he becomes the child of a woman and accepts the lowly state of ordinary people. He would push his lowliness and likeness to us to the point of joining us in sin if his dignity as Son of God were not incompatible with sin. He is born a Jew, "a servant to the circumcised" (Rom 15:8). Consequently, he spends his earthly life observing the Law. By doing so, he fulfilled it perfectly but also put an end to it. The Law had to be thus perfectly fulfilled before it could disappear.[16]

By sinning, we became "enslaved to the elemental powers of the world" (Gal 4:3). The Lord therefore had to take "the form of a slave" (Phil 2:7) in order to rescue us from enslavement.

Evidently we are constantly in touch with the paschal mystery as we meditate on these texts from the Christmas liturgy. Thus, when the Church asks, in the collect for Mass on the sixth day within the octave of Christmas, that we might be freed "from the yoke of sin," she is thinking of the newborn Child as the King and Servant who comes into the world so that he might be obedient unto death and thereby serve his Father and do his will. But the cross, though a torment reserved for slaves, will also be the means whereby Christ is exalted and all creation is gathered into unity after sin and guilt and death have been done away with.

12. THE CHRISTMAS PASCH

In the preceding chapter we were constantly reflecting on paschal themes. What is "King and Servant," after all, but one expression of the paschal mystery? The fathers of the Church are always reminding us of a point they evidently consider absolutely basic: "The Son of God became human in order that humans might become God," and this, of course, is a theme both of Christmas and of the paschal mystery. The world has been renewed, and we have become new creatures, but the coming of the Son of God in the flesh is the starting point of these transformations. St. Irenaeus writes: "The Word of God became human, and the Son of God became a Son of Man, so that humans, united to the Word of God, might through adoption become children of God."[1] We would be mistaken if we tried to find in the liturgy a metaphysics of the incarnation, and especially one that would be offered for its own sake. Scripture does not take such a narrow approach to Jesus. It sees the incarnation as part of the mystery of our redemption. Paul does not even dwell on the earthly life of Jesus: "[E]ven if we once knew Christ according to the flesh, yet now we know him so no longer" (2 Cor 5:16). He is aware, of course, that the earthly life of Jesus is the necessary starting point, but it is precisely that—a starting point—and derives its meaning from the goal, which is our salvation and our transformation as new creatures. If, then, Christ became human, he did so in order to redeem us: "But when the fullness of time had come, God sent his Son, born of a woman, born under the law, to ransom those under the law" (Gal 4:4-5). He came in order to offer the sacrifice that would ransom us: "and found human in appearance, / he humbled himself, / becoming obedient to death, even death on a cross" (Phil 2:7-8). The Letter to the Hebrews gives clear expression to this theology of the incarnation as directed to sacrifice: "Sacrifice and offering you did not desire, / but a body you prepared for me; / holocausts and sin offerings you took no delight in. / Then I said, 'As is written of me in the scroll, / Behold, I come to do your will, O God'" (Heb 10:5-7). While directed toward sacrifice, the incarnation must lead ultimately to resurrection and victory, or it would be a venture that had failed. Everyone knows, at least from the liturgy, St. Paul's words in his Letter to the Philippians:

> Because of this, God greatly exalted him
> and bestowed on him the name
> that is above every name,
> that at the name of Jesus
> every knee should bend,
> of those in heaven and on earth and under the earth,
> and every tongue confess that
> Jesus Christ is Lord,
> to the glory of God the Father. (Phil 2:9-11)

On January 1, the Solemnity of Mary, Mother of God, the Church sings in the first antiphon for Vespers, "O marvelous exchange!" In her eyes, this exchange is the intended issue of the incarnation. Of all the fathers, St. Cyril of Alexandria and St. Gregory the Great have given perhaps the clearest expression to the nature of this "marvelous exchange." To bring the meaning home to Christians is one of their main concerns.

St. Cyril writes, "The Son who was truly begotten of the Father, the Word of God who is Life, set out upon the way to death and became human like us. He did not introduce into his earthly nature any change emanating from his divine nature (for he did retain his divine nature entire with all its attributes), but simply assumed an earthly body and a rational soul."[2] In another passage, after describing the "exchange," St. Cyril points out its ultimate consequences: "He who exists eternally was born according to the flesh, taking to himself what is ours, so that the offspring of the flesh, that is, we who are subject to corruption and damnation, might abide in him who made his own what is ours and made ours what is his."[3]

The thoughts of Scripture and of the fathers on the incarnation have found vital expression in the liturgy. It is striking that in the East the feast of Christmas should be announced as "A Pasch, a three-day festive holiday."[4]

The West does not have any such explicit title for Christmas, but we need only run through the Scripture texts and liturgical compositions of the Christmas liturgy to see that the West shares the idea. It took a long time for theologians to turn back to Scripture, the fathers, and the liturgy; to stop limiting themselves to speculation; and to engage in the study of the mysteries as parts of the divine plan of salvation. Moreover, the change of attitude in Western theology is something quite recent. Here we have evidence of the extent to which the liturgy had been carried out without being truly experienced or becoming part of life. The liturgy had become simply a ceremony in the course of which texts were read and antiphons were sung; Christians seemed to have lost any sense of the value that these texts and antiphons had for Christian life.

From the Vigil Mass of Christmas on, the liturgy of the season has a clearly paschal character. Three stages in God's plan of salvation are mentioned several times. In the entrance antiphon, the Lord's coming is linked to salvation, and salvation in turn to the Lord's glory. We have already seen the messianic and eschatological significance of that "glory." "Today you will know that the Lord will come, and he will save us, and in the morning you will see his glory." The choice of text (cf. Exod 16:6-7) reveals the theological outlook of a whole age.

The second reading presents Christ, the Son of David, as Savior of Israel (Acts 13:16-17, 22-25), while the gospel, taken from St. Matthew, contains the illuminating sentence: "She will bear a son and you are to name him Jesus, because he will save his people from their sins" (Matt 1:21). The collect of the Mass dispels any doubt: "we joyfully welcome your Only Begotten Son as our Redeemer."

The first coming of Christ, at his human birth, is thus closely bound up with our salvation, and precisely because it is a step toward the paschal mystery, it must have as its ultimate goal the last day and the second coming of Christ. There are several temporal stages involved here and we cannot consider them all simultaneously, but we must bear in mind that the liturgy always celebrates the totality of these mysteries. Rightly so, for they are indeed inseparable.

The Liturgy of the Hours also brings out the redemptive finality of the incarnation. Thus, the first responsory in the Office of Readings says, "Tomorrow the wickedness of the earth will be destroyed, and the Savior of the world will rule over us." And the third antiphon at Lauds (in the Latin Office): "Tomorrow salvation will be yours, says the Lord of hosts."

Thus, beginning on the Vigil Mass of Christmas, we have a clear statement of the finality of the incarnation and its connection with our salvation.

Redemptive Incarnation

As we have already had occasion to remark, we should not go to the liturgy for a treatise on dogma; as a matter of fact, there is always danger of attempting to impose too much of a systematic structure on what we do and experience in the liturgy. Nonetheless, for the sake of greater clarity, we shall recall here the paschal themes taken over by the Roman liturgy for Christmas; we must be on guard, however, not to force the texts.

The theology of the incarnation that is to be found in the Offices and Masses of the season can be expressed as follows. Christ came to earth and assumed our nature in order to save us. Salvation consists above all in our being forgiven and given a new life, becoming sharers in the divine nature. Because of and through that sharing, we bear in ourselves, once again, the image in which we were originally created. In the final analysis, then, the unity of human beings and the renewal of all creation will depend on the incarnation of the Word. At the end, when the new creation achieves its mature perfection, Christ will come again as supreme Judge, and the definitive entry into the promised land will take place. Humanity will return to the paradise from which the first humans were expelled because of sin.

There are many texts that tell us that the purpose of the Son's incarnation was our salvation. Thus, the third antiphon at First Vespers on Christmas confronts us with the fact of redemption: "The eternal Word, born of the Father before time began, today emptied himself for our sake and became man," while the ancient hymn "Christ, Redeemer of all" puts the same thought in more lyrical form: "The present day, as it comes round every year, bears witness to this—that you, the only-begotten of the Father, have come as savior of the world. The heavens, the earth, the sea and every creature under heaven greet him with a new song as the author of new salvation."[5]

In the Office of Readings, St. Leo the Great tells us: "[A]ll share the same reason for rejoicing. Our Lord, victor over sin and death, finding no man free from sin, came to free us all."[6] The first responsory in the same Office of Readings reminds us that "today, for our sake, the King of heaven chose to be born of his virgin mother, to reclaim lost men for the heavenly kingdom."

One of the hymns for Morning Prayer, the ancient "From where the sun rises" (*A solis ortus cardine*), sings of the same deliverance:

"The blessed maker of the world assumed a servant's form so as to free humanity by becoming human and not to lose those whom he had created."[7]

The liturgy thus reflects the theology of the fathers and affirms that our salvation has already been effected in the birth of Christ. Such a statement means, for these writers, that Christ's birth is an intrinsic part of the work of redemption, to the point that it is not simply a condition or indispensable beginning but already contains our deliverance in germ.

In a passage from his ninth sermon on the Nativity, St. Leo the Great explains the concrete significance for Christian life of the mystery that is being celebrated. The salvation inaugurated by Christ's birth is a salvation that is always of this present moment:

> [The prophets] teach us not so much to recall the Lord's birth, in which he became flesh, as though it were past, but to gaze upon it as present to us. . . . We retain in the ears of our heart, as though they were spoken at today's celebration, the words of the angel: "I bring you good news of a great joy which will come to all the people; for to you is born this day in the city of David a Savior, who is Christ the Lord."[8]

A New Creation

The birth of Christ destroys the effects of death and causes new life to be reborn in us; humanity is regenerated by Christ's coming in the flesh. This new life consists in our sharing the divine nature.

Here again, the Church in her liturgy has been guided by the theology of the fathers. In the patristic reading for the Office of Readings on Christmas, St. Leo bids us thank God through his Son, in the Holy Spirit, because "in his great love for us he took pity on us, *and when we were dead in our sins he brought us to life with Christ,* so that in him we might be a new creation." He then utters the well-known exclamation: "Christian, remember your dignity, and now that you share in God's own nature, do not return by sin to your former base condition."[9]

The liturgy links the birth of Christ with a *renovatio,* or renewal, with our *generatio,* or birth, and with a *novitas,* or newness of life, as opposed to a *vetustas,* or decrepitude (the state of one who is worn, decayed, old, and feeble).

The liturgy uses these terms because they were current in the language and writings of the fathers, who themselves had found them implicit in Scripture. Thus St. Paul says that we have become "a new creation" (2 Cor 5:17). On the octave of Christmas, a passage is read from the Letter to the Galatians in which Paul explains that we have become adopted children of God, being interiorly transformed to the point where we can say "Abba, Father!" (Gal 4:4-7). Many of the Eastern liturgies use this passage in the one Mass they celebrate on Christmas. The popularity of the pericope shows how the Christian world has understood Christmas as the celebration of a renewal and an adoption. Christmas anticipates Easter and the paschal mystery. Just above, we heard St. Leo saying that in Christ we are "a new creation," a new work of God's hands. Such language, we repeat, was current among the fathers.

In the Missal of Pius V, there used to be interesting traces of that language in the collect and secret for the Christmas Mass during the Day. In these prayers the expression *nova nativitas*, "new birth," occurred. In the collect, there was a contrast between the *nova*, the new, that which renews, and the *vetusta*, the old, the earlier; the *nova nativitas*, the new birth of Christ that makes new, was opposed to the *vetusta servitus*, the ancient slavery of humankind due to original sin. The birth of Christ in our flesh liberates us who had been captive under the yoke of sin.

The postcommunion prayer for the Mass at Dawn, again in the Missal of Pius V, is to be found for the first time in the Gelasian Sacramentary. In the meantime, however, it had been rewritten.[10] In its original form it read, "Lord, may the newness of this mystery of birth constantly restore us, for its singular nobility has cleansed humankind of all decrepitude."

In his fifth sermon for Christmas, St. Leo had used almost identical language: "The Word of God . . . through his birth called humankind back from its decrepitude to a new beginning."[11]

A New World

The birth of Christ shares with the paschal mystery the power to bring the created world together in unity.

St. Ambrose saw the Church as coming into existence at the very moment of Christ's birth: "Christ is born and the shepherds begin their watch, gathering into the Lord's house his flocks, that is, the nations that hitherto had been living like beasts."[12] The second antiphon at Morning Prayer makes use of Luke 2:13, putting the words of the heavenly host into the mouth of a single angel: "The angel said to the shepherds: I proclaim to you a great joy; today the Savior of the world is born for you, alleluia." The antiphon for the *Magnificat* at Second Vespers has angels, archangels, and the just of the earth joining together in song.

The renewal that Christ's birth produces is not to be thought of as restricted to intelligent beings. The whole of creation benefits from the re-creation that is the fruit of Christ's suffering and resurrection and that is already implicitly contained in his birth. St. Paul told the Ephesians that the aim of God's love-inspired plan was "to sum up all things in Christ, in heaven and on earth" (Eph 1:10).

But Christ's coming also contains an element of eschatological judgment. That is how St. Ambrose sees it when commenting on Luke 2:34: "Simeon prophesies that the Lord Jesus Christ has come for the downfall and resurrection of many, that is, in order to distinguish the deserts of the just and the unjust, and, as a true and just Judge, decree punishment or rewards as our deeds deserve."[13]

A New Jerusalem

Finally, Christ's birth is linked to the return to paradise. The Office of Readings on Christmas alludes to this idea in the first responsory: "Today, for our sake, the King of heaven chose to be born of his virgin mother, to reclaim lost men for the kingdom of heaven."

In the patristic reading, St. Leo speaks of the angels' joy as they see the heavenly Jerusalem being formed of all the nations of the earth. He bids the Christian "remember that you have been rescued from the power of darkness and brought into the light of God's kingdom."[14] St. Gregory the Great, commenting on Luke 2:1 in his eighth sermon on the Gospel of Luke, explains the reason for the census taken by Caesar Augustus: "Why is a census of the world made just when the Lord is about to be born, except to show that he who was coming in the flesh would enroll his chosen ones in eternity?"[15]

Evidently, then, the subheading to this section is not an exaggeration but rather brings out the unity permeating the Church's entire liturgy, centered as it is on the mystery of death and life.

In the Byzantine liturgy for the Vigil of Christmas, there is a processional antiphon that brings out quite clearly the paschal character of Christmas: "Rejoice, Jerusalem! All you lovers of Sion, share our festivities! On this day the age-old bonds of Adam's condemnation were broken, paradise was opened for us, the serpent was crushed, and woman, whom he once deceived, lives now as Mother of the creator. . . . Let all creation dance and thrill with joy, for Christ has come to call it home and to save our souls."[16]

Incarnation and Cosmos

In one of his visions that are, surprisingly, favorites even today, Isaiah writes: "One cried out to the other: / 'Holy, holy, holy is the LORD of hosts! / All the earth is filled with his glory!'" (Isa 6:3). This theme, which has become part of the eucharistic liturgy, is the best expression we have of the glorification of the cosmos. The whole of creation, and not humanity alone, experiences the regenerative power of the incarnation.

The "unconquered Sun" idea, as we pointed out earlier, is at the origin of the feast of Christmas.* In a sermon that often used to be attributed to St. Ambrose, St. Maximus of Turin wrote, "The people are quite right, in a way, when they call this birthday of the Lord 'the new sun.' . . . We gladly accept the name, because at the coming of the Savior not only is humanity saved but the very light of the sun is renewed."[17]

Toward the end of the third century, an anonymous writer, intent on showing the perfection of Christian worship as compared with the pagan cults, gave us this important text:

> They call [this day] "the birthday of the unconquered [sun]." But is the sun so unconquered as our Lord who underwent death and overcame it? Or they say it is "the birthday of the sun." But is our Lord not the Sun of righteousness of whom the prophet Malachi said: "For you who fear my name, the sun of righteousness shall rise, with healing in its wings"?[18]

A renewal of the world takes place, and it begins with the incarnation of the Word. As a matter of fact, the choice of a cosmic phenomenon as a reference point for determining the date of the feast of

* See comments on p. 54.

Christ's birth suggests that we consider the repetition of the Christmas cycle as intimately linked with creation itself. The feast we celebrate interests not humans alone but the whole created world. We should not be surprised, therefore, that the fathers often mention the connection between the birth of Christ and the cosmic renewal that takes place at the winter solstice. We may well feel some regret that the readings chosen for the Christmas Offices have not given sufficient attention to this aspect of the feast, especially since it is both important in itself and one to which our generation is quite sensitive.[†]

It is easy to see in the emphasis on the renewal of the sun's light a connection with the primal light at the creation of the world. How beautifully Genesis brings out the harmony that marks God's creation of the world! We can sense the writer's deep emotion in the face of so many splendid things: the earthly paradise that forms the setting, the bodily beauty of man and woman, the light of the stars; the author is overwhelmed by it all and tries to give us a glimpse of the beauty seen. Then the catastrophe comes and puts an end to this marvelous harmony.

Christmas, linked as it is with the winter solstice, comes as the re-creation of the world according to the original plan and its original beauty.[‡] The coming of the Word and his entry into the world were not geared, as it were, to sheer efficiency; they were not dull and prosaic. God's plans are never narrow. The Word made flesh will indeed live his life in a particular region of the world, among a particular kind of people, in the climate of the country where he was born; he will speak one human language and submit to the rhythm and laws that govern human life. At the same time, however, we must realize that his presence is a consecration of the world. The world was, of course, already consecrated to a degree, since God was the one who had made it, but the presence of the Word within the cosmos restores its dignity and gives it the possibility of rebuilding itself with the elements already at its disposal.[19]

It was of this consecration that Isaiah was speaking when he reported his inaugural vision. In the collect of the Mass during the Day on Christmas—one of the oldest Christmas prayers we know of, now restored to its proper place—the Church bids us say: "O God, who

---

[†] Nocent limits his perspective to the northern hemisphere.
[‡] In the antipodes it coincides with the glorious warmth of summer.

wonderfully created the dignity of human nature and still more wonderfully restored it, grant, we pray, that we may share in the divinity of Christ, who humbled himself to share in our humanity."

If we were to think of this restoration as applying only to humans, we would be forgetting the context and framework of the celebration. The world too is being restored. A sermon of St. John Damascene on the transfiguration brings this out clearly:

> The benevolent will of the Father united all things in his only begotten Son. Humanity is already a microcosm that unites in itself all things visible and invisible. The Lord, whose good will created and governs all, determined that in his only begotten consubstantial Son, divinity and humanity, and therewith all other created things, should be united, so that God might be all in all.[20]

The Greek fathers have much more to say on this subject than do the Latin Fathers. They are also more interested in the restoration of the entire world as part of redemption, and they see the incarnation as the first step to the restoration. Here is another text, a magnificent one from St. Gregory of Nyssa:

> Today the darkness begins to grow shorter and the light to lengthen, as the hours of night become fewer. Nor is it an accident, brothers and sisters, that this change occurs on the solemn day when divine life is manifested to all. Rather, to those who are attentive, nature manifests through visible things a hidden reality. . . . I seem to hear her saying: "Realize, as you observe these phenomena, that the invisible is being manifested to you through the visible. You see, do you not, that night has reached its greatest length, and since it can advance no farther, comes to a halt and withdraws? Think, then, of sin's deadly night that was lengthened by every evil act and had reached its highest pitch of wickedness, but on this day was cut short and allowed to creep no farther; it is now being forced to lessen and will finally be completely eliminated. Do you see that the beams of light are more intense and the sun higher than it has been? Realize that the true light is now here and, through the rays of the gospel, is illumining the whole earth."[21]

An Ambiguous Longing

Everyone without exception wants to be free. Such a yearning is exalting, it possesses beauty and grandeur, but it is also ambiguous. For what does "freedom" mean? There is no point here in dwelling on the false interpretations of freedom. A married man is not totally "free" where his wife and children are concerned. A friend is not totally "free" where the friend is concerned. A Christian is not totally "free" as regards the Body of the Church of which he or she is a member. No individual is totally "free." Certainly humanity, which has been redeemed from the bondage of sin, is not totally "free" from God.

If freedom is to be an authentic, that is, genuinely liberating freedom, it must make room for the other, for fidelity to people and even more to God. Free people must have respect for themselves as well as for others. Consequently, we must say that there is a yearning for freedom that is infantile or unbalanced, stupid or even perverse, a yearning that is just literary romanticism or unwitting egoism.

But there is also a yearning for freedom that is a desire to escape both servitude and false freedoms. Christmas is an efficacious celebration of this freedom, which might also be called peace.

Once again, it is impossible to speak of this authentic freedom to anyone who is unwilling to look at things through God's eyes, that is, through the eyes of faith.

Freedom through Humble Obedience

The incarnation was a self-humbling for the Word of God, and the first step toward the death that would be his sign of acceptance and self-giving to the Father. The incarnation thus represents more than the now-real possibility of redemption; it is in itself an event that liberates. Karl Rahner once wrote on this point: "The incarnation is the acceptance of the flesh of sin; in its passible state, which itself is an expression of human guilt, the flesh is destined for death. . . . Thus the incarnation is already a soteriological event in the proper sense of the term, and not simply a condition for the possibility of redemption."[22]

The second preface for Christmas in the new missal gives succinct expression to this and the previous point: "so that, raising up in himself all that was cast down, he might restore unity to all creation and call straying humanity back to the heavenly Kingdom." Moreover, because of the Son's obedience we become so free that we will live forever, as the third of the Christmas prefaces tells us: "For through him the holy exchange that restores our life has shone forth today in splendor: when our frailty is assumed by your Word not only does human mortality receive unending honor but by this wondrous union we, too, are made eternal."

Eternal life—that is what we are promised in the incarnation of the Word. It is an idea that deeply impressed the earliest Christian writers. One of the earliest of whom we have knowledge, St. Ignatius of Antioch, wrote a letter to the Ephesians that contains a whole theology of our liberation. It is cast in a literary form that is somewhat alien to us, but the message is clear:

> A star burned in the sky more brightly than all the others; its light was indescribable, its newness marvelous, and all the other stars, along with the sun and the moon, formed a chorus around this star, the light of which reached farther than that of any other. . . . Then all magic was destroyed, and every bond wrought by wickedness was broken, and the ancient kingdom was razed. When God appeared in human form to bring the newness of eternal life, his counsel began to be fulfilled.[23]

In his second Christmas sermon, St. Leo the Great develops the same theme. We were fallen, expelled from paradise, and living in an exile that would never end. Life was hopeless, but suddenly everything changed:

> Of old you were cast off and driven from your thrones in paradise. You were dying in your long exile and turning to dust and ashes; you had no hope of life. Then, through the incarnation of the Word, you received power to return from afar off to your Creator and to acknowledge your Father, to become a free person instead of a slave, a child and no longer a stranger.[24]

Our freedom is the effect of the Son's obedience in the humility of the flesh. The continuous reading of Isaiah during Advent has familiarized us with the theme of liberation. We will recall this passage brimming with enthusiasm: "Arise, shake off the dust, / sit enthroned, Jerusalem; / Loose the bonds from your neck, / captive daughter Zion" (Isa 52:2).

Perhaps it is not a simple matter, even for the baptized, to believe that they have been liberated. The more we learn of human physiology and psychology, the more humans seem subject to pressures that stifle freedom. It remains true, nonetheless, that we can achieve genuine freedom, but only by a dramatic effort that brings much suffering.

The incarnation liberates us, but it does not work by magic; the incarnation is the origin of the Christian's sacramental life, but the sacraments are not magical ways of avoiding a struggle. They are efficacious means, if properly used, of entering into the boundless kingdom of freedom and peace.

Such is the experience of the saints. We cannot claim that our age is not having the same experience. The violence that has become habitual will provide for it, if it wishes, the chance to get beyond the simplistic challenges and the overly facile means of drowning out the inner feeling of enslavement. The artificial means of oblivion as a way of escaping moral struggle and moral obligation have never yet had results that were not far more disastrous than what the users were trying to avoid. Escape is really impossible. Once individuals have the courage to enter on the path to freedom offered them by Christ and his incarnation, they will become certain that liberation is indeed to be won through suffering and humiliation.

This takes an act of faith. No apologetics can convince someone that entry upon the path of liberating humility that the incarnation has opened to people is indeed an effective means to freedom. We are confronted here with the mystery of God's gift. But there are perhaps moments of abrupt dislocation and keen suffering when God can suddenly lay hold of individuals and bring them, amid continued suffering that is, however, permeated with a certain sweetness, into the way already traveled by the Son in his redemptive incarnation; then they will experience a hidden joy as they go.

The Christmas Virgin

Nothing is more frequent in the fathers than the parallel between Eve and Mary; at times this seems so important to them that it becomes somewhat forced. Their excuse is that they had discovered, and were intensely aware of, Mary's special part in the liberation of humanity.

The Church father who has perhaps placed the greatest emphasis on the parallel is St. Irenaeus of Lyons (second century), as he endeavored to show how the Virgin collaborated in her Son's redemptive work:

> Eve disobeyed, and did so while still a virgin. But while Eve, wife of Adam but still a virgin . . . disobeyed and became the cause of death for herself and the whole human race, Mary, spouse of a predestined man but still a virgin, obeyed and became the cause of salvation for herself and the whole human race.[25]

It is odd that the Roman liturgy has not developed the Eve-Mary parallel or contrast, which was such a favorite of patristic tradition. A good occasion for it would have been January 1, now that the feast concentrates once more on its original object: Mary, Mother of God. Other liturgies, like the Ambrosian, as we shall point out later, made good use of the striking contrast between Eve and Mary in their celebrations. A splendid preface in the Ambrosian liturgy expresses it with vigor and balance; we quoted it in our brief remarks on Advent at Milan.[26]

In addition to the parallel between Eve and Mary in the Christmas liturgy, we occasionally find the fathers confronting, rather than paralleling, the Virgin with Adam. St. Ephraem, for example, writes, "Mary wove a garment of glory and gave it to her father, Adam, who was naked among the trees. He donned this chaste robe and became beautiful. His wife led him to a fall; his daughter supported him; he arose to be a hero."[27]

All these texts endeavor to state the collaboration of the Blessed Virgin in the work of redemption; the incarnation provides an occasion for doing so. Mary's *Fiat* made it possible for Christ to be born as a human and thus to restore Adam, via the New Adam, to his original dignity. Mary made it possible for the Savior to be the new human who gives the rest of humankind a share in his status. Mary obeyed in order to save us; by her obedience, she made up for the harm done by the first disobedience.

The texts are prudent in their expression, but they are nonetheless significant of the devotion the fathers had to Mary within the context of the Christmas celebration. The Roman liturgy at a very early date chose rather to establish a special feast in honor of the Virgin Mother of God. Its date was January 1; it was soon turned into the feast of the circumcision, but its original object and purpose have now been restored. This was the oldest feast of Mary in the West. In fact, we should note that the Church chose January 1 well before this day was designated as the first day of the year. In her celebration we hear again the accents of the fathers. Thus, the collect of the Mass emphasizes Mary's role in the incarnation: "O God, who through the fruitful virginity of Blessed Mary bestowed on the human race the grace of eternal salvation, grant, we pray, that we may experience the intercession of her, through whom we were found worthy to receive the author of life, our Lord Jesus Christ, your Son."

The preface of this same Mass likewise speaks of Mary's part in the work of salvation: "For by the overshadowing of the Holy Spirit she conceived your Only Begotten Son, and without losing the glory of virginity, brought forth into the world the eternal Light, Jesus Christ our Lord."

Structure and Themes of the Christmas Liturgy

13. THE INCARNATION TODAY

The Appointed Time Has Come (December 24)

The Advent season is at its end, and the Church, which is responsible for the expectation of the world and of people and knows their weakness and impatience (for all creation groans as its awaits its redemption; Rom 8:22-23)—the Church cries out: "Come quickly, we pray, Lord Jesus, and do not delay, that those who trust in your compassion may find solace and relief in your coming."

Thus does the Church speak in the collect at Mass on the morning of December 24. If we are at all familiar with the Roman liturgy, we will be surprised to hear a prayer addressed, not to the Father, but to Christ himself, in the manner of the Spanish or Frankish liturgies. Why did the new Missal choose this mode of prayer, which is alien to Roman usage? Perhaps those who composed the new Mass realized that the celebration of Advent has by now made the faithful impatiently desirous of liberation: "Oh, that you would rend the heavens and come down" (Isa 63:19).

In proclaiming the gospel on this day, the Church speaks through the mouth of John the Baptist's father, Zechariah. The latter is filled by the Holy Spirit, recovers his lost powers of speech, and prophesies concerning Christ and his own son (Luke 1:67-79). The Lord has "visited" his people, says Zechariah, using a familiar Old Testament way of expressing God's interventions.[1] The New Testament also uses the term in other passages besides the present one, and it is especially dear to Luke, who alone seems to use it in this precise Old Testament form (see 7:16; 19:44).

Readings for the Feasts and Sundays of the Christmas Season

	Prophet	*Epistle*	*Gospel*
Vigil of Christmas	The Lord takes delight in you; Isa 62:1-5	Paul testifies that Christ is son of David and Son of God; Acts 13:16-17, 22-25	Genealogy of Jesus; Matt 1:1-25
Christmas: Midnight	A son is given to us; Isa 9:2-7	God's grace has been revealed to all people; Titus 2:11-14	Today a savior has been born for you; Luke 2:1-4
Christmas: Dawn	Your savior is born; Isa 62:11-12	God's compassion has saved us; Titus 3:4-7	The shepherds find Mary, Joseph, and the child; Luke 2:15-20
Christmas: Day	The world shall see God's salvation; Isa 52:7-10	God has spoken to us through his Son; Heb 1:1-6	The Word became flesh and dwelt among us; John 1:1-18
Holy Family	Fear of God and love of parents; Sir 3:2-6, 12-14	The life of a Christian family; Col 3:12-21	A. The flight into Egypt; Matt 2:13-15, 19-23 B. Jesus grew in age and wisdom; Luke 2:22-40 C. Jesus among the doctors; Luke 2:41-52
Mary, Mother of God (January 1)	I will bless Israel; Num 6:22-27	The Son of God, born of a woman; Gal 4:4-7	The child is named Jesus; Luke 2:16-21
Second Sunday after Christmas	The wisdom of God in our midst; Sir 24:1-2, 8-12	We are predestined to be adopted children in Jesus; Eph 1:3-6, 15-18	The Word was made flesh; John 1:1-18

Readings for the Weekdays

	Epistle	*Gospel*
December 29	Brotherly love and the light within us; 1 John 2:3-11	The light that enlightens the nations; Luke 2:22-35
December 30	Doing God's will; 1 John 2:12-17	The witness of Anna; Luke 2:36-40
December 31	We are anointed in Christ and have all knowledge; 1 John 2:18-21	The Word was made flesh; John 1:1-18

Scripture Readings in the Liturgy of the Hours

Vigil of Christmas	Isa 51:17–52:2, 7-10
Christmas	Isa 11:1-10
Holy Family	Eph 5:21–6:4
Mary, Mother of God (January 1)	Heb 2:9-17
December 29	Col 1:1-14
December 30	Col 1:15–2:3
December 31	Col 2:4-15
January 2	Col 2:16–3:4
January 3	Col 3:5-16
January 4	Col 3:17–4:1

The Lord's "visit" here refers to his active intervention as he comes to free the house of David by raising up within it a liberating force. The prophecies are being fulfilled, and the Lord's mercy is taking concrete form as he shows his fidelity to the covenant. Evil will have no more power over us, and for the rest of our days we will be able to sing of our liberation and our covenant with the Lord, in prayer and in celebration of his worship. And we shall worship, not in slavish attachment to external rites, but "in holiness and righteousness."

This last expression occurs only twice in the New Testament to signify the attitude we should have of complete devotion to the Savior during this time of our salvation. Like Luke, Paul uses it in his Letter to the Ephesians (4:24) to characterize the outlook of the new person. Plato, in this a true Greek, defines holiness as the knowledge of the right behavior toward the gods. The New Testament, however, considers holiness to be an effect of rebirth in God through water and the Spirit.

John the Baptist will tell the world of its liberation, thus preparing the way for Jesus to reveal to his people that they are saved and that their sins are forgiven. Such is "the tender compassion of our God."

In all this the Lord himself has taken the initiative. The first reading for Mass on December 24 emphasizes the point: "I took you from the pasture and from the care of the flock to be commander of my people Israel" (2 Sam 7:8). The Lord then goes on to say (still speaking through Nathan the prophet), "I will give you rest from all your enemies. The LORD also reveals to you that he will establish a house for you" (2 Sam 7:11). God is here setting David's line apart, for in it the Christ will be born.

Psalm 89 is a response of awed jubilation to these wondrous things the Lord is doing; in it God now speaks in the Church to the assembled faithful:

> "With my chosen one I have made a covenant;
> I have sworn to David my servant:
> I will establish your descendants forever,
> and set up your throne through all ages." . . .
> He will call out to me, "You are my father,
> my God, the rock of my salvation." . . .
> I will keep my faithful love for him always;
> with him my covenant shall last. (Ps 89:4-5, 27, 29)

The Eucharist we celebrate is the tangible proof that God has indeed intervened; the communion antiphon gives a sacramental reference to the words we just heard in the Gospel: "Blessed be the Lord, the God of Israel! He has visited his people and redeemed them."

"In the Morning You Shall See the Glory of the Lord" (Vigil Mass)

The Vigil Mass on December 24 stands between the end of Advent and the coming of Christ in the flesh. In what better way could we spend these final moments of waiting than by meditating on his genealogy? How moving this list of Christ's ancestors is! How vividly it shows him to be a member of our race, truly one of us, a son of David (Matt 1:1-25)!

At the same time, the Church seems to have feared that the simple proclamation of the genealogy might have fostered too human a view of Christ. She therefore goes on and tells the faithful of the words the angel spoke to Joseph, who was disturbed by his fiancée's condition: "For it is through the Holy Spirit that this child has been conceived in her. She will bear a son and you are to name him Jesus, because he will save his people from their sins" (Matt 1:20-21). Jesus is Emmanuel: "God with us." With these words added to the genealogy, we have Christ presented to us according to his full reality: he is the incarnate God.

With the coming of Christ, a long history is ended. And yet is this really an end? Or is it not rather the beginning of a new history, the history of a world that is renewed and of people who find a new life and move on toward the definitive fulfillment? The Israel that had been chosen, the Jerusalem that had been preferred—these are now to be identified with the Church to which we now belong and to which all belong, at least in desire, who honestly seek the right way.

The first reading at this Vigil Mass (Isa 62:1-5) shows us this Jerusalem, that is, the Church of yesterday, today, and tomorrow. She is "a glorious crown in the hand of the LORD, / a royal diadem held by your God," and her names are "My Delight" and "Espoused." Such is the reality brought into being by the incarnation and God's visitation. The Lord himself rejoices at it in the responsorial psalm (Ps 89):

> He will call out to me, "You are my father,
> my God, the rock of my salvation." . . .
> I will keep my faithful love for him always;
> with him my covenant shall last.

Today, as once in the synagogue at Antioch, St. Paul presents the Lord Jesus to us: "From this man's [David's] descendants God, according to his promise, has brought to Israel a savior, Jesus. John heralded his coming by proclaiming a baptism of repentance to all the people of Israel" (Acts 13:23-24).

The Alleluia verse sums up the spirit of the Vigil celebration: "Tomorrow the wickedness of the earth will be destroyed: the Savior of the world will reign over us." Christmas is part of the paschal mystery.

"Today I Have Begotten You" (Mass during the Night)

We must not mistake the real spirit of the account of Christ's birth that is read in the gospel at the Mass during the Night (Luke 2:1-14). It can be read simply as a moving story, and many have so read it. Think of all the tender poems, all the paintings, whether realistic or abstract! But the real meaning of the gospel is indicated by the two readings that precede it: Isaiah 9:2-7, which tells us that a son is given to us, and Titus 2:11-14, which tells us that God's grace has been revealed for the salvation of all humankind.

The central theme of the celebration is also expressed in the Alleluia song that accompanies the procession with the Gospel: "I proclaim to you good news of great joy: today a Savior is born for us, Christ the Lord." The same message may also be sung after the first reading, in place of the "new song" (Ps 96) to which the good news in the first reading gives rise. The whole earth sings a new song to the Lord; his glory must be proclaimed to the nations and the peoples, for "he comes to judge the earth" (Ps 96:13).

Oddly enough, the communion antiphon for this Mass during the Night does not use a verse from the gospel but instead takes a verse from St. John's Prologue in order to comment on the reading from Luke and to draw attention to the real mystery being celebrated: "The Word became flesh, and we have seen his glory."

The preface, for its part, says: "we recognize in him God made visible" (first Christmas preface). This holy night marks the beginning of the Church's and the Christian's sacramental life. Henceforth, we experience God through signs, and the signs are efficacious because of the incarnation of God, who thereby allowed himself to be seen and touched. We see his glory. The Eucharist we celebrate, the bread we eat, and the wine we drink are the signs through which we touch God. Because the Word became a man, he was able to give his life for us. Thus, there came into existence those sacred signs of the paschal mystery, which enable us to live henceforth in sacramental union with the Lord.

There might be value in commenting on this passage of Luke with the help of all the recent studies on its authenticity, its sources, Luke's objectivity, the value of the information he provides, etc. The scientific literature on the passage is indeed extensive. We shall not cite it, however, for we can surely understand that while it is of great importance, it has nothing to do with Luke's attitude of faith and with the Church's attitude of faith at the moment of this celebration.

"A Light Will Shine on Us This Day" (Mass at Dawn)

The solemnity of the texts and chants at the Mass during the Night are followed by a full vision of life-giving joy in the Mass at Dawn. This Mass sings of the light that radiates from the newborn Savior. St. Luke continues his account by telling us of the shepherds who hasten to find out what has happened and what the Lord would have them know. They want to see, and "to see" in this context means to verify God's love for humanity. The glory of God is somehow linked to the peace on earth that originates in the good pleasure of the God who has come to save humanity. The joy that fills the message to the shepherds is foretold in Isaiah (62:12), "They shall be called the holy people, / the redeemed of the LORD, / and you shall be called 'Frequented,' / a city that is not forsaken." The responsorial psalm echoes this joy: "Light shines forth for the just one, / and joy for the upright of heart" (Ps 97:11).

The good will of God toward the people he has determined to save is the theme of the second reading (Titus 3:4-7). Here, the true basis for the Christian's behavior finds expression: we live not by law but by the fact of the incarnation and the gift of renewal that has been given to us. Renewal through water and the Spirit is the foundation of the Christian's action and of the baptized person's value judgments on people and things. Having become just, that is, having been made just by the Lord's grace, we now live in hope of eternal life. But all this has for its foundation the incarnation of our God, for the incarnation is the starting point of a new history for humanity.

In living this new history that moves to fulfillment every day and especially every time we celebrate the Eucharist as an efficacious sign of our liberation and as a pledge of our salvation, we experience a joy that the communion antiphon tries to express: "Rejoice, O Daughter Sion; lift up praise, Daughter Jerusalem: Behold, your King will come, the Holy One and Savior of the world."

A Newborn Child, Our Messenger from God
(Mass during the Day)

It is in these terms that the entrance antiphon for this Mass presents Jesus to us: "A child is born for us, and a son is given to us; his scepter of power rests upon his shoulder, and his name will be called Messenger of great counsel."

After such an entrance antiphon, no better gospel passage could be chosen than St. John's Prologue (1:1-18). For this little child that is born for us is the Word of God, the incarnate Word of the Lord himself. This is the one John the Baptist proclaims. Now that this Word has become flesh, the whole world will see the salvation of our God. Such is the theme of the first reading (Isa 52:7-10). The Letter to the Hebrews then specifies that after speaking in many other ways, God has finally spoken through his Son whom he has sent among us (Heb 1:1-6).

The whole Liturgy of the Word at this Mass focuses on the message of God, that is, on the knowledge of his saving plan that he makes known to us in his Son. Henceforth, the "mystery" will be not what we do not understand but, on the contrary, what God has revealed to us about his plan of salvation through the Son he has sent among us (Col 1:25-29). The child just born is a messenger "announcing peace, bearing good news, / announcing salvation"; in the person of this child, "The LORD has bared his holy arm / in the sight of all the nations; / all the ends of the earth will behold / the salvation of our God" (first reading).

As the Church meditates on this astonishing yet ever-present and wonderful fact, she sings her enthusiastic response in Psalm 98, "The LORD has made known his salvation, / has shown his deliverance to the nations. . . . / All the ends of the earth have seen / the salvation of our God."

All of this marks the final stage of a very long history. It reaches its climax in the sending of God's own Word, after God's fruitless attempts to enter into a dialogue with us through other messengers. God did doubtless speak to our fathers through the prophets, in fragmentary and varied ways; but now, in the final age, literally, "in these last days," he has spoken to us through his Son (Heb 1:2). "In these last days": we should take these words quite as they stand. God speaks now, to us, today: to us who celebrate Christmas as a "today" that is part of the paschal mystery. This is neither poetry nor simply a "manner of speaking." God speaks to us now through his Son and reveals to us, now, his plan of salvation.

Encountering Christ

Christmas, then, is far from being just a feast of tender love or a marvelous poem of childhood. What it really means for the world and for us is that we encounter Christ in person, with all the specific consequences such an encounter involves. Christmas puts an end to the mythological notion of a far-off God who has no experience of our lives. It puts an end to the God-of-the-gaps, to whom people have recourse in the difficulties of life. It puts an end to the idea of God as a refuge, the God who comforts us and solves our riddles.

Our God is indeed God, but he is also a human who is all that we are, except that he is not a sinner. The Church at an early date had to deal with the Nestorian tendency to regard Jesus as simply a human being, even though a very special one whose mere presence sanctifies things human. Such a view would have meant that Christianity aimed not at transforming human life into a divine life but at "divinizing" the lives of humans without really changing them in any significant way. Humanity saved would be humanity "transformed" in Christ, in the sense that the mystery of Christ would cast an aura over humanity without making it different interiorly.

In modern terms, Nestorianism is a form of "horizontals." It is enough to see God and the sacred in one's neighbor. Social love is salvation. Why do we really need anything else—for example, sacramental signs, especially sacramental signs that are not exact duplicates of what we do in our everyday lives? The ideal eucharistic celebration is simply an ordinary meal at which the whole emphasis is put on the equality of those present. But in this view, of course, people forget that the Supper was never at any time an ordinary meal, for it was chosen by Christ because it was already a ritual meal actualizing the first Passover and the departure from slavery.

At the other extreme from Nestorianism is Eutychianism: the tendency to deny the humanity of Christ and to see in him only God, whose presence among us rouses us from our torpor. Consequently, those sacred signs, the sacraments, should be as remote from us as possible and be completely esoteric, since they are, after all, the signs of an encounter with the inaccessible God. Everything in the liturgy should be different from our everyday lives: the language should be unintelligible, the garments strange, the gestures unusual and inexplicable. It is essential that all these should be alien to us. Moreover, we should maintain the most extreme possible view of the institution of the sacraments, namely, that Christ instituted them without taking any human context into account and without paying any heed to anthropology and history. In this view, it approaches heresy to think that Christ could have used preexisting forms and filled them with a new content, thus putting himself into the stream of history.

These two very ancient tendencies are always around; we meet them today in many fervent Christians who are hardly conscious of them. Have such people ever understood the liturgy of Christmas? Have they ever had any inkling that their views have nothing in common with a valid conceptual theology of the person of Christ and with a theology expressed in a more vital fashion through the liturgy?

According to St. Leo the Great, in his well-known first sermon for Christmas, the fact of the incarnation has completely changed human life. The joy a Christian experiences on this feast is deeply rooted, for the Lord has come to destroy sin and death; he finds no one free of sin and comes to set everyone free. The holy person should rejoice, because his reward is near; the sinner should rejoice, because forgiveness is offered to him; the pagan should take courage, because he is being called to true life.[2]

The most famous passage of the sermon is, however, the following; "Christian, recognize your true worth, and, having once become a sharer of the divine nature, do not again live an evil life and thus return to your former base condition. Remember who your Head is and of whose body you are a member."[3] This is the sermon we read in the Office of Readings on Christmas Day. Our encounter with Christ, then, transforms us. It is not merely a psychological encounter, such as may be achieved in prayer, but ever since the incarnation, it is a sacramental encounter through the Church and her signs. Through these, "we recognize in him God made visible."[4]

14. MEDITATIVE CELEBRATIONS
OF CHRISTMAS

The Byzantine Liturgy

The Byzantine liturgy, to which we have ready access these days, contains some truly meditative celebrations of Christmas.

The calendar notes that the Sunday before Christmas is dedicated to "the memory of all the Fathers who pleased God, from Adam to Joseph, the spouse of the most holy Mother of God." Moreover, the five days before Christmas are, as it were, an extended "eve" of the feast. Then, finally, the calendar for December 25 says: "Birth according to the flesh of our Lord, God, and Savior, Jesus Christ. Passover."

It is rather striking that despite St. Francis and the Franciscan missions in the East, the celebration of Christmas there never incorporated the folklore of the Christmas crib. In addition, the feast (which includes the birth, the adoration of the shepherds, and the adoration of the Magi) is focused on the Word rather than on the lowly condition he accepted in order to carry out the Father's will. In private, personal prayer, the Western Christian likes to concentrate on Jesus, the Son of Mary; the Eastern Christian prays rather to the only Son of God.

First Vespers contains a series of *stichera*, each with its own melody; these are *troparia*, or sung poems, that are intercalated between the final verses of the psalms at the end of Vespers or between the four last verses of Psalm 150 at the end of Matins. Then come eight readings from the Old Testament. The third and sixth of these readings are followed by another *troparion*.

The list of readings is an interesting one: Genesis 1:1-13; various verses from Numbers 24; Micah 4:6-7 and 5:1-3; Isaiah 11:1-10; Baruch 3:35 and 4:4; Daniel 2:31-36, 44-45; Isaiah 8:3-6; and Isaiah 7:10-16; 8:1-4, 9-10. These are followed in turn by New Testament readings: Hebrews 1:1-12 (with an Alleluia) and Luke 2:1-20.

On the vigil of a great feast such as Christmas, a further Office called a "Vigil" is celebrated between Vespers and Matins. This additional Office consists of *troparia* and numerous other hymns, with their own melodies, that sing of the mysteries associated with the Nativity.

In Matins, the psalms are from the Ordinary, but they are accompanied by nine odes, each containing its own *heirmos* (a model strophe at the beginning of an ode or group of *troparia*) and *troparia*.

Here are some of these texts. From the first song of the Vigil Office: "Heaven and earth today rejoice with a prophetic joy. We men, and the angels, should rejoice spiritually, since God has been born of a woman and has appeared in the flesh for the sake of those who sit in darkness and the shadow of death." "Heaven and earth are one today, for Christ is born. Today God has come to earth, and man has returned to heaven. Today he who is by nature invisible is visible in the flesh—for man's sake!"

In Matins, the second *heirmos*, or model strophe, of the fourth Ode: "In his songs the prophet Habakkuk of old predicted the new creation of the human race, for he was judged worthy to contemplate its ineffable image. The little Child who has come forth from the mountain that is the Virgin is the Word, who comes to restore the nations."

During the liturgy (i.e., the celebration of the Eucharist), the *Trisagion* (the triple "Holy," i.e., the *Sanctus*) is replaced by these words: "All you who have been baptized in Christ have put on Christ." The words indicate to us the kind of theology that characterizes this rich liturgy. The readings for this same Mass are Galatians 4:3-7 and Matthew 2:1-12.

The Holy Family of Christ

Devout Christians wanted a special celebration for the Holy Family of the Lord, though it is highly probable, of course, that the conditions of the times also played an important role in the insistence of Pope John XXIII on this feast. The feast concentrates on the three persons whose life together should be an influential model for all families today. Each of the three lived for God and for the others, with that true heroism that is always simple and unassuming. The collect of the Mass shows the Church's main concern on this feast, which is a prolongation of the feast of Christmas: "grant that we may imitate [the Holy Family] in practicing the virtues of family life and in the bonds of charity."

At first sight, such a celebration may seem somewhat childish and of value only to the simple; hardly a celebration for educated Christians! But it would be a mistake not to see in it a new manifestation of the fact that Jesus has come among human beings and entered into the kind of life we all live. And it would be a sign of superficiality if we failed to grasp the importance of the unpretentious behavior of Mary and Joseph for the unfolding of that sacred history that will reach its climax in the paschal mystery.

The new lectionary has provided a three-year cycle of gospel readings for this feast. All three focus on the way the parents of Jesus act in regard to him: the flight into Egypt and the return to Nazareth, with Joseph's docility to the Lord's commands and his care to protect the child (A: Matthew 2:13-15, 19-23); the child's growth in age and wisdom, and his parents' surprise at what others say of their child, especially when the old man Simeon tells prophetically of the significance of his life (B: Luke 2:22-40); Jesus discovered among the teachers as he listens and asks questions (C: Luke 2:41-52).

In the reading of Year A, we will note the parallelism between the two passages (vv. 13-15 and vv. 19-23). We need only read them carefully and we will find a striking similarity of literary structure. We may note especially the emphasis on the fulfillment of prophecy. In the first section (vv. 13-15), the prophecy is that of Hosea: *"Out of Egypt I called my son"* (11:1). In the background there is also the account in Genesis 46:2-15, where God bids Jacob set out for Egypt: "Do not be afraid to go down to Egypt, for there I will make you a great nation. I will go down to Egypt with you and I will also bring you back here." Note too that, while in the genealogy Jesus is called "son of David" (1:1), here he is called Son of God: *"Out of Egypt I called my son."*

For the Israelites, Egypt was the land of slavery; they had experienced it and the Lord had delivered them. Now Jesus is the deliverer. There is a striking parallelism between Exodus 4:19-20 and verses 19-21 of this gospel reading, with Jesus appearing as the new Moses. Joseph probably did not grasp all that we are now able to see, but he was nonetheless a faithful servant, faithful to the Lord's commands and determined to carry out the Lord's plan of salvation.

In Year B, the gospel passage from Luke (2:22-40) shows us the presentation in the temple and the meetings with Anna, the prophetess, and with the elderly Simeon, who points to Jesus as Savior, Light of the world, Glory of Israel, and Deliverer of Jerusalem. Yet salvation will in fact be given only to those who believe (Luke 20:17-18). As believers, Simeon and Anna are able to recognize and proclaim the Messiah. Mary receives from Simeon a revelation of her son's role in the salvation of all, but at the same time she learns of his tragic destiny as he comes to save Israel but is not received with faith. At this point, Joseph and Mary take over the rearing of the child who is to save the world.

Luke 2:41-52, the reading for Year C, speaks of the relationship between Jesus and his parents. The passage does more than preserve an anecdote, for it reveals the wisdom of Jesus as he shows us how he understands God's will. The divine will is not simply something he learns; rather, his whole life is focused on devotion to his Father's affairs. His parents respect this mystery of their son that will be fully revealed in the paschal mystery, when hidden things become clear in Christ.

The first two readings for this feast are the same every year. The first is an exhortation to respect our parents: "Whoever reveres his father will live a long life; / he who obeys his father brings comfort to his mother" (Sir 3:2-6, 12-14). Psalm 128 then sings of the happiness of a family that worships the Lord. Finally, St. Paul, in his Letter to the Colossians, exhorts his hearers to the domestic virtues (3:12-21): mutual love and forgiveness, a spirit of thanksgiving, submission of wives to their husbands, love of husband for wife, obedience on the part of the children. This may seem to be an idyllic vision of the Christian family, but it is in fact realistic, since the Holy Family gives us an example of it, and the Lord enables us to imitate that example in our daily lives.

Mary, Mother of God (January 1)

On January 1, the octave day of the nativity, we have the oldest celebration of the Virgin in the Roman Church. The modern Church has decided to revive that celebration of Mary, the Mother of God, without, however, forgetting either the beginning of the new year or the circumcision of Jesus or his reception of the name Jesus. The entrance antiphon expresses briefly the focus of the Church's thoughts during this liturgy: "Hail, holy Mother, who gave birth to the King who rules heaven and earth for ever."

The gospel is the same passage as is read in the Mass at Dawn on Christmas. Here again we can observe how the gospel must be interpreted in connection with the first and second readings of the feast being celebrated. On Christmas, the gospel was emphasizing the coming of the Word made flesh; in this new context, the emphasis is on the role of the Virgin Mother of God. For this reason the second reading is taken from St. Paul's Letter to the Galatians (4:4-7), where we read that God sent his Son to be born of a woman. The preface for this day also celebrates the motherhood of Mary, who conceived her Son when the Spirit overshadowed her. "[W]e glory in the beginnings of your grace."[1]

The Church also remembers today the giving of the name Jesus to the Virgin's child (in the gospel). It is a powerful name when invoked over the beginning of the new year; that is the point of the first reading, Numbers 6:22-27.

The Word and Wisdom among Us

The Second Sunday after Christmas continues the Church's contemplation of the mystery of the Nativity. The gospel is that read at the Mass during the Day on Christmas. The other readings emphasize two aspects of the coming of the Word among us. One is that with his coming the Wisdom of God has now taken up its abode in its own people (Sir 24:1-2, 8-12). The other is that we are predestined to become children of God through Jesus (Eph 1:3-6, 15-18). Both aspects are important.

We can hardly believe that in the eyes of the Old Testament writers, Wisdom was a person. The liturgy nonetheless uses this text to describe the person of Jesus. The reading acquires its full Christian meaning once we identify the incarnate Son of God with the Wisdom that comes to dwell among humans. Such a rereading and an identification of Christ with Wisdom is possible and legitimate in a liturgical celebration, although a strictly exegetical reading could not justify such an interpretation.

The second reading unveils to us God's plan of salvation. We were chosen before the creation of the world to become holy and blameless in the Lord's sight; we were predestined in advance to become children for God through Jesus the Christ. It is the Spirit who now makes us discern God's wisdom and conforms us to the image of the Son.

We thereby learn how, through the mystery of the incarnation, we enter into the life of the Trinity. From all eternity God has loved us; he never gets discouraged but, despite our sins, loves us so much that he sends his Son. This Son dies for us and redeems us, while the Spirit creates in us the image of the Son so that when the Father sees us, he can see his Son in us.

This marvelous plan of God reuses Paul's wonder and admiration. He prays that the Spirit may open our hearts and that we may be able to grasp the hope that springs from the invocation of the Father and the priceless and glorious heritage that we share with all believers.

15. CHRISTMAS IN THE LITURGIES OF THE PAST

1. Christmas in the Early Roman Liturgy

Readings

There is a wide variety of readings for the Christmas season to be found in the lectionaries of earlier times. We must, however, limit ourselves to a selection of these, since too long a list would be cumbersome and less useful. In addition, there are many similarities between the various lectionaries. The reader can peruse the table that follows; there is no need for us to comment on it.

There are other lectionaries from the Roman tradition that we might also have noted; for example, the Chartres Lectionary, compiled around 740,[1] or the Epistolary of Corbie,[2] or the Verona Lectionary.[3]

Prayers

The wealth of prayers in the sacramentaries, and especially in the *Verona*, or *Leonine*, *Sacramentary*, is truly remarkable, and a whole book would be required for an adequate study of the material. The Verona Sacramentary, for example, contains eight formularies of Masses for Christmas.[4] St. Leo the Great is a chief source of these formularies, which show a close similarity to his other writings.

Some prayers from the Verona Sacramentary have been taken over in the new Missal of Paul VI. There is, for example, a collect for Christmas in the Verona Sacramentary that in the past served in the Roman Rite (and still does, though in modified form) as a blessing of the water to be added to the chalice at Mass but has now also been restored to its proper function as the collect for Mass on Christmas Day; "O God, who wonderfully created the dignity of human nature and still more wonderfully restored it, grant, we pray, that we may share in the divinity of Christ, who humbled himself to share in our humanity."[5] Another prayer from the Verona Sacramentary serves

	1	2	3	4	5	6
Vigil of Christmas		Isa 62:1-4			Rom 1:1-6	Rom 1:1-6
		Rom 1:1-6	Matt 1:18-21		Matt 1:18-21	Matt 1:18-21
Christmas Midnight		Isa 9:2-7			Isa 9:2-7	
	Titus 2:11-15	Titus 2:11-15				Titus 2:11-15
			Luke 2:1-14		Luke 2:1-14	Luke 2:15-20
Christmas Dawn					Isa 61:1-3; 62:11-12	
	Titus 3:4-7				Titus 3:4-7	Titus 3:4-7
			Luke 2:15-20		Luke 2:15-20	Luke 2:15-20
Christmas Day					Isa 52:6-10	
	Heb 1:1-12	Heb 1:1-12			Heb 1:1-12	Heb 1:1-12
			John 1:1-14		John 1:1-14	John 1:1-14
Mary, Mother of God, January 1					Titus 2:11-15	Titus 2:11-15
			Luke 2:21-32		Luke 2:21-32	Luke 2:21
Sunday after Christmas	Gal 4:1-7	Rom 12:6-16			Gal 4:1-7	Gal 4:1-7
				Matt 2:19-23	Luke 2:33-40	Luke 2:33-40

1 = The Würzburg Epistolary (ca. 560–90). Edition: G. Morin, "Le plus ancient lectionnaire de l'Eglise romaine," *Revue bénédictine* 27 (1910): 41–74. For its history, see Vogel, *op. cit.*, 309–10, 313–14, 321–25.

2 = The Comes or Epistolary of Alcuin. The manuscript is from the ninth century, but it is thought to represent a Roman lectionary of the year 626, which Alcuin simply modified. Edition: A. Wilmart, "Le lectionnaire d'Alcuin," *Ephemerides liturgicae* 51 (1937): 136–97. See Vogel, *op. cit.*, 310–12.

3 = The Würzburg Evangeliary (ca. 645), a pure Roman document. See Vogel, *op. cit.*, 313–14.

4 = A pure Roman evangeliary of around 740, described in Vogel, *op. cit.*, 314.

5 = The Murbach Lectionary, composed at Murbach, France, toward the end of the eighth century; it is later followed at Rome, and the Missal of Pius V makes extensive use of it. Edition: A. Wilmart, "Le Comes de Murbach," *Revue bénédictine* 30 (1913): 26–69. See Vogel, *op. cit.*, 318–19.

6 = Missal of Pius V.

as the prayer after communion of the Mass during the Night.[6] A number of other prayers in the new Missal have been inspired by those of the Verona Sacramentary.

We shall limit ourselves here, however, to some especially interesting prayers of the Verona Sacramentary that have not been taken over into the new Missal. The postcommunion prayer in the first Christmas Mass is important for a theology of the liturgy as actualization in time of the mysteries of Christ: "Lord, grant your servants a deeper faith and a greater freedom from anxiety, so that your children, who rejoice at the birth of your Son, our Lord, may through your providential governance not experience the opposition of the world and may enjoy in eternity what they yearn to celebrate in time."[7]

The mystery of Christmas is regarded as a paschal renewal: "Lord, you have restored human nature to a more wonderful condition than that in which you first created it. Complete what the divine generation of your Word created in us and what his glorious birth as man has now made new."[8]

The prayers taken over into the new Missal from the older sacramentaries are also quite rich. The Masses for Midnight and Dawn emphasize the theme of light in relation to the meaning of Christmas. Thus the collect of the Mass during the Night: "O God, who have made this most sacred night radiant with the splendor of the true light, grant, we pray, that we, who have known the mysteries of his light on earth, may also delight in his gladness in heaven." This prayer is taken from the Gelasian Sacramentary,[9] where it is likewise used as the collect of the Mass during the Night; it brings out the paschal aspect of the feast, since the grace of the latter is an intensification of the illumination received in baptism.

The first of the Christmas prefaces in the new Missal likewise stresses the theme of light: "For in the mystery of the Word made flesh a new light of your glory has shone upon the eyes of our mind, so that, as we recognize in him God made visible, we may be caught up through him in love of things invisible." The second preface concentrates more on the sacramental aspect of the incarnation: "though invisible in his own divine nature, he has appeared visibly in ours." The third preface emphasizes the wonderful exchange that has taken place: "when our frailty is assumed by your Word not only does human mortality receive unending honor but by this wondrous union we, too, are made eternal." The prefaces in the Verona Sacramentary were of great theological depth. We cannot cite them all, but we may at least note how the first of them makes Christmas the basic celebration of the Christian year: "All that a devout Christian faith celebrates has its origins in this feast and is already contained in the mystery we celebrate in this liturgy."[10]

2. The Celebration of Christmas at Milan

We shall simply list the readings given in the Sacramentary of Bergamo[11] and in the present Ambrosian Missal:

	Sacramentary of Bergamo	*Ambrosian Missal*
Vigil of Christmas	Heb 10:37-39	Heb 10:38-39
	Matt 1:18-25	Matt 1:18-25
Christmas: Midnight	Gal 4:4-6	Gal 4:4-6
	John 1:9-14	John 1:9-14
Christmas: Dawn		1 Cor 9:13-23
		Luke 2:15-20
Christmas: Day		Isa 9:1-7
	Heb 1:1-12	Heb 1:1-8
	Luke 2:1-14	Luke 2:1-14
Sunday after Christmas		Isa 8:10-18
	Rom 8:3-11	Rom 8:3-11
	Luke 4:14-22	Luke 4:14-22
Octave of Christmas (January 1)		Bar 6:1-2, 4-6
		Jer 51:47-48, 58
		Phil 3:1-8
	Luke 2:21-32	Luke 2:21-32

The Sacramentary of Bergamo contains no prayer that is unusually rich in content that is not also found elsewhere.

3. The Celebration of Christmas in Merovingian Gaul

The celebration of Christmas in Merovingian Gaul provides us with some interesting readings. We may note, for example, the custom of reading a passage from a father of the Church during the Vigil Mass (see the Lectionary of Luxeuil). Another point worth noting is the originality shown in the choice of readings from Scripture; this may be seen by comparing them with those of Rome, Milan, and Spain.

4. The Celebration of Christmas in Spain

Christmas	*January 1*
Isa 7:10-16; 9:1-7	Gen 21:1-8
Heb 1:1-12	Rom 15:8-13
Luke 2:1-20	Luke 2:21-40

For Christmas Day the Spanish *Liber sacramentorum* has a prayer that is of special interest:

> Lord, in fidelity to your gifts and your precepts, we place on your altar holocausts of bread and wine. We ask you, in your loving mercy that is given so abundantly, that the undivided Trinity would consecrate these gifts by the power of the same Spirit through whom the spotless Virgin conceived you in the flesh. Then, when we have received these gifts with fear and reverence, whatever militates against the soul will be destroyed, and whatever has been destroyed will not gain power over us again.[12]

	L	S	S¹	B	P
Vigil of Christmas	Isa 41:26-42 Isa 44:23-46 Sermon of Augustine Isa 54:1-56 Mal 3:1-4, 6 John 1:1-14	Isa 9:1-7	Gal 3:24–4:7	Isa 9:6-7 Heb 1:1-5 Matt 1:1-2, 6	
Christmas Day	Isa 7:10–9:7 Heb 1:1-12 Luke 2:1-20	Isa 9:1-7	Gal 3:24–4:7	Isa 9:1-7 Heb 1:1-5 Matt 1:1–2:6	Luke 2:1-20
Sunday after Christmas	Ezek 43:18–44:4 Eph 1:3-14		2 Cor 6:12-18		
January 1	Isa 1:10-18 1 Cor 10:14-31 Luke 2:21-40	Isa 45:18-24	1 Cor 10:17-31		

L = Lectionary of Luxeuil. P. Salmon, ed., *Le Lectionnaire de Luxeuil* (Collectanea Biblica 7 and 9; Rome, 1944 and 1953). See Vogel, *op. cit.*, 291.

S = Lectionary of Sélestat. A Merovingian lectionary, ca. 700; originally from northern Italy. Partial edition by G. Morin, "Un lectionnaire mérovingien de Sélestat avec fragments du texte occidental des Actes," *Revue bénédictine* 28 (1908): 161–66. See Vogel, *op. cit.*, 292.

S¹ = Fragment of a lectionary from Sélestat, indicating readings from Third Sunday of Advent on. Edited in G. Morin, *art. cit.*, 166. See Vogel, *loc. cit.*

B = The eighth-century Bobbio Missal, preserved at Paris. Edited by E. J. Lowe and J. W. Legg, *The Bobbio Missal* 1: *Facsimilie*; 2: *Text* (Henry Bradshaw Society 53 and 58; London, 1917–20). See Vogel, *op. cit.*, 293.

P = Marginal notations in the seventh-century Evangeliary of Saint Dénis. Edited by P. Salmon, "Le texte biblique de l'Evangéliaire de Saint-Dénis," *Miscellanea Mercati* 1 (Rome, 1946), 103–6. See Vogel, *op. cit.*, 295.

Noteworthy, too, is the preface of the Mass for the beginning of the new year:

> God our Father, he who was born of you before time began and who with you and the Holy Spirit created time, has deigned to be born within time from the womb of the Virgin Mary. Yet he is eternal and fixed the course of the years through which the world goes its way. . . . Fill the earth with fruits; free our souls and bodies of sickness and sin; eliminate scandals; crush our enemy.[13]

The
Epiphany
Mystery

Biblico-Liturgical Reflections on the Epiphany

16. THE EPIPHANY: A MYSTERY OF PLENTY

Two Celebrations of the Same Mystery?

The Epiphany may at first sight seem to be a superfluous feast, one that originates in the desire to emphasize the dogma of the incarnation. As a matter of fact, there is a certain validity to this view, since the Epiphany certainly did owe its existence to the desire of making the mystery of the incarnate Word better appreciated and of relating it to Christian life.

The purpose of the feast, however, is not to dwell on the details of stories from the life of Jesus but to highlight his incarnation and manifestation. The folklore surrounding the crèche since the time of St. Francis, the medieval Christmas legends, and an excessive curiosity about the details of Christ's life have all contributed to a loss of the vision of the overall mystery of Christmas and Epiphany. The feasts of Christmas and Epiphany depend for their proper understanding on the paschal mystery, the incarnation of the Word being the first stage in the carrying out of the work of our redemption. The collect for the Mass on Christmas Day, taken from the Verona Sacramentary, is significant in this respect; its whole atmosphere is that of the paschal mystery.[1]

The best way to grasp the connection between Christmas and Epiphany, and at the same time their different objects, is by a comparison of the Roman prefaces for the two feasts.

The Verona Sacramentary contains eight Mass formularies and eight prefaces for Christmas. The sixth of these prefaces sums up the object of the feast in a luminous way:

> It is truly right and proper, fitting and conducive to salvation that we should always and everywhere give you thanks, holy Lord, almighty Father, eternal God, for the magnificent exchange that restores our

nature has now been manifested. From the old human a new human arises and from mortality immortality, as the human condition is healed with a remedy wrought from that same human condition; and from a race subject to sin a child innocent of all sin is born. Not only is undying honor done our weak nature when your Word makes it his own, but through his marvelous sharing with us we ourselves become eternal.[2]

This beautiful preface should be compared with the prayer, mentioned just above, that is likewise found in the Verona Sacramentary and now appears in the Mass for Christmas Day. Christmas brings with it the gift of a new nature; so intimate now is our communion with the Word that "we ourselves become eternal." The incarnation is presented as the start of the process of redemption, since the restoration of our nature consists essentially in this, that "from the old human a new human arises."

The mystery of Christmas is seen essentially in the perspective of the paschal mystery:

It is truly right and proper, fitting and conducive to salvation that we should always and everywhere give you thanks, holy Lord, almighty Father, eternal God, as we offer you the unceasing sacrifice of praise. Abel the just one prefigured it with his sacrifice; the lamb prescribed by the law was its type; Abraham celebrated it; and the priest Melchisedech showed it forth, but only the true Lamb and eternal priest, the Christ born this day, made it a reality.[3]

Finally, the three prefaces now used for Christmas likewise make our transformation their theme.

Since our restoration comes about through intimate contact with the Godhead, the nuptial theme was felt to be appropriate. The sixth preface of the Verona Sacramentary suggests it, as we saw above. The first of the Verona prefaces makes it its major theme as it speaks of our present union with Christ, that is, the union of Christ and his Church that is to deepen and reach its fullest form at the end of time:

All that a devout Christian faith celebrates has its origin in this feast and is already contained in the mystery we celebrate in this liturgy. It was made known even to the parents of the human race, as the Apostle tells us when speaking of the first human beings: "This is a great mystery, and I mean in reference to Christ and the church." The patriarchs pointed to it in various words and deeds; the observance of the law prefigured it; all the prophets foretold it in their oracles. In it the ancient ceremonies are brought to their perfect form. In it heavenly grace is now bestowed upon us and the promise of blessings to come. For since what was predicted is evidently fulfilled in it, we may rightly and surely expect that what was promised will also come to pass.[4]

The Christmas prefaces, then, speak of our restoration through the incarnation and our resultant close communion with the incarnate Word.

In the Mass for the Vigil of the Theophany (a frequent Eastern name for our Epiphany), the Gelasian Sacramentary has a preface that appears later on in the Gregorian Sacramentary as the preface for January 6; it was also the preface for the Epiphany in the Roman Rite until the recent reform and still forms part of the new preface for the Epiphany: "For, when your only-begotten Son appeared in the reality of our mortal nature, he restored us by the newly manifested radiance of his immortal being."[5]

The theme of renewal or restoration evidently is basic in this preface, but in one respect it is new, inasmuch as it is through an illumination or enlightenment that we are made new. Christ comes as the light that sheds light into our darkness and makes us new. The theme is clearly Johannine.

The other prayers in this Gelasian Mass develop the same theme. Thus, the collect reads: "Lord, let the radiance of the coming feast enlighten our hearts, so that we may be liberated from the darkness of this world and reach the fatherland where eternal light shines."[6] The postcommunion prayer continues in the same vein: "Lord, enlighten your people and inflame their hearts with your radiant grace so that the birth of the world's Savior, heralded by the star, may be ever revealed to their minds, and that the understanding of it may grow in them."[7]

On the feast day itself, January 6, the same Gelasian Sacramentary has a preface that aptly highlights the meaning of the feast:

> It is truly right and proper, fitting and conducive to salvation, that we should praise you, our God, who are marvelous in all the works by which you have revealed the mysteries of your kingdom. A star announcing the virginal birth shone in advance of this feast and told the wondering Magi that heaven's Lord was born on earth. Thus God was manifested to the world by a heavenly sign, and he who was born in time was revealed through temporal signs.[8]

The preface is supplemented by a *communicantes* prayer: "In union with the whole Church we celebrate the sacred day on which your only-begotten Son, who shares your eternal glory, appeared as one truly born of our flesh."[9]

The star is a focus of attention in the liturgy, insofar as it manifests the incarnate Word. In other words, the eternal generation of the Word is revealed by earthly manifestations. The preface quoted above tells us that earthly, temporal signs pointed to him who is born in time. The earthly, temporal signs that thus manifest the birth of the Word are the star, but especially the baptism in the Jordan and the marriage feast of Cana.

The feast of Christmas, then, celebrates the incarnation of the Son of God, while the feast of the Epiphany emphasizes the earthly manifestations of his eternal birth. In the one feast we celebrate the birth in the flesh; in the other we concentrate on the earthly manifestations of the eternal generation of the Word. At Christmas we begin with the eternal generation of the Word and go on to celebrate his earthly incarnation. On Epiphany we recall and celebrate the earthly manifestations that tell us that the newborn child is the eternally begotten Word.

The same theology will be at the center of the liturgical celebrations that follow the Epiphany, and we shall find it especially emphasized on February 2, the feast of the Presentation or, as the Eastern Church calls it, the Meeting of the Lord.

"Three Mysteries"

The feast of the Epiphany is truly a feast of plenty, especially in the East, where the *tria miracula*, the "three mysteries" of Christ's life, are celebrated together, with the emphasis on the wealth of teaching they contain. The antiphon for the *Magnificat* at Second Vespers on Epiphany speaks of these three mysteries that are the object of the day's liturgical celebration: the star that leads the Magi to the crib; the miraculous wine at the marriage feast of Cana; the baptism of Jesus in the Jordan.

We shall see in some detail just what these three events of our salvation mean to us. First, however, in order better to grasp the way the various Churches celebrate Epiphany, we must review, even if only briefly, the history of the feast.

The Epiphany in History

St. Paul uses the word "epiphany" (*epiphaneia*) three times in his letters. He uses it of the first coming of Christ: "the grace . . . now made manifest through the appearance [*epiphaneias*] of our savior Christ Jesus, who destroyed death and brought life and immortality to light through the gospel" (2 Tim 1:9-10). The other two texts speak rather of Christ's triumphant return to his own: "as we await the blessed hope, the appearance [*epiphaneian*] of the glory of the great God and of our savior Jesus Christ" (Titus 2:13); "And then the lawless one will be revealed, whom the Lord [Jesus] will kill with the breath of his mouth and render powerless by the manifestation [*epiphaneia*] of his coming" (2 Thess 2:8).

The Greek words *epiphaneia* and *theophaneia* signify the coming of a king or emperor; the Latin word for this "coming" is *adventus*. The same words are also used, however, for the self-manifestation of a god or for his miraculous intervention. The words were perhaps applied first to the gods and later to sovereigns.

For a better grasp of the history of Epiphany, we should look at it first in the East, then in the West.[10]

In the East, the feast of Epiphany (January 6) was instituted before the feast of Christmas was. At the end of the fourth century, the object of the feast of the Epiphany at Jerusalem was the birth of Christ.[11] Christmas seems to have been introduced around 430, but only for a while, since a sixth-century document shows that at Jerusalem Jesus' birth was celebrated on Epiphany, while December 25 was the feast of Sts. David and James. During the years 567 to 578 the feast of Christmas was reintroduced and set alongside Epiphany.

At Constantinople and in Asia Minor there is no trace of Epiphany before the end of the fourth century. When Epiphany was introduced, it was called *Ta Phota*, the feast of "lights," and it celebrated the birth of Christ. Once Christmas was also introduced, the feast of lights took for its object the baptism of Christ.

In Syria, January 6 continued to be the feast of the incarnation until around 486, when St. John Chrysostom introduced the feast of Christmas at Antioch. From then on, Epiphany became the feast solely of the baptism of Christ.

The feast of Christmas thus originates in Rome and is adopted everywhere throughout the East during the fifth century, except perhaps in Armenia. Once Christmas is introduced, the baptism of Jesus becomes the most important and, in some instances, the only object of the celebration on January 6.

Why was January 6 chosen as the date for Epiphany? A letter of St. Epiphanius suggests that in various cities of Egypt and Arabia a feast was celebrated on January 6 in honor of the birth of *Aion*, daughter of the virgin *Kore*, and in connection with the winter solstice. In addition, pagan writers like Pliny and Christian writers like St. Epiphanius and St. John Chrysostom report certain wonders connected with January 5: spring water changed into wine; water that never turned foul, because it had been drawn on that day. It looks, then, as if the Church wanted to christianize both the pagan feast and the prodigies.

In the West, the feast of Christmas was celebrated at Rome as early as 336, but there is no trace of Epiphany. Throughout the rest of Italy, Epiphany was being celebrated around 383, but not everywhere, and where it was celebrated, it was not regarded as being of the same importance as Christmas. As for Gaul and Spain, the feast of Epiphany seems to have been introduced there around 384 and 400, respectively.[12] In fact, it may have been celebrated in Gaul before Christmas was, whereas in Rome and in Africa the feast of Christmas antedates that of Epiphany.

Though Epiphany came from the East to the West, it has a threefold object in the West—the visit of the Magi, the baptism of Christ, and the marriage feast of Cana—whereas in the East today, Epiphany is the feast only of the baptism of Jesus.

The Epiphany and Ourselves

Despite all this background and explanations, we may well continue to think that Epiphany is simply a feast that sheds further light on Christmas, a continuation of a meditation that is already rich but is now enriched still more. The questions we must ask ourselves are evidently these: What are the Magi to us? What meaning can Christ's baptism have for us today? How can we relate to the marriage feast of Cana? It is difficult for us to overcome the impression that the Church is simply expanding our view of Christmas and spreading before us treasures that further enrich her catechesis of the incarnation.

Even if we have no further need of proofs and no difficulty in admitting both the full divinity of Christ and the integrity of his human nature, we may retain the impression of an Epiphany liturgy that, for all its richness of detail, has more to do with poetic evocation than with any new concrete demands made upon us as soon as we seek to participate in the celebration in an authentic way. Liturgical development under the influence of varied cultures may seem to have turned the feast into a great theatrical display.

The difficulty we may feel, then, is not so much with the general problem of the actualization of the mysteries being celebrated; by what has been said already, we may have been convinced that such actualization is indeed important. Our problem with the Epiphany may be not the "today" aspect in the abstract but the "today" relation of this particular feast to our daily lives. It is easy to see the relevance of Christmas, but what are we to make of the "three mysteries"?

17. THE MAGI OF OLD AND THE "MAGI" OF TODAY

St. Matthew's gospel was the one the early Christians liked best. For all its variety, it possessed a profound unity, and readers saw this. There can be no doubt, of course, that this gospel, like John's, is shaped by the intention of teaching and defending a point of view or, in other words, that it has a "thesis." But to admit this does not mean, for Matthew any more than for John, that we are to be suspicious or doubtful about the authenticity of the facts recorded in the narrative. Research and discoveries have shown that John's gospel, often called the "spiritual" gospel, is perhaps the most accurate of the four in its localization of events.

Exegetes universally see in the First Gospel the Gospel of the kingdom. That is Matthew's "thesis": the establishment of the kingdom in our world. Within this framework, however, the point that Matthew emphasizes most forcefully is that the teaching and works of Jesus prolong and "fulfill" the Old Testament.[1]

Whether we see the gospel as a seven-act play[2] or as five books with a prologue (the infancy narrative, chaps. 1–2) and an epilogue (the resurrection, chap. 28),[3] the doctrinal unity of the whole work is evident. Not for a moment does St. Matthew forget his essential concern, which is to show the Jews that the Old Testament has been fulfilled. The formula, "All this took place to fulfill what the Lord had said through the prophet" (Matt 1:22), occurs ten times or more.

Cerfaux points out that the infancy narrative

> is a perfect prelude to the Gospel, while the solemn apparition of Jesus on a mountain in Galilee . . . is a very fitting conclusion: the apostles are now sent out to the nations (and not just to the towns of Israel, as on their first mission); they are to teach all of Jesus' commandments, and he will be with them until the end of the world.[4]

Now we have the context and perspective in which we must read the story of the magi's visit (chap. 2). Their coming fulfills the prophetic proclamation that the nations will acknowledge the God of Israel.

The book of Numbers had spoken of a leader who would emerge from the midst of Israel and assert his power:

> I see him, though not now;
>   I observe him, though not near:
> A star shall advance from Jacob,
>   and a scepter shall rise from Israel,
> That will crush the brows of Moab,
>   and the skull of all the Sethites,
> Edom will be dispossessed,
>   and no survivor is left in Seir.
> Israel will act boldly,
>   and Jacob will rule his foes. (Num 24:17-19)

The power and divinity of the king here predicted are signified by a star, which, in the East, was a sign of divinity. St. Matthew, always bent on his apologetic purpose of showing the continuity between the Old and New Testaments, gives us the genealogy of Jesus and stresses the connection between him and his ancestors, Abraham and David. The star, therefore, may, in Matthew's view, be the Davidic monarchy to which he has linked Jesus in the genealogy.

The evangelist here emphasizes once again that a prophecy has been fulfilled (he is only beginning the second chapter of his gospel, yet this is the second prophecy he sees being fulfilled!). The prophecy in this case is a prophecy of Micah:

> But you, Bethlehem-Ephrathah
>   least among the clans of Judah,
> From you shall come forth for me
>   one who is to be ruler in Israel. (Mic 5:1; Matt 2:6)

Matthew is aware, however, of other prophecies that are even more decisive, and he alludes to these in the course of his story. Thus, the magi prostrate themselves before Jesus. In so doing, they fulfill a prophecy of Isaiah:

> Kings shall be your guardians,
>   their princesses your nursemaids;
> Face to the ground, they shall bow down before you
>   and lick the dust at your feet.
> Then you shall know that I am the Lord,
>   none who hope in me shall be ashamed. (Isa 49:23)

Matthew also alludes to chapter 60 of Isaiah, which will play an important part in patristic commentaries on the Epiphany and in the liturgy of the feast:[5]

> Arise! Shine, for your light has come,
>   the glory of the LORD has dawned upon you.
> Though darkness covers the earth,
>   and thick clouds, the peoples,
> Upon you the LORD will dawn,
>   and over you his glory will be seen.
> Nations shall walk by your light,
>   kings by the radiance of your dawning.
>
> Raise your eyes and look about;
>   they all gather and come to you—
> Your sons from afar,
>   your daughters in the arms of their nurses.
> Then you shall see and be radiant,
>   your heart shall throb and overflow.
> For the riches of the sea shall be poured out before you,
>   the wealth of nations shall come to you.
> Caravans of camels shall cover you,
>   dromedaries of Midian and Ephah;
> All from Sheba shall come
>   bearing gold and frankincense,
>   and heralding the praises of the LORD. (Isa 60:1-6)

The prophecies of Psalm 72 (Vulgate 71) are likewise fulfilled according to Matthew's narrative. This psalm is another passage that the fathers and the liturgy make great use of; it provides the responsorial psalm for the feast of Epiphany in the new Missal:

> The kings of Tarshish and the islands
> shall pay him tribute.
> The kings of Sheba and Seba
> shall bring him gifts.
> Before him all kings shall fall prostrate,
> all nations shall serve him.
> For he shall save the needy when they cry,
> the poor, and those who are helpless.
> He will have pity on the weak and the needy,
> and save the lives of the needy.
> From oppression and violence he redeems their souls;
> to him their blood is dear.
> Long may he live!

May the gold of Sheba be given him.
They shall pray for him without ceasing,
and bless him all the day. (Ps 72:10-15)

He Wished to Be Known by All

St. Leo the Great fully comprehended the theological meaning of the event. The real issue is the founding of the kingdom throughout the world, the preaching of the gospel, the establishment of God's kingdom, the healing of the sick, the working of miracles.

> It was important to the whole human race that the Mediator between God and humanity should be made known to the whole world, even while he was still a child and living in a small town. For though he had chosen the people of Israel and, within that people, a single family in which to make his own the nature all humanity shares, he did not wish his birth to pass unnoticed within the narrow confines of his mother's house. Rather, he wished to be known straightway by all, since he had deigned to be born for the sake of all.[6]

Later in this same sermon, St. Leo points out the symbolism of the magi's gifts (a theme dear to the fathers): "To God they offer the incense, to the human the myrrh, and to the king the gold. They are conscious of honoring the divine nature and the human nature as united in a single being. For what was proper to each nature was not divided in the exercise of power."[7]

St. Leo's second sermon on the Epiphany emphasizes the proclamation to the entire world of the Savior's coming:

> Thus the heavens were already proclaiming the glory of God, and the voice of truth was being heard over the whole earth when the army of angels told the shepherds of the Savior's birth, and a star went on ahead to guide the Magi as they came to worship him. Thus from east to west the birth of the true King was splendidly manifested, since the kingdoms of the east learned the truth through the Magi, while it was not hidden from the Roman empire.[8]

Further on in this second sermon, St. Leo cites Genesis 49:10 and comments:

> "The scepter shall not depart from Judah, nor the ruler's staff from between his feet, until he comes to whom it belongs; and to him shall be the obedience of the peoples." With regard to these peoples: the

blessed patriarch Abraham had been given the promise of a countless posterity, begotten not by the flesh but by a fruitful faith. This posterity was compared to the stars, in order to show that the father of all the nations hoped for a heavenly, not an earthly, posterity. When the time came for the birth of the promised posterity, the heirs signified by the stars were alerted by the rise of a new star; thus he to whom the heavens had borne witness received from heaven homage and service.[9]

Manifestation to the World

St. Gregory the Great likewise saw that the point of the magi's visit was the recognition by the entire world of the Savior's kingship. He goes a step further, however, and sees not only humans but the very elements acknowledging their Lord:

> All the elements bore witness that their Maker had come. In terms customary among us, we may say that the heavens acknowledged this man as God by sending the star; the sea acknowledged him by turning into a solid support beneath his feet; the earth acknowledged him by quaking as he died; the sun acknowledged him by hiding its rays; the rocks and walls acknowledged him by splitting at the moment of his death; hell acknowledged him by surrendering the dead it held.[10]

The Epiphany as understood by the fathers and the liturgy is truly what St. Matthew meant it to be: a manifestation to the world. As we shall see, this aspect of manifestation is equally important in the other two events of Jesus' life that are commemorated by this feast: his baptism and the marriage feast of Cana. The whole world is already enlightened by the manifestation of the Savior at these three moments of his human life, even before he enlightens it by his preaching.

St. Matthew, who so much likes to emphasize the fulfillment of prophecy, evidently has in mind (as we have already pointed out) the prophecies of Isaiah. And in fact it seems clear that Isaiah was the first of the prophets to foretell unambiguously "the extension of eschatological salvation to the entire world."[11] The will of Yahweh, who is concerned with the whole world, is made clear as early as chapter 14:

> The LORD of hosts has sworn:
> As I have resolved,
>   so shall it be;

As I have planned,
    so shall it stand:
To break the Assyrian in my land
    and trample him on my mountains;
Then his yoke shall be removed from them,
    and his burden from their shoulder.
This is the plan proposed for the whole earth,
    and this the hand outstretched over all the nations. (Isa 14:24-26)

By destroying Assyria, Yahweh crushes the peoples who form the empire of Sennacherib, that is, for practical purposes (in the author's view), the whole earth.

But an oracle in chapter 2 (which is almost identical with one in Mic 4:1-3) gives even better expression to Yahweh's action in relation to the whole world, and not simply to Israel or the "small remnant":

In days to come,
The mountain of the LORD's house
    shall be established as the highest mountain
    and raised above the hills.
All nations shall stream toward it.
    Many peoples shall come and say:
"Come, let us go up to the LORD's mountain,
    to the house of the God of Jacob,
That he may instruct us in his ways,
    and we may walk in his paths."
For from Zion shall go forth instruction,
    and the word of the LORD from Jerusalem.
He shall judge between the nations,
    and set terms for many peoples.
They shall beat their swords into plowshares
    and their spears into pruning hooks;
One nation shall not raise the sword against another,
    nor shall they train for war again.
House of Jacob, come,
    let us walk in the light of the LORD! (Isa 2:2-5)

Doubt has been cast upon the authenticity of this passage from Isaiah. The presence of the same text in both Isaiah and Micah is good reason for judging the prophecy to be of eighth-century origin. But it seems that Micah, usually a pessimist, is here dependent on Isaiah, one of whose favorite themes is the universal power of Yahweh.[12]

Furthermore, Isaiah 2:2-5 is paralleled by Isaiah 11:1-9; 32:1-5; and 32:15-20, all of which express the same idea that peace is the fruit of the knowledge of Yahweh.[13]

We may be surprised that St. Matthew, like the fathers of the Church after him, has taken nothing from Amos, even though this prophet was so open to universalism. The reason for this is that Isaiah, though not slavishly repeating his predecessor, is nonetheless deeply influenced by the latter's teaching. At the same time, he is influenced by the prophet Hosea, with his greater sensitivity to the special covenant that Yahweh had made with Israel. It is to be expected, therefore, that Isaiah, synthesizing as he does the tendencies of both Amos, with his universalism, and Hosea, with his greater interest in Israel, should be a favorite of the fathers and the liturgy.

The Magi of Today

The Church's evident intention is to show us the magi of yesteryear so as to make of us in turn the magi of today. St. Leo the Great makes this point clearly in his second sermon on the Epiphany:

> Beloved, let us therefore recognize in the Magi who adored Christ our forerunners in calling and in faith, and with great joy let us celebrate in them the blessed beginnings of our own hope. For it was at that time that we began to enter into our everlasting inheritance; it was at that time that the mysterious passages of Scripture relating to Christ opened their meaning to us.[14]

In his third sermon on the Epiphany (now the second reading in the Office of Readings for Epiphany), St. Leo recalls the prophecies of Isaiah and concludes:

> This came to be fulfilled, as we know, from the time when the star beckoned the three wise men out of their distant country and led them to recognize and adore the King of heaven and earth. The obedience of the star calls us to imitate its humble service: to be servants, as best we can, of the grace that invites all men to find Christ.
>
> Dear friends, you must have the same zeal to be of help to one other; then, in the kingdom of God, to which faith and good works are the way, you will shine as children of the light.[15]

It is in his fifth sermon for Epiphany, however, that St. Leo becomes most insistent:

> Thus, beloved, the mystical content of those events continues to exist, and what began in symbol becomes authentic reality. The star of grace shines in heaven, and in every nation the three Magi, summoned by the brilliant light of the gospel, hasten to adore the power of the supreme King. . . .
>
> Keep the lamps of your souls ever burning, and let no darkness dwell in your hearts, for, as the Apostle says, "once you were darkness, but now you are light in the Lord; walk as children of the light." Make real in yourselves what you see in the figures of the Magi, and "thus let your light shine before others, so that, seeing your good deeds, they may glorify your heavenly Father."[16]

In a sixth sermon, St. Leo adds:

> The gifts of God are multiplied, and we in our time experience all that the first believers did. For though the Gospel account tells us only of the days when three men, untaught by prophetic preaching or the testimonies of the Law, came from the distant East in order to know God, yet we see the same thing happening now even more clearly and on a far larger scale in the enlightenment of all who are called.[17]

These long quotations from Pope St. Leo are valuable. Better than many other commentaries, they tell us what the Church aims to accomplish in us when she celebrates the three magi and their coming. For in them we are to see "our forerunners in calling and in faith." To them, the star is the sign of the great King. As the third antiphon at First Vespers for Epiphany expresses it: "The star burned like a flame, pointing the way to God, the King of kings; the wise men saw the sign and brought their gifts in homage to their great King."

The departure of the magi from their homelands, as soon as they saw the star, has always been a symbol of the response of faith. The magi very early acquired a place in Christian iconography because they were seen as models for the faithful; as soon as they were called, they responded with faith. A fresco in the catacombs of St. Priscilla (early second century) at Rome shows the magi in Persian dress. This is rather odd, since the gifts the magi bring seem to come rather from Arabia, where they were typical offerings. But just as the fathers of the Church, without any serious historical basis and in dependence rather on Psalm 72:10-11, think of the magi as kings, so too, for no special historical reason, they think of them as being Persians.

The immediate response of the magi to the call mediated by the star is rewarded by an illumination, which is an anticipation of our faith. The hymn for Second Vespers in the Latin *Liturgia Horarum* shows the light of the star helping the magi to find the true Light they seek: "The Magi went on their way, following the lead of the star they had seen. By its light they go in search of the Light and their gift of incense owns Him to be God."[18]

Recall the passage in which St. Leo emphasizes the present actuality of the "mystery" of the magi: "The mystical content of those events continues to exist, and what began in symbol becomes authentic reality." In the sixth sermon he makes the same point even more strongly: "That day has not so completely passed away that the power, then revealed, of God's action has passed with it or that the only thing to have reached us is the report of what happened so that faith might accept it and memory honor it. No, the gifts of God are multiplied, and we in our time experience all that the first believers did."[19]

The feast of the Epiphany, then, draws us into a journey toward the Lord whereby we may more fully acknowledge his divinity and fulfill our creaturely task by an offering to our God.

The prayer over the offerings in the Epiphany Mass during the Day mentions the gifts offered by the kings of Arabia and Seba as they prostrated themselves before the Lord. Our own gifts of bread and wine become the Body and Blood of the Lord—a mysterious transformation prefigured by the wine at Cana. But our offering, which replaces the gold, frankincense, and myrrh of the magi, must also be an offering of our very selves as human beings grafted onto Christ, who alone can make an efficacious offering. The prayer over the offerings gives expression to this theology, according to which the action of the magi is perpetuated through time by Christ, who himself acknowledges the sovereign power of the Father: "Look with favor, Lord, we pray, on these gifts of your Church, in which are offered now not gold or frankincense or myrrh, but he who by them is proclaimed, sacrificed and received, Jesus Christ."

Here, once again, we find, in the Epiphany, the paschal mystery of Christ. The light that shines at the Epiphany has renewed our souls; it enables us, as a people fed with the Body and Blood of Christ, to journey toward the meeting with our God, who is sovereign Master of all things.[20]

A Difficult Role

Every Christian, we have learned, is to be a magus for this day, in search of the Light and guided by it in the life of faith, while drawing the nations along.

As we meditate on these truths, it is difficult not to feel a painful distance between what ought to be and what is. The magi were the first in a procession of countless people who have journeyed toward the Lord. But we must always be asking ourselves: Are we really magi for today? We ought to be, since the light, once received, cannot be hidden under a basket but must be set upon the lampstand! What a heavy responsibility every Christian bears!

Christians must let the divine light within them shine through to others. They have sought the light and have been guided by it; now, because of the light that is in them, the world must in turn go in quest of the Light. The apostles were magi for their own time, and the apostles of every age become magi in their turn: people called by the star, led by it, leading the nations in turn to the King. Many Christians do not believe in their role, and therefore they cease to be lights amid the world's darkness, yet it remains their duty to point to the star.

The Christian role has undoubtedly become a difficult one, yet was it ever anything but foolishness in the world's eyes? It consists, after all, in showing the world "the sign of the great King,"[21] that is, the Lord's cross! *That* is the sign we must show the world and toward which we must lead the world so that through it the world may find true life. The cross is the paschal mystery, the central mystery of Christianity, which no baptized person can evade; it promises no earthly success in this life, not even apostolic success, but it does lead to the glory of risen life with Christ.

The individual Christian is not the only one called to point out this sign. The Church of every age, illumined by the Spirit of her Christ, has likewise as her essential role to show this light. Christ "manifested" himself, and the Church, as his spouse and the agent of his continuing work on earth, also "manifests" him. For her as for the magi, the most effective way to manifest him is to worship him. It is Epiphany, we may say, that assigns to the Church, once she has been gathered by the Spirit of Pentecost, her activity of unending contemplation. Pentecost is the feast of the Church, because on that day she receives the Spirit of Christ, but Epiphany too is in a sense the feast of the Church, because it is the annual celebration of the Lord's self-manifestation to his kingdom. Like the Gospel of St. Matthew, the feast of the Epiphany asserts that the prophecies concerning the kingdom have been fulfilled. To this self-manifestation of Christ corresponds the Spouse's adoration of her Lord.

Her essential act of adoration is to offer bread and wine, Christ's Body and Blood. But in this very act that embodies her adoration, the Spouse also exercises most effectively her apostolate of showing Christ. For in eating the bread and drinking the cup, she proclaims to the world the Good News of the death and resurrection of the Lord—and thus of our salvation—until he comes again.

The Church of our day, then, is prefigured by the magi. At the same time, the nations that come and acknowledge the Church are also "magi" who become aware of the self-manifestation of Christ and journey toward his cross so that they may rise to new life and meet the Lord face-to-face.

18. THE JORDAN: "OUR JORDAN"

We have just seen that the feast of the Epiphany, like that of Christmas, is a paschal feast. One object of the Epiphany commemoration, the baptism of Christ (which has now become the object of a special celebration of its own), leads us even more deeply into the paschal mystery. For the baptism of Christ in the Jordan manifests the fact that salvation is now given to all: sin is destroyed and adoption is bestowed upon the living who have been rescued from sin. At his baptism Christ is proclaimed God's Son and the Lamb of God who removes the world's sin, and he is anointed as messianic King. These themes, which are developed by the Eastern fathers and the Eastern liturgy, make Christ's baptism the focal point of the theophany.

If we study Christian baptism in the New Testament, we soon realize that the basis for the tradition concerning baptism is the account of the baptism of Jesus himself. The Synoptic Gospels all record it (Matt 3:13-17; Mark 1:9-11; Luke 3:21-22); St. John presupposes the event and refers back to it (John 1:33-34). The scene at the Jordan is also one of those most frequently found in Christian iconography.[1]

It is not a matter of indifference that the Jordan was the place where John baptized. In sheer point of fact, of course, it is the only river in Palestine, yet the fathers saw in it, as they did in the Red Sea, a type of baptism. Origen writes:

> That we may be convinced of this interpretation of the Jordan as the river that appeases thirst and is full of grace, it will be useful to recall Naaman the Syrian who was cured of leprosy. . . . Just as no one is good but one, namely, God the Father, so among rivers none is good but the Jordan, which is able even to cleanse from leprosy anyone who with faith washes his soul in Jesus.[2]

Origen thus connects the purifying power of the Jordan with Old Testament events. St. Luke had already referred to the same incident in 2 Kings (5:14) and had written: "Again, there were many lepers in Israel during the time of Elisha the prophet; yet not one of them was cleansed, but only Naaman the Syrian" (Luke 4:27). In his homilies on the Third Gospel, Origen pursues the same line of thought when he comes to comment on this verse of Luke.[3]

Origen's attention is also drawn by Elijah's and Elisha's crossing of the Jordan (in 2 Kgs 2:8).

> We must note that at the moment when Elijah is to be taken up into heaven by the whirlwind, he takes his cloak, rolls it up, and strikes the water, which parts and allows the two men, Elijah and Elisha, to pass between. Elijah was better prepared for his being taken up by being baptized in the Jordan; "baptized," because Paul, as we saw above, calls the miraculous passage through the water a baptism.[4]

The crossing of the Red Sea and the crossing of the Jordan were two traditional figures of baptism.[5] The New Testament, however, does not mention the parallel when it comes to speak of the baptism of Jesus, as it does when speaking of Elijah. The fathers nonetheless saw in Joshua's crossing of the Jordan the same idea of deliverance that finds expression in the crossing of the Red Sea. As Joshua was a figure of Jesus (Joshua-Jesus), so his crossing of the Jordan became a type of baptism. In his address on baptism, St. Gregory of Nyssa writes:

> You have been for a long time wallowing in the mud: hasten to the Jordan, not at the call of John, but at the voice of Christ. In fact, the river of grace runs everywhere. It does not rise in Palestine to disappear in the neighboring sea; but it envelops the entire world and plunges itself into Paradise, flowing against the course of the four rivers that come down from there, and carrying back into Paradise things far more precious than those which came out. For those rivers brought sweet perfumes, and the cultivation and semination of the earth: but this river brings back people, born of the Holy Spirit. Imitate Joshua, the son of Nun. Carry the Gospel as he carried the Ark. Leave the desert, that is to say, sin. Cross the Jordan. Hasten toward life according to Christ, toward the earth that bears the fruits of joy, where run, according to the promise, streams of milk and honey. Overthrow Jericho, the old dwelling-place, do not leave it fortified. All these things are a figure [*typos*] of ourselves. All are prefigurations of realities that now are made manifest.[6]

The Jordan here represents the baptism of which Joshua's crossing is a type.

A Baptism That Led to the Forgiveness of Sins

The Gospel of St. John does not tell the story of Jesus' baptism; it simply alludes to it, but the allusion is highly significant. We may note, in passing, that the reference to "Bethany across the Jordan" (John 1:28) has been the subject of much debate. Such a "Bethany across the Jordan" is simply unknown. Father Abel, in his discussion of the place venerated as the spot where Christ received baptism, thinks it must have been known to Israelites around the time of Christ as *Beth 'Abarah*, "place of passage," in memory of the crossing of the river by the Hebrews.[7]

In practicing baptism, the Precursor was using a rite totally new to his contemporaries. Jewish tradition was familiar with washings intended as ritual purifications. The books of Leviticus, Numbers, and Deuteronomy speak often of "clean" and "unclean" and of the regulations governing these two states. The "cleanness" or purity in question was of the ritual order, that is, it was achieved by the performance of a rite, usually a washing.

When, however, Isaiah tells the people of Israel, "Wash yourselves clean!" he adds, "Put away your misdeeds from before my eyes; / cease doing evil; / learn to do good" (Isa 1:16-17). Here there is evidently no question of a real ritual bath; the latter simply provides an image of something deeper. The ritual washing could give only a ritual purity, and the Israelite did not expect anything more of it. The intention was to symbolize a purity of heart but not to try to produce it by an outward rite. In their struggle with Judaism, the fathers of the Church made much of this distinction, seeing in it the essential difference between Jewish ritual washing and Christian baptism.[8]

Among the Essenes, there was an increased emphasis on ritual purification, with daily ritual washings being practiced. The Qumran finds show that the Community Rule prescribed many ritual purifications. Yet it was clear to all that these washings could not bring about an interior purification. For that, people must await the day of the Lord's visitation, when he would breathe upon them a spirit of holiness.[9]

The baptism practiced by John was quite different from these ritual washings. It aimed at interior purification: "Repent, for the kingdom of heaven is at hand!" (Matt 3:2). Many Jews were willing to be baptized by John, "as they acknowledged their sins" (Matt 3:6). And when Pharisees and Sadducees came forward for baptism, John spoke to them very frankly: "You brood of vipers! . . . Produce good fruit as evidence of your repentance" (Matt 3:7-8). There could no longer be question of evading God's anger by mere outward ritual; people must produce fruits of genuine repentance if they were not to be cut down and thrown into the fire (Matt 3:10). John's baptism was thus one of "repentance for the forgiveness of sins" (Mark 1:4; Luke 3:3), or, as John puts it in Matthew's gospel, "I am baptizing you with water, for repentance" (3:11).

Three marks thus distinguish John's baptism from other ritual washings practiced by the Jews. The first of these marks is external: the Jews purified themselves, but John baptized others (and he must have done a great deal of baptizing, since his contemporaries named him "the Baptist").

A second distinguishing mark was that when John administered his baptism, he acted as a prophet who proclaimed the coming of the Messiah: "the one who is coming after me is mightier than I. I am not worthy to carry his sandals" (Matt 3:11). The Messiah's coming would bring judgment with it: "Even now the ax lies at the root of the trees. Therefore every tree that does not bear good fruit will be cut down and thrown into the fire" (Matt 3:10).

The third and final mark of John's baptism is that while it is a baptism that is a sign of conversion and leads to the forgiveness of sins, it is also a preparation for a further baptism: "I am baptizing you with water, for repentance, but the one who is coming after me is mightier than I. . . . He will baptize you with the holy Spirit and fire" (Matt 3:11; Luke 3:16).

Purification by fire is already used in the Old Testament as an image of God's intervention,[10] and judgment by fire is a frequent theme.[11] As for purification by the Spirit, John knew that this had been promised: "Until the spirit from on high / is poured out on us" (Isa 32:15); "I will give you a new heart, and a new spirit I will put within you. I will remove the heart of stone from your flesh and give you a heart of flesh" (Ezek 36:26); "It shall come to pass / I will pour out my spirit upon all flesh. / Your sons and daughters will prophesy, / your old men will dream dreams, / your young men will see visions. / Even upon your male and female servants, / in those days, I will pour out my spirit" (Joel 3:1-2).

We have thus dwelt on John's baptism in general because it will enable us better to grasp the meaning of the baptism Jesus will receive at the hand of his Precursor.

The Sign of the Spirit

Given this background, however, we cannot but be surprised by Jesus' receiving baptism from John. John himself felt exactly the same way: "I need to be baptized by you, and yet you are coming to me?" (Matt 3:14). Jesus' answer soothes him: "Allow it now, for thus it is fitting for us to fulfill all righteousness" (3:15). St. Matthew is the only one to record the Baptist's hesitation, but the whole first Christian generation must have been puzzled by Jesus' baptism.

Jesus' answer is that the "righteousness" he is fulfilling is that proper to the messianic kingdom. In fact, the baptism that Jesus will receive will be the outward sign of his investiture as Messiah: "behold, the heavens were opened [for him], and he [Jesus] saw the Spirit of God descending like a dove [and] coming upon him. And a voice came from the heavens, saying, 'This is my beloved Son, with whom I am well pleased'" (Matt 3:16-17; see also Mark 1:9-11; Luke 3:21-22).

John the Evangelist does not report the scene, but he does bring out its theological meaning: "The next day he [John] saw Jesus coming toward him and said, 'Behold, the Lamb of God, who takes away the sin of the world. He is the one of whom I said, "A man is coming after me who ranks ahead of me because he existed before me." I did not know him, but the reason why I came baptizing with water was that he might be made known to Israel.' John testified further, saying, 'I saw the Spirit come down like a dove from the sky and remain upon him'" (John 1:29-32).

What happened at Jesus' baptism completed John's enlightenment. He had indeed known that the Spirit would descend upon, and remain in, the Messiah, who in turn would baptize in the Spirit: "I did not know him, but the one who sent me to baptize with water told me, 'On whomever you see the Spirit come down and remain, he is the one who will baptize with the holy Spirit.' Now I have seen and testified that he is the Son of God" (John 1:33-34).

It was from Isaiah that John would know the Spirit was to descend and rest on the Messiah: "But a shoot shall sprout from the stump of Jesse, / and from his roots a bud shall blossom. / The spirit of the LORD shall rest upon him" (Isa 11:1-2). John the Evangelist must have had this passage of Isaiah in mind as he wrote his first chapter. This is confirmed when, in verse 34, he has the Precursor say: "Now I have seen and testified that he is the Son of God." These words are undoubtedly an allusion to Isaiah 42:1, "Here is my servant whom I uphold, / my chosen one with whom I am pleased. / Upon him I have put my spirit; / he shall bring forth justice to the nations."

The fact that the Synoptics have replaced "servant" with "Son" does not cause any real problem. We have already had occasion to note that the Greek word *pais* can mean both "servant" and "son."

This is not the place to go into the content of the word "Spirit," which in the Old Testament means the "breath" of Yahweh. At the beginning of creation itself, we see the "Spirit" at work, sweeping over the waters, and his action continues to be felt throughout all subsequent history. The sign of the Spirit serves to make Messiah Jesus known to John the Baptist and all the disciples. Once this sign has been given, no further doubt is possible: "Now I have seen and testified that he is the Son of God" (John 1:34).

"My Beloved Son"

The Synoptics report the words heard from heaven at the moment after Jesus' baptism: "This is my beloved Son, with whom I am well pleased" (Matt 3:17 and parallels). Though John the Evangelist does not cite these words, he has the Baptist say their equivalent: "he is the Son of God."

The Synoptic statement is of tremendous importance for the Jewish people, since it concerns the divine sonship of an individual human being. The Old Testament had often spoken of God as a Father, but only in relation to the Chosen People as a whole. In this fatherhood of God, moreover, the Old Testament saw a favor bestowed with complete freedom by God.

Jeremiah makes Yahweh speak of himself as a Father: "I am a father to Israel, / Ephraim is my firstborn" (31:9). Again, when Yahweh speaks to Israel, his unfaithful spouse, he says to her: "But because you have a prostitute's brow, / you refused to be ashamed. / Even now do you not call me, 'My father'?" (Jer 3:3-4). In Isaiah we find a similar expression: "For you are our father" (Isa 63:16). And again: "Yet, LORD, you are our father" (64:7).[12]

The book of Deuteronomy implies that if we are to have God for our Father, we must imitate his holiness and become like him in some fashion: "You are children of the LORD, your God. . . . the LORD, your God, has chosen you from all the peoples on the face of the earth to be a people specially his own" (Deut 14:1-2).[13]

In all these passages, however, it is always the people who have God for Father. At the baptism of Jesus, on the other hand, the heavenly voice addresses a single individual as "Son." Jesus is the chosen One, the Servant, the Son. In fact, St. John will give the name "Son" to no one but Jesus and will speak of him as the "only begotten"; the rest of us are called only "children."[14]

The baptism of Jesus consecrates him in the world's eyes as the "Son," as we listen to the first of those dialogues between the two divine Persons, Father and Son, that provide the essential framework of the gospels, and especially of the Fourth Gospel. Later, as the final Passover draws near and Jesus foretells his glorification, he addresses the Father once again, and once again, as at the baptism, a voice is heard from heaven: "I have glorified it [my name] and will glorify it again" (John 12:28).

At the baptism, the Spirit too is present. His special role is to show the world who Jesus is. He anoints Jesus as Messiah and Son of God. The Son and the Father meet in the Spirit, and the Spirit unites them in love: "This is my beloved Son, with whom I am well pleased" (Matt 3:17 and parallels).

The Lamb of God

The Spirit has descended and remained on Jesus, the Messiah; now Jesus can in turn transmit the Spirit to others. He will be able to do so, however, only after his death and resurrection. Consequently, we find once again, this time in connection with the baptism of Jesus, the paschal theme being voiced. The Precursor himself has already alluded to it, when, on seeing Jesus coming toward him, he exclaims: "Behold, the Lamb of God, who takes away the sin of the world" (John 1:29).

The word "Lamb" has not been easy for exegetes to handle. Some of them suggest that the Evangelist has put the word into the Baptist's mouth. The word calls to mind the Passover lamb, whose annual immolation not only reminded the Israelites of Exodus 12 but, by the time of Christ, also had an expiatory function. If this is what John the Baptist had in view, he was thinking of Jesus as one who comes to make expiation, like a Passover lamb. But the word also calls to mind the prophecy of Isaiah about the Suffering Servant of Yahweh. In

Isaiah 53:7 we have a comparison intended to emphasize the resigna-
tion shown by the Suffering Servant.

Since the baptism of Jesus was also his anointing as Messiah, we
may choose to think that "Lamb" (a term often used of Jesus in the
book of Revelation) was a messianic title used by the Precursor.

A third hypothesis has been proposed. An original Aramaic text
referred to the "servant of God" of Isaiah's prophecy. In Aramaic,
however, the word *talia* meant both "lamb" and "servant." Under
the influence of Christianity and the typology of the Passover lamb,
the Greek translator of the Fourth Gospel translated *talia* as "lamb"
rather than as "servant." According to this interpretation, then, the
gospel gives a Christian coloring to John's words, but this is the doing
not of the Evangelist but of his translator.[15]

We must also observe that the Greek verb *airein* in John 1:29 can
mean either "carry" or "take away." It is possible, therefore, to interpret the words as referring to Isaiah 53:4 and the lamb who "bears"
our infirmities or to Exodus 12:23 and the Passover lamb, whose
blood, in the Christian interpretation, "takes away" sins. Pursuing
this double interpretation, we might claim that John the Baptist interpreted his own words in the light of Isaiah, while John the Evangelist read into them a further Christian reference to the Passover
lamb. Such a double meaning for a word is quite in accordance with
John's methods. Recall, for example, the use of the verb "lift up" (in
John 3:14 and 12:32), which may mean both to be lifted up onto the
cross and to be lifted up or exalted in victory.

"I Have a Baptism to Be Baptized With"

How, then, can we sum up the theology of Jesus' baptism as seen
by the evangelists? They see in the baptism a clear statement of his
messiahship and the solemn, public reception of both his title and
his mission. Henceforth, Jesus can baptize people in the Spirit that
he himself has received: the Spirit who gives the strength to walk in
the right path and who takes sin away.

Thus, when all is said and done, the baptism of Christ confronts
us with the cross and the paschal mystery. The fathers of the Church
were not caught up in the problems of exegesis and did not doubt
that the "Lamb" signified Jesus offering his life in order to expiate
the sins of the world. They grasped the close connection between the

baptism of Jesus and cross, and, in fact, between every baptism and the cross. Their spiritual insight made them see in the account of Jesus' baptism a prediction of his passion and his redemptive role. The Latins interpreted the text in the light of the Passover lamb typology, the Greeks in the light of Isaiah's prophecy of the Suffering Servant. Both Latins and Greeks, however, think of the baptism of Jesus as closely connected with his cross.

At his baptism, Jesus is anointed Messiah and Redeemer, and his answer to the Precursor who is surprised to see him coming is highly meaningful: "for thus it is fitting for us to fulfill all righteousness" (Matt 3:15). Commentators have often remarked on the explicit juxtaposition of the baptism and the passion in Mark and Luke. "Can you drink the cup that I drink or be baptized with the baptism with which I am baptized?" says Mark 10:38. St. Matthew records the same conversation but mentions neither cup nor baptism (20:20-23). In St. Luke, the linking of baptism and passion is equally emphasized: "I have come to set the earth on fire, and how I wish it were already blazing! There is a baptism with which I must be baptized, and how great is my anguish until it is accomplished!" (12:49-50).

The baptism of Jesus thus introduces us into the mystery of his death and resurrection. It is in the latter mystery that his baptism will be fully real, and it is then that he will pour out the Spirit. Peter's discourse on Pentecost shows us how fully the apostles understood all this, once the Spirit had descended on them:

> Jesus the Nazorean was a man commended to you by God with mighty deeds, wonders, and signs, which God worked through him in your midst, as you yourselves know. . . . [Y]ou killed [him], using lawless men to crucify him. But God raised him up. . . . Exalted at the right hand of God, he received the promise of the holy Spirit from the Father and poured it forth, as you [both] see and hear. . . . Therefore let the whole house of Israel know for certain that God has made him both Lord and Messiah, this Jesus whom you crucified. (Acts 2:22-36)

According to Peter, then, it was after the mystery of his death and resurrection had been accomplished that Christ, now exalted to the Father's right hand, poured out the Holy Spirit he himself had received.

Such is the teaching of the New Testament about the baptism of Jesus: that the baptism, which is a manifestation of Jesus as Lord and

Messiah, is also a manifestation of him as Lord and Savior by reason of his cross and resurrection.

Patristic Commentaries

The fathers rival each other in commenting on these two aspects of the baptism of Jesus. We shall limit ourselves here to the second aspect, since it is the one emphasized in the Roman liturgy for the feast of the Savior's baptism. The Church has chosen for the Office of Readings a homily of St. Gregory Nazianzen:

> I cannot restrain my joy; my heart is deeply moved and filled with delight. Forgetting my weakness, I long to undertake the mission of the great John the Baptist; though I am not the Precursor, I have indeed come from the desert!
>
> Christ receives the sacrament of enlightenment, or rather he enlightens us with his brilliance. He is baptized; let us go down into the water with him so that we may also come up with him. John is baptizing, and Jesus comes to him. Christ certainly sanctifies the man who now baptizes him, but his purpose is chiefly to bury the old Adam in the waters and, above all, to sanctify the waters of the Jordan by his baptism in them so that just as he was spirit and flesh, those who would later be baptized might be sanctified by the power of the Spirit and by water.
>
> John refuses; Jesus insists. "It is you that should be baptizing me!" says John. The torch addresses the Sun, the voice speaks to the Word.
>
> Jesus comes out of the water, drawing the world with him, as it were, and raising it up when it had hitherto been sunk in the abyss. He sees the heavens, not being rent, but opening of their own accord. The first Adam had of old closed heaven to himself and us, just as he had seen the earthly paradise being closed to him, with a fiery sword barring access.
>
> The Holy Spirit bears witness. Here all is in perfect harmony, for the testimony comes from heaven, just as he to whom the Spirit bears witness has come from heaven.[16]

In a homily on the baptism of Christ, St. John Chrysostom asks why Jesus had himself baptized. The first reason, he says, is that all might learn from Jesus' baptism that the baptism administered by John was meant for repentance and as a way of leading people to believe in the One who would come after John (see Acts 19:4).

> The other reason is the one he himself [Jesus] gave. What is it? When John had said, "I should be baptized by you—and do you come to me?"

he replied: "Let be. For it befits us in this way to fulfill all justice" (Matt 3:14-15). . . . But what does "fulfilling all justice" mean? Justice is to be understood as the carrying out of all God's commandments. . . . Now, since all were obliged to fulfill this justice and since no one in fact fulfilled it perfectly, Christ came to accomplish it. . . . When he came and found us debtors, he paid the debt, fulfilled the obligation, and liberated those who could not pay the debt and thus liberate themselves.[17]

The fathers do not fail to note that the baptism of Jesus, which is a sign of our salvation, also reveals the Trinity to us. A homily attributed to St. Maximus of Turin, and certainly very old, expresses both of these aspects:

"Behold the Lamb of God, behold him who takes away the sins of the world." John is here saying: Cease now to ask for my baptism, which leads to repentance; here is a Baptist who takes sins away! Seek no longer to be baptized by me, your fellow servant, now that the Lord of us all is here. . . .

How marvelous the mystery in which our Lord Jesus, by mere bodily contact or the mere passage of his glory, sanctifies and gives life and light to his creature at every moment! For by being baptized he sanctifies the water; by being buried he sanctifies the earth; by rising he raises the dead; he glorifies everything in heaven by ascending to heaven and sitting at the right hand of God the Father.[18]

The Jordan, Our Jordan

We must explain a little more fully how Jesus' baptism in the Jordan concerns us. It is undoubtedly the type of our own baptism; it is undoubtedly the proclamation of Christ's role as the Messiah who gives his life in order to reintegrate the broken world. But is not all that still rather remote from us?

We must go back briefly to a basic aspect of Jesus' baptism in the Jordan, referring the reader, as we do so, to the pages that have preceded. We saw that John the Baptist speaks of Christ as the "Lamb of God," and we tried to grasp the theological meaning of this expression. It tells us clearly that the role that now officially belongs to Jesus is to give his life for the redemption of the world.

There is a further point. When the Father speaks and presents his Son to us, each of his words is important, and each takes on its full meaning, with all its implications, only in the context of the statement as a whole. Thus, we cannot correctly understand who and what the "Son" is unless we add that he is "my beloved." Moreover, for a complete understanding of the Father's words, we must read them together with those that the Father speaks at the transfiguration, when he adds, "listen to him" (see Matt 17:1-8; Luke 9:28-36).

We are confronted here with the "only begotten" Son, and our thoughts immediately go back to Isaac, the only son of Abraham. Such a connection already tells us a great deal about the way the Father conceives the role of his only Son. As we pointed out earlier, the word "Son" here has several resonances. Tradition sees it as meaning "servant" or "slave" as well as "child."

Elsewhere in John's gospel, we find a theme very dear to him: doing the Father's will. That is the mark of the true Son, as many texts assure us (John 4:32-38; 7:17; 14:31). The last words of Jesus on the cross, "It is finished" (John 19:30), serve as a perfect description of the Son: he is the one who has accomplished his Father's will. That is why the Father loves the Son, and that is why we must listen to him, that is, follow him along the road that he has shown to be the only true way to the Father.

If we broaden our vision and move a little further along this line, we find ourselves confronted with the history of salvation, with God's plan for reconstruction, and with our participation in his work. In what does that work consist?

The work of the Spirit is to rebuild and restore the world that was created as a unified whole for the glory of the Father but was then shattered by sin. The attempts at reconstruction in the Old Testament did not succeed. Then, when the time is ripe, the action of the Spirit turns history upside down, for he provides the eternal Word of God with a human nature. The fathers connect the whole sacramental life with the activity of the same Spirit. According to them, we are to see in the Spirit's action on the water of baptism our own new creation and our entry into the life of God. The same Spirit who effected the coming of the eternal Word in the flesh also effects our birth in God.

In the life of Christ, the action of the Holy Spirit specifies the role of Christ, at his baptism in the Jordan and later at his transfiguration. We can say that at his baptism in the Jordan, Christ was officially appointed Prophet, Messiah, King, and Priest. May we not also think of our own confirmation, which is the sacrament of Christian "perfection" (i.e., completion), as corresponding to the Spirit's action at the

Jordan, which is closely connected with his action at Pentecost and in which, like Christ, we are appointed to our role as prophets, messiahs, kings, and priests? After all, the anointing conferred upon us immediately after our baptism designated us as members of a priestly people.

When did Christ carry out the mission to which he was appointed? He did it when he brought to a successful end his paschal mystery, that is, his death, resurrection, ascension, and sending of the Spirit. At this moment he completed the work for which he had come among us and to which he was officially appointed. By preaching the word and giving his life in such a glorious way, Christ succeeded in restoring the world (in principle) to unity so that his Father might therein be glorified. When do we accomplish our own mission? We do it every time we celebrate the Eucharist, which renders present and active among us the paschal mystery of Christ. When we eat the bread and drink the cup, we proclaim the Lord's death until he comes again.

The baptism of Jesus in the Jordan is, therefore, indeed, relevant to us. For in Jesus our own role is clearly specified, and in addition we learn what our own attitude should be as children of God who have been born again of water and the Spirit. We understand the close connection between the three sacraments of Christian initiation: baptism, the sacrament of birth; confirmation, the sacrament in which we are appointed to our proper function; and the Eucharist, in which we share in the work of rebuilding the world as we proclaim the paschal mystery and the end of time.

There can be no real confusion between the different priesthoods. In point of fact, there is but one priesthood, that of Christ. But there are two essentially different ways of sharing in it, both of them fully real: the ordained or ministerial priesthood, which, through the intervention of the Spirit, makes the paschal mystery efficaciously present; and the baptismal priesthood, which, once the mystery of the world's restoration has thus been rendered present, actively collaborates with Christ, who brings his work to completion with our help. There is thus an essential difference between the two priesthoods, and yet they complement each other.

There is no point in discussing in greater detail how the Jordan of Christ's baptism is also our Jordan and how our whole attitude to it depends on that of Christ.

19. CANA

Christmas, the visit of the magi, and the baptism of Jesus have proved to be, not isolated episodes in the life of Christ, but links in the chain that is the paschal mystery. We have seen how in each of these liturgical celebrations the Church looks to the one center of the Christian year: the death and resurrection of Christ, with his return at the end of time. We find now the same preoccupation as we turn to the third facet of Epiphany, the marriage feast at Cana.

In celebrating these various events, the liturgy for Epiphany follows the sequence in the Fourth Gospel: first comes the manifestation of Christ at the Jordan and the witness of the Precursor, then a new manifestation to the disciples at the marriage feast of Cana (John 2:1-11).

In these opening chapters of the Fourth Gospel we get the impression that we are being presented with a catechesis. In the Prologue, John writes: "And the Word became flesh / and made his dwelling among us, / and we saw his glory, / the glory as of the Father's only Son, / full of grace and truth" (1:14). This statement is immediately followed by the Precursor's witness to Christ: "The one who is coming after me ranks ahead of me because he existed before me" (1:15). The Baptist will repeat his testimony after the baptism of Jesus, which is the latter's anointing as Messiah and represents the firstfruits of our redemption. Finally the Evangelist tells us: "On the third day there was a wedding in Cana. . . . Jesus did this as the beginning of his signs . . . and so revealed his glory, and his disciples began to believe in him" (2:1-11).

The baptism of Jesus and the wedding feast at Cana are both of them manifestations of Jesus' glory. Moreover, they are not two totally separate manifestations, each isolated from the other, but they complete each other and overlap.

> On the third day there was a wedding in Cana in Galilee, and the mother of Jesus was there. Jesus and his disciples were also invited to the wedding. When the wine ran short, the mother of Jesus said to him,

"They have no wine." [And] Jesus said to her, "Woman, how does your concern affect me? My hour has not yet come." His mother said to the servers, "Do whatever he tells you." Now there were six stone water jars there for Jewish ceremonial washings, each holding twenty to thirty gallons. Jesus told them, "Fill the jars with water." So they filled them to the brim. Then he told them, "Draw some out now and take it to the headwaiter." So they took it. And when the headwaiter tasted the water that had become wine, without knowing where it came from (although the servers who had drawn the water knew), the headwaiter called the bridegroom and said to him, "Everyone serves good wine first; and then when people have drunk freely, an inferior one; but you have kept the good wine until now." Jesus did this as the beginning of his signs in Cana in Galilee, and so revealed his glory, and his disciples began to believe in him. (John 2:1-11)

If we read this second chapter of St. John carefully, we will be struck by the ambiguity of certain terms, and we may even feel a certain uneasiness as we attempt to interpret them. I am not referring only to the famous verse 4, where the exegetes flounder in their effort to rescue the respect that every Christian feels is due to the Mother of God. No, there are a number of points where the exegesis is difficult, if one wishes to be objective.

From the opening words it seems clear that the Evangelist wishes his account to carry a fairly precise overall meaning. "On the third day" a marriage took place at Cana. This manner of dating the event is not accidental; it not only situates the event in an immediate temporal context but also shows St. John's desire to turn our thoughts toward the definitive "sign" of Christ's glory, namely, his resurrection. In other words, the wedding at Cana is not simply a sign of Christ's present glory but a sign also of that future glory that is his "on the third day" after his death. It has been rightly noted that this phrase "on the third day" could not but remind the early Christians of the resurrection.[1] For St. John, then, the first sign, the changing of water into wine, prepares for, and is linked with, the supreme sign, the resurrection on the third day. Thus, from the very first words of the account, we glimpse the paschal significance that John intends the account of the wedding at Cana to have.

The central point in the whole account, namely, the changing of water into wine, brings us even closer to the paschal theme. In fact, the whole episode is so rich in signs that proclaim and prefigure the mystery of the passion, the resurrection, our redemption, and the parousia that we must take them one by one, despite the fact that each is inseparable from the others and complements them.

The "Hour" of Christ

Christ's surprising reply to his Mother—literally, "Woman, what to me and to you?"—has often preoccupied the exegetes more than the next words: "My hour has not yet come." And yet, if we are to understand Jesus' strange answer to his Mother, it is on these next words that we must focus our attention. The statement "My hour has not yet come" shows us that God's plan is set and that Jesus must conquer evil and be supremely glorified after a death that destroys sin.

"My hour has not yet come" is one of the expressions that turn this whole account into a proclamation of the paschal mystery. It is a statement St. John puts on the lips of Jesus at several points in his gospel. When Jesus, at Jerusalem, emphasizes his own divine origin, his enemies try to arrest him, but "no one laid a hand upon him, because his hour had not yet come" (7:30). Then, when he bears witness to himself while teaching in the temple, "no one arrested him, because his hour had not yet come" (8:20). When he tells his disciples that his death and glorification are at hand, he does so by saying that his "hour" has at last come: "The hour has come for the Son of Man to be glorified" (12:23). And when he is troubled by this thought, he prays: "I am troubled now. Yet what should I say? 'Father, save me from this hour'? But it was for this purpose that I came to this hour. Father, glorify your name" (12:27-28).

When the time comes for the Last Supper, John introduces it by saying: "Before the feast of Passover, Jesus knew that his hour had come to pass from this world to the Father" (13:1). And Jesus himself, in his high-priestly prayer, addresses his Father: "Father, the hour has come. Give glory to your Son, so that your Son may glorify you" (17:1). The "hour" of Christ is the hour of his death but also the hour of his passing to the Father (13:1), from whom he will receive the glory that crowns his victory.

We must not overlook the phrase John uses in 13:1, where he says that Jesus is to "pass" from this world to the Father. Exodus 12:11 had used the word "Passover" in the sense of "passage of the Red Sea."

Once again, then, in chapter 2 of John, the phrase "hour of Jesus" turns our thoughts to the paschal mystery of Christ's death, resurrection, and glorification.

"Woman, How Does Your Concern Affect Me?"

How are we to understand these words: "Woman, how does your concern affect me? My hour has not yet come." There seems to be a lack of logic in the sequence of events. Jesus says his hour has not yet come, and he gently reproaches his Mother for not having grasped this clearly, and yet he accedes to his Mother's implicit request by changing water into wine! Some exegetes see in his action a proof of his abasement and of the effectiveness of his Mother's prayer: because she asks him, he pushes his hour forward. This solution may satisfy devotion, but it seems inadequate. After all, the "hour" of Jesus had been fixed from eternity by the divine plan of redemption; it is difficult to understand how the plan could be modified.

How, then, are we to understand Jesus' statement that the moment for his glorification has not yet come, when he proceeds to perform a miracle that is precisely a sign of that glory? The Mother of Jesus realized that despite his answer, he is going to do the miracle, for she tells the servants: "Do whatever he tells you." Her instructions contradict her Son's negative answer to her. Jesus has answered: My hour has not yet come for performing a sign that will reveal my glory and anticipate my definitive glorification. Yet his Mother here and now expects a sign that will be revelatory of that glory. Signs, as we know, were meant to prove that a prophet's mission was authentic. Moreover, at the end of the account, the evangelist specifically says, "[He] revealed his glory."

Some exegetes have sought to solve this difficult problem by supposing that Jesus was really asking a question: "Has my hour not come?"[2] The interpretation offered by some of the fathers leans in this direction, but it finds no support in the rest of the gospel, since whenever Jesus wishes to say that his hour has come, he always does so by using the indicative, not the interrogative, form: "The hour has come" (17:1; etc.).

In fact, however, no solution of the text is possible at the level at which the problem is too often placed. The account of the feast at Cana is not an anecdote whose every detail is to be examined with a magnifying glass and whose logic is to be carefully analyzed. The whole Gospel of John has a thesis, and it is a catechesis. Its unifying concept is the progressive manifestation of the glory of Jesus; its intent is not to present a sequence of stories, each of them obeying a human logic that is faithful to material facts. The facts serve simply as points of departure; in addition to providing historical anchorage, they have a special religious meaning that will emerge more and more clearly through the course of Jesus' life and in the narratives chosen by John.

Christ gently reprimands his Mother, and there is no reason for trying to soften the rebuke, any more than we should be shocked by the address "Woman," once we understand how it was used at that time. Is Jesus inconsistent with himself when he refuses to respond to his Mother's request yet then performs the miracle? It does not seem that he is—provided we abandon our concern for the isolated episode and enter into the spirit that permeates the Gospel of John.

What Jesus is refusing is to manifest himself in his definitive (Easter) glory. In that sense, his hour has not yet come; it will come only in his death, resurrection, and ascension. But while refusing this complete manifestation of his glory, he does give an anticipatory sign of it, by reason of which the evangelist can say: "[He] revealed his glory." The miracle at Cana is, then, an anticipatory glorification, a first stage in the glorification of Jesus and one that, being a sign, is closely linked to the definitive glorification of Christ and his full self-revelation to the world at the end of time.

The sign of Christ's victory through death and resurrection is the Eucharist, which is prefigured in, and signified by, the changing of water in wine. At the same time, the Eucharist proclaims the triumphant death of the Lord until he comes again, and it is a figure of the messianic banquet.

Overlapping Signs

Evidently we are dealing with signs that point to, and are connected with, one another. The wedding feast of Cana stands at the beginning of the linked series. In the mind of Jesus, to change water into wine is to prefigure the Last Supper. But the Supper is in turn the sign of the death and victory of Christ and, at the same time, of the eternal wedding feast that will begin when the Lord comes again. The eucharistic celebration hastens the Lord's return by prefiguring the banquet that will begin on that day.

Now, against the background of these linked prefigurations that are so typical of St. John, we will be able to understand better the intervention of the Virgin at Cana. Jesus addresses her as "Woman," just as he will later on from the cross (19:26) at the moment when Mary is appointed the new Eve, Mother of all the living (cf. Gen 3:15-20). At that moment she will represent the Church and all of us. When we return to the Mary who intercedes with Jesus to obtain an anticipatory sign, are we indulging in exaggeration if we see in her the Church that celebrates the Eucharist and thereby hastens the return of Christ and the full revelation of his glory? Mary hastens this manifestation by asking for a sign, just as the Church hastens it by proclaiming the death and glorification of the Lord.

Such are the profound theological implications of the wedding at Cana. The wedding, like the resurrection, is celebrated "on the third day." Water is changed into wine, and sinful humanity passes, by way of baptism, from the law of Moses to the law of the Spirit. At the same time, the water changed into wine foretells the cup, that is, the hour of Jesus, namely, his passion. It prefigures the Supper that will be repeated and will make present in space and time the death and resurrection of Jesus. The wedding feast, like the Supper, also prefigures and leads to the eschatological banquet of the triumphant Christ, the wedding feast of the Lamb, which will be the wedding feast of God and human beings reunited in a restored world.

The Key to the Symbols

A narrative so rich in implications could not fail to attract the attention of the fathers, and they study and comment on the wedding feast in all its aspects. We shall cite, to begin with, a relatively rare yet very meaningful kind of reflection on the wedding; it comes from Tertullian's treatise on baptism. Instead of dwelling on the miracle of the water changed into wine, Tertullian is interested more in the presence of the water and in the baptismal symbolism it has for him:

> What grace water has, before God and his Christ, for bringing out the meaning of baptism! Christ is never unaccompanied by water. He himself is baptized in water, and when he is invited to a marriage, he uses water in making his first show of power. . . . His witness to baptism continues right up to his Passion.[3]

In Tertullian's view, then, Cana is a prefiguration of baptism. Such an interpretation deserves notice, especially when we remember that the Roman liturgy celebrates on January 6 not only the self-manifestation of Jesus to the magi and the world but also his baptism and the wedding feast at Cana. We should remember too that the blessing of baptismal water in the Roman Rite (until the recent revision of the baptismal rite), as in the liturgies of Milan and Syria, connected the baptism of Jesus with the wedding feast at Cana.

The fathers generally concentrate, however, on the more basic meanings symbolized in the Johannine narrative. Cyril of Alexandria, for example, picks up the words "on the third day" and comments: "The wedding is celebrated on the third day, that is, in the last age of this present world, for the number three signifies to us the beginning, middle, and end." He then quotes Hosea 6:2-3, a prophecy of the resurrection, and explains in a forceful way how Cana is a sign of Christ's triumphant resurrection and of our own transformation into Christ: "He also cured those afflicted with corruption and death, and did it on the third day, that is, not in the first nor in the middle, but in the last age, when, having become human, he healed human nature, raising it totally from the dead in himself."[4]

The eucharistic and nuptial aspect of Cana is the one most fully developed by the fathers. In their view, the wedding at Cana prefigures the marriage of Christ and the Church. The nations are invited to the wedding feast, since wine has now been substituted for the water of Jewish purifications. St. Cyprian, for example, writes:

> The Jews lacked spiritual grace, and therefore wine as well, though the house of Israel was meant to be the vineyard of the Lord of hosts (Isa 5:7). Then, to teach clearly that the Gentiles were succeeding to the position the Jews had lost and that later on we too would succeed to it by faith, Christ changed water into wine. He showed thereby that after the Jews had defected, the Gentiles would flock in even greater numbers to the marriage of Christ and the Church.[5]

St. Cyril of Jerusalem, in one of his *Catecheses*, likewise interprets the wedding feast at Cana as a type of the Eucharist and of the marriage of Christ and his Church:

> At Cana of Galilee, he [Jesus] changed water into wine. Is he not to be believed, then, when he changes wine into Blood? When invited to an

earthly marriage, he did this marvelous deed. Shall we not profess our faith even more readily when to the companions of the Bridegroom he makes a present of the enjoyment of his Body and Blood?[6]

Structures and Themes of the Epiphany Season

20. EPIPHANY: HOMAGE TO THE LORD

Contemplating the Glory of the Lord

The central theme of the gospel reading, in the context provided by the other two readings, is the manifestation of the Lord's glory to all peoples. The passage (Matt 2:1-12) twice makes explicit the purpose of the magi in coming from their home in the East: to prostrate themselves before the Lord.

The danger in the account of the Epiphany, with its element of the marvelous, is that we may be led astray into the exegesis of facts and signs. The number and names of the magi, the star, the gifts, and many connected problems have, of course, a certain importance, and they cannot be simply ignored, but in choosing this passage for the liturgy, the Church presupposes the research of the scholars and has her eye on an aspect of the passage that is far more meaningful and important.

The principal interest of the account, in its liturgical context, is the manifestation of Christ the Lord to the whole world and the world's adoration of the infant King. Even here, however, the important thing is not the past but the present and the future that will emerge from the present. In other words, when the account is read in the liturgy, it is proclaimed as an actualization of the past event here and now, a dynamic actualization that is meant to lead the nations to the worship of the Lord and the acknowledgment of his glory.

The liturgy, then, has an eschatological vision of this worship of the glory of the God who is revealing himself; it is within that framework that the Church proclaims this gospel. She sees the present people of God and, indeed, the entire world journeying toward the moment when God will definitively reveal his glory and the world will adore that glory in a perfect way. That, after all, is the objective of the paschal mystery: to reunite and rebuild the world for the worship of the Lord of glory. The proclamation of this gospel can be for us a striking example of the true function of the liturgical celebration of the word as an act in which the Lord himself actualizes a past event so as to lead us toward something definitive and everlasting.

As a matter of fact, in this same liturgy Isaiah has already offered us an eschatological vision when he describes the nations walking toward the light and the kings advancing toward the light of the coming dawn. At the same time, this passage from Isaiah gives us a sense of God's presence in the Jerusalem where all people will ultimately be made one race again. Jerusalem is the mother of the scattered sons and daughters we see being gathered again. All the nations, even the Gentile ones, come to Jerusalem; all of them seek to reach Jerusalem and the Lord in his glory.

The theme of the final reunion is, of course, found often in the Old Testament, for example, in Isaiah 2:1-4 and 66:18-21 and in Zechariah 14:16. In the city the prophets speak of, we Christians too find our heavenly Jerusalem; in today's Mass St. Paul speaks of that city and tells us she is our mother (Gal 4:26). Thus, even in this opening phase of the paschal mystery, the Church already has an apocalyptic vision of the new heavens and the new earth, and "the holy city, a new Jerusalem, coming down out of heaven from God, prepared as a bride adorned for her husband" (Rev 21:2). The glory of God is the city's light, and the Lamb is its lamp: "The nations will walk by its light, and to it the kings of the earth will bring their treasure" (Rev 21:24).

Readings for the Eucharist in the Epiphany Cycle

	Prophet	*Apostle*	*Gospel*
Epiphany	Isa 60:1-6	Eph 3:2-3, 5-6	Matt 2:1-12
Baptism of the Lord	Isa 42:1-4, 6-7	Acts 10:34-38	A. Matt 3:13-17 B. Mark 1:7-11 C. Luke 3:15-16, 21-22
January 7		1 John 5:14-21	John 2:1-12

Readings for the Liturgy of the Hours

Epiphany	Isa 60:1-22
Baptism of Christ	Isa 42:1-9; 49:1-9
January 7	Isa 61:1-11

Psalm 72, the responsorial psalm for the Epiphany Mass, sings of this future reality as having already begun in a present that is the actualization of the past:

> *Lord, every nation on earth will adore you.*
> The kings of Tarshish and the islands
> shall pay him tribute.
> The kings of Sheba and Seba
> shall bring him gifts.
> Before him all kings shall fall prostrate,
> all nations shall serve him.

The Mystery Revealed to All

In the second reading of the Mass we are offered the knowledge of the mystery of Christ. St. Paul tells us that the favor God has given him consists in the revelation to him of this mystery (Eph 3:2-3), and he in turn reveals it to us on this feast of the Epiphany. Through him, the Lord makes the mystery of Christ known to us.

The journey into the mystery requires faith. The star is a sign to the magi, who put aside all further questioning and set out for the place where they will prostrate themselves and do homage. But the same sign produces quite different effects, according to what we are told in the gospel. To the magi, the star is a revelation, and they promptly set off to glorify God. But the sign leads Herod deeper into blindness; its light does not illumine the dark places that his passions have created, and he sees it as a threat to his kingdom, whereas the magi, being people of faith, see it as a guide that will lead them to the goal that every human being wants. The magi bring the Lord their homage in the form of the traditional gifts.

The attitudes of the magi are meant to be ours as well: to see the star, not to flee from its light, to believe in the sign God has given, to set out with the purpose of prostrating and adoring and offering ourselves under the sign of the eucharistic gifts that are intended to represent our self-giving for the glory of the Lord.

The Epiphany is thus not a triumphalist celebration. No, Epiphany is a feast of humility, for when the Church sees the bright light of the star, she is forced to ask herself whether she is constantly journeying to adore the Lord, whether that is her central and predominant concern, and whether all individual Christians see it as their essential purpose to surrender everything, in a spirit of faith, so that they may set out to adore and offer themselves to the Lord. This kind of examination of conscience can be very realistic. All of us must search our own hearts; the point at issue is the very meaning of Christian life.

The Nations Shall Advance toward Jerusalem

The gospel, then, as proclaimed in the liturgy, presents us with an eschatological vision, just as the first reading does (Isa 60:1-6). The new Sion of which Isaiah speaks is the lasting city, and so intent is the liturgy upon this eschatological vision that it adds the word "Jerusalem" to the text (in Isa 60:1). The addition of the word "Jerusalem" to the opening exhortation, "Arise, shine," gives a direction to our reading of the passage and thus indirectly to our reading of the gospel as well.

St. Paul received the gracious light given to him and communicated it to us; that was his essential mission. But it is also the mission of every baptized person. By being baptized in Christ Jesus, we receive the knowledge of his mysteries. Moreover, every sacrament is an epiphany, a star, a sign of the one mystery. The light of the revelation of Christ's mysteries that has been given to us must be passed on, so that the Gentiles share in the same inheritance as the Jews. All of us are called to share the same promise of a definitive regathering in the heavenly Jerusalem, where we shall all pay homage to the glory of the Lord.

We already pay this homage when we celebrate the Eucharist. As the communion antiphon for the Mass during the Day says, "We have seen his star in the East, and have come with gifts to adore the Lord." The prayers of the Mass make the same connection between present and future: "O God, . . . grant in your mercy that we, who know you already by faith, may be brought to behold the beauty of your sublime glory" (collect), and "[may we] perceive with clear sight and revere with true affection the mystery in which you have willed us to participate" (prayer after communion).

Christ, the Light of the Nations

The preface for the Epiphany speaks of the enlightenment that has been brought to the peoples of the world. This preface is of Roman

inspiration and is in harmony with the rest of the liturgy in emphasizing the same aspect of the Epiphany: its manifestation of Christ
and revelation of his mystery to all the nations. What is special to the
preface is its stress on the manner in which Christ manifests himself:
through our human nature.

Here, of course, we have something that is supremely important
for the Church and for all who seek Christ. It is the basis for the whole
sacramental life of the Church, since Christ himself is already the
sacrament of our meeting with God, and this epiphanic light continues to shine in and through the Church. In addition, in revealing
himself by making our mortal flesh his own, Christ also re-created
us. That is why we celebrate Epiphany, not as a simple memorial, but
as a "sacrament," that is, the actualization of a mystery that we are
thereby enabled to enter profoundly here and now and that is inseparable from the paschal mystery of the reconstruction of the world.

The preface says: "For today you have revealed the mystery of our
salvation in Christ as a light for the nations, and, when he appeared
in our mortal nature, you made us new by the glory of his immortal
nature." Since we are here emphasizing the paschal aspect of Epiphany, it is worthwhile noting the original Latin text of the second
clause: *cum in substantia nostrae mortalitatis apparuit, nova nos immortalitatis eius gloria reparasti*. A new glory, and not just a new light, was
manifested at the Epiphany.

The entrance antiphon for the Mass during the Day sings: "Behold,
the Lord, the Mighty One, has come; and kingship is in his grasp,
and power and dominion." *That* is the glory manifested. It is from
his vision of glory that the light comes, when the nations see "his
glory, / the glory as of the Father's only Son" (John 1:14).*

---

* The third edition of the Roman Missal added a Vigil Mass for the Epiphany.
Nocent's commentary predates the existence of these texts, but the reader will find
many of their themes covered already.

21. THE BAPTISM OF THE LORD

The Three Evangelists

The entrance antiphon for the feast of the Lord's baptism pinpoints the central theme of the celebration: "After the Lord was baptized, the heavens were opened, and the Spirit descended upon him like a dove, and the voice of the Father thundered: This is my beloved Son, with whom I am well pleased."

In some manuscripts, only St. Luke, in the passage used for today's gospel in Year C (Luke 3:15-16, 21-22), has the words: "You are my beloved Son; today I have begotten you."[1] In Mark and Luke, the Father addresses the Son directly; in Matthew he speaks of the Son in the third person: "This is my beloved Son." Mark and Matthew, moreover, have the Father use words reminiscent of Isaiah 42:1, "Here is my servant whom I uphold, / my chosen one with whom I am pleased, / upon whom I have put my spirit; / he shall bring forth justice to the nations," while Luke, according to the better manuscript tradition, has the Father use Psalm 2:7, "You are my son; / today I have begotten you."

As we noted earlier, the Father speaks the same words as at the baptism (as reported by Matthew and Mark). Thus, while the facts reported are authentic, the text of the account of the baptism has been revised and shows, like many other passages of the gospel, the reactions of the early Church. Luke's text uses, on the Father's lips, a verse from a psalm that indicates the messiahship of Jesus. The other two evangelists prefer to follow the text in Isaiah, but in so doing, they also situate Jesus in a messianic context; in addition, they point out his role as Messiah: the role of "servant."

We also noted earlier that the expression "only [or: only begotten] Son" contains a reference to Genesis and the account of the sacrifice of Isaac that was required of his father, Abraham. The words "only son" occur three times in the account: "Take your son Isaac, your only one, whom you love" (Gen 22:2); "you did not withhold from me your son, your only one" (22:12); "in not withholding from me your son, your only one" (22:16).

The words "only" and "whom you love" are enough to tell us what a terrible sacrifice God was demanding. The same holds for the baptism of Jesus. It is no exaggeration, therefore, to speak of the baptism as being his investiture as Messiah. That, surely, is what the evangelists are emphasizing. They use the same Old Testament text at the transfiguration; this latter event, coming as it did at a point nearer in time to the Passover sacrifice Christ was to offer by offering himself, made all the clearer the specific character of Jesus' messiahship: he is the Servant who does the Father's will.

Every aspect of the gospel account of the baptism is undoubtedly of interest, but we must observe, once again, how the liturgy uses the passage with a particular end in view; it does not scorn the other elements in the account, but it does highlight one of them, not all.

The Servant

For the first reading the liturgy has Isaiah 42:1-4, 6-7, the very passage that is closely related to the words put on the Father's lips at the baptism in the accounts of Matthew and Mark. Isaiah has, "Here is my servant whom I uphold, / my chosen one with whom I am pleased" (42:1), while Mark has, "You are my beloved Son; with you I am well pleased" (1:11). Isaiah goes on to say, "upon whom I have put my spirit," while the evangelist tells us that the Spirit descends on Jesus like a dove.

A Christian reading of Isaiah 42 turns our thoughts to God's action in the history of salvation, that is, to the love of the Father, who, through Christ and in the Spirit, renews the world.

The role that the Servant receives at the Jordan is spelled out for us in Isaiah 42. His first and foremost task is to reunite the people to God: "I formed you, and set you / as a covenant of the people" (42:6). But at the same time he is Messiah and Servant for all humankind: "I formed you, and set you / as . . . a light for the nations." His task is to enlighten and set free: "to open the eyes of the blind, / to bring out prisoners from confinement, / and from the dungeon, those who live in darkness" (42:6-7).

The responsorial psalm (Ps 29) sings of the Lord's "voice," the voice we shall shortly be listening to in the gospel: "The God of glory thunders. / . . . In his temple they all cry, 'Glory!' "

Anointed by the Spirit

With this heading we come to the point that St. Luke (in Acts 10:34-38) regards as the most important thing about Jesus' baptism in the Jordan: through his baptism Jesus was anointed by the Spirit and filled with the Spirit's power. In the discourse of which this passage is a part, St. Peter does not speak of the event as though it were cut off from the course of history. On the contrary, it is a real historical event, with a real historical context: "You know . . . what has happened all over Judea, beginning in Galilee after the baptism that John preached, how God anointed Jesus of Nazareth" (Acts 10:37-38). Similarly, Luke tells us in his gospel that Jesus went about preaching in Galilee and Judea (Luke 23:5). Thus, the anointing of Christ is situated in a definite historical context: his mission is beginning, and that of John is drawing to its end.

Jesus is anointed with the Spirit and his power. This description from Acts (10:38) reminds us of Isaiah's words in chapter 61:1, "The spirit of the Lord GOD is upon me, / because the LORD has anointed me; / He has sent me to bring good news to the afflicted, / to bind up the brokenhearted."

God has chosen Jesus as recipient not only of the Spirit but of power as well. This "power" should be understood not as something distinct from the anointing of the Spirit but rather as part of the gift of the Spirit. St. Luke (in Peter's discourse) further specifies the effects of this anointing: "He went about doing good and healing all those oppressed by the devil" (Acts 10:38).

The anointing makes of Jesus a prophet who brings the glad tidings of salvation, and Luke further observes that Jesus goes about doing good and healing those in Satan's power. These various effects, as we noted several times in our study of Advent, are a sign that the kingdom is present. Once again, then, the coming of the Spirit in the form of a dove is a sign of messianic investiture.

We can understand now why the Eastern liturgy celebrates the baptism in the Jordan on Epiphany. The baptism is a basic sign of our salvation in Jesus and tells the entire world that he is the Servant who has come to do the Father's will.

22. EPIPHANY IN THE LITURGIES OF THE PAST

1. Epiphany in the Early Roman Liturgy

The table given below of the readings for Epiphany in the early Roman liturgy shows that a firm tradition had been established by the time of the surviving lectionaries.

There are very few variations. The Missal of 1570 introduces one by substituting Galatians 4:1-7 for Titus 3:4-7 as the first reading for Mass on the Vigil of Epiphany.

The tradition is less unified for the feast of the Lord's baptism. John 1:29-34 appears by itself in two of the old lectionaries, but the Evangeliary of Würzburg offers a choice.

As for prayers, the Gelasian Sacramentary has an interesting preface for Epiphany that gives us an insight into this sacramentary's conception of the season:

> It is truly right and proper . . . that we should praise you as the God who are wonderful in all the works wherein you have revealed the mysteries of your kingdom. For a star pointing to the virginal birth preceded this feast and told the astonished Magi that the Lord of Heaven had been born on earth. Thus the God who was to be revealed to the world was announced by heavenly signs and, being born in time, was made known also by the help of temporal signs.[1]

	1	2	3	4	5	6
Vigil of Epiphany	Titus 3:4-7	Titus 3:4-7			Titus 3:4-7	Gal 4:1-7
Epiphany	Isa 60:1-6	Isa 60:1-6	Matt 2:19-23 Matt 2:1-12	Isa 60:1-6	Matt 2:19-23 Isa 60:1-6 Matt 2:1-12	Matt 2:19-23 Isa 60:1-6 Matt 2:1-12
Baptism of Jesus			John 1:29-34	Mark 1:1, 4-11 John 1:29-34 Matt 3:1-17	Isa 25:1 or 12:3-5 John 1:29-34	Isa 60:1-6 John 1:29-34
Sunday after Epiphany	Rom 12:1-5	Rom 12:1-5	Luke 2:42-52		Rom 12:1-5 Luke 2:42-52	Rom 12:1-5 Luke 2:42-52

1 = The Würzburg Epistolary. See p. 142 above.

2 = The Comes or Epistolary of Alcuin.

3 = The Würzburg Evangeliary, reconstructed earlier form. See G. Morin, "Liturgie et basiliques de Rome au milieu du VIIe s. d'après les listes d'évangiles de Wurzbourg," *Revue bénédictine* 28 (1911): 296–330.

4 = The Würzburg Evangeliary, later stage.

5 = The Murbach Lectionary. See p. 143 above.

6 = Missal of Pius V (1570).

2. The Celebration of Epiphany at Milan

The Milanese liturgy shows no originality in its choice of readings for the Mass of Epiphany. In fact, the readings proposed in, for example, the Bergamo Sacramentary are to be found in the other liturgies.

Vigil of Epiphany	Epiphany	Sunday after Epiphany
Titus 3:3-7 or 2:11–3:2	Titus 2:11–3:2	Eph 4:23-28
Matt 3:3-17	Matt 2:1-2	Luke 2:42-52

The Bergamo Sacramentary does, however, have some prayers that are original. Here, for example, is the preface for the Vigil of Epiphany, with its mention of the *tria miracula*, or "three mysteries," so dear to the Eastern Church:

> . . . for by his birth from heaven [Christ our Lord] introduced into the world the marvelous signs of his majesty: he showed the Magi the star they were to venerate; after a time the same Jesus Christ changed water into wine, and by his baptism sanctified the waters of the Jordan.[2]

The preface for Epiphany concentrates on the baptism:

> . . . eternal God who revealed yourself from heaven in the sound of thunder over the river Jordan in order to make known the Savior of the world and show yourself the Father of eternal light. You opened the heavens, blessed the air, purified the water-springs, and pointed out your only Son by sending the Holy Spirit in the form of a dove. The fonts today received your blessing and removed the curse that lay on us, offering to believers purification from all their sins and giving them birth into eternal life as adoptive children of God.[3]

3. The Celebration of Epiphany in Merovingian Gaul and in Spain

We limit our choice here to a few books that give the most characteristic readings. The table below shows the abundance of texts provided for the Merovingian liturgy in the Luxeuil Lectionary, the Wolfenbüttel Palimpsest, and the Bobbio Missal. We shall not cite any of the prayer texts, since those of the Bobbio Missal are not of any special interest.

The readings listed could be of help in constructing a Liturgy of the Word by way of preparation for the feast or as a meditation on the mystery celebrated in the feast of Epiphany.

For Spain, we note only the readings found in almost all the Spanish lectionaries, namely, Numbers 24:3-9, 15-18; Titus 2:11–3:7; Matthew 2:1-15.

Readings for the Epiphany Cycle in Merovingian Gaul

	L	W	S	S¹	B
Epiphany	Isa 60:1-16	Isa 59:21-60	Isa 60:1-6		
	Titus 2:11–3-7	Titus 2:11–3:7		Eph 5:20-33	Titus 2:11-13
	Matt 3:13-17	Matt 3:13-17			Matt 3:13-17
	Luke 3:23	John 2:1-11			Luke 3:23
	John 2:1-11	Matt 15:29-31			John 2:1-11
		John 6:1-2			
		John 6:5-14			
Sunday after Epiphany	Isa 6:1-10				
	1 Cor 10:26-31				
	Luke 4:16-22				

L = Lectionary of Luxeuil. See p. 148 above.

W = Wolfenbüttel Palimpsest, ca. 500. Edited in A. Dold, *Das älteste Liturgiebuch der lateinischen Kirche* (Texte und Arbeiten 26–28; Beuron, 1936). See Vogel, *op. cit.*, 290.

S = Lectionary of Sélestat. See p. 150 above.

S¹ = Fragment of a lectionary from Sélestat. See p. 150 above.

B = The Bobbio Missal. See pp. 148–49 above.

4. The Celebration of Epiphany in the East

The Eastern liturgy for Epiphany concentrates mainly on the baptism of Jesus; its formularies and texts are quite rich.

"Devotion" to the Jordan was so important that baptism was often so named, while even in our day baptismal fonts are still called "Jordan" in the East. Bede the Venerable (675–735) saw with his own eyes the wooden cross erected on the spot where John was supposed to have done his baptizing; the cross was as tall as a man and was submerged when the waves were high. A bridge crossed the Jordan at this point, connecting on the other side with a monastery dedicated to St. John the Baptist. St. Jerome tells us that catechumens preferred to be baptized in the Jordan and sometimes imprudently delayed their baptism until they could have their wish. St. Ambrose reacts against such a custom, telling his hearers that Christ is everywhere and that wherever Christ is, there the Jordan is as well.[4]

The Byzantine Rite is, for most Western Christians, the most accessible of the Eastern rites. We shall therefore go into it in some detail.

On January 5, preparation begins for the feast of the holy Theophany. In the Office of Prime a troparion expresses the theology of Christ's baptism as elaborated by the fathers:

> The Jordan once ran backward toward its source at the touch of Elisha's mantle after Elijah had been taken up, and the waters parted. Under his feet the river became a solid pathway and a realistic figure of baptism that enables us to cross the shifting waters of life. Christ manifested himself in the Jordan in order to sanctify the waters.[5]

The first part of this troparion is very reminiscent of a passage in Origen's commentary on the Fourth Gospel:

> We must observe again that Elias, when he was about to be carried to heaven by a hurricane, having taken his sheepskin and spread it out, struck the water with it, which opened on either side, and they went through one after the other; I mean himself and Eliseus. So he was made fit to be taken up to heaven, after having been baptized in the Jordan.[6]

The waters of Jordan are a figure of a "vehicle" that takes a road to heaven. St. Gregory Nazianzen uses the image: "Baptism is . . . the destruction of sin, the vehicle to carry us to God,"[7] and St. Cyril of Jerusalem uses the same expression.[8]

An *idiomelos* (hymn with its own melody) based on a poem attributed to St. Sophronius (ca. 560–638), patriarch of Jerusalem, sings of Jordan's waters being sanctified for the forgiveness of our sins:

On this day the element of water is consecrated; Jordan stops flowing
and holds back its waters as it sees the Savior purifying himself in
them. . . . O Christ, our King, as a human you went down into the
river, hastening because of our sins to receive from the Precursor the
baptism meant for slaves.[9]

In this hymn the paschal theme is announced. The baptism of Jesus
prefigures our redemption and continues the incarnation in which
the Savior took "the form of a slave" (Phil 2:7), for in his baptism he
received a rite meant for slaves.

The choice of readings is illuminating for a grasp of the Eastern
theology of the feast. The first reading is from Isaiah 35:1-9, which
contains these verses:

Here is your God,
    he comes with vindication;
With divine recompense
    he comes to save you.
Then the eyes of the blind shall see,
    and the ears of the deaf be opened;
Then the lame shall leap like a stag,
    and the mute tongue sing for joy.
For waters will burst forth in the wilderness,
    and streams in the Arabah.
The burning sands will become pools,
    and the thirsty ground, springs of water. . . .
A highway will be there,
    called the holy way;
No one unclean may pass over it,
    but it will be for his people;
    no traveler, not even fools, shall go astray on it.
No lion shall be there,
    nor any beast of prey approach,
    nor be found.
But there the redeemed shall walk. (Isa 35:4-7a, 8-9)

This passage is especially appropriate. It announces salvation in
terms that Jesus himself will use in answering the question of John
the Baptist's disciples whom John had sent to Jesus from prison: "Go
and tell John what you hear and see: the blind regain their sight, the
lame walk, lepers are cleansed, the deaf hear" (Matt 11:4-5). The passage also develops the theme of the highway that we met in the
troparion quoted earlier.

With regard to this highway Isaiah mentions a point not taken over in the New Testament. It is that on this highway, which the Jordan becomes, there are lions and beasts of prey, but henceforth they are excluded so that the redeemed may walk there free. What the liturgy is focusing on at this point is the theme of ransom from the devil; the ransoming is effected by water, after the latter has itself been freed from the domination of evil powers.

There are numerous other references to the crossing of the Jordan as being a victory over infernal powers. When Isaiah describes the end of time and the new creation it brings, he sees Yahweh crushing the dragon of the sea: "On that day / The LORD will punish with his sword / that is cruel, great, and strong, / Leviathan the fleeing serpent, / Leviathan the coiled serpent; / he will slay the dragon in the sea" (Isa 27:1). Closer to the reading in the liturgy is another passage from Isaiah: "Was it not you who crushed Rahab, / you who pierced the dragon? / Was it not you who dried up the sea, / the waters of the great deep, / You who made the depths of the sea into a way / for the redeemed to pass through?" (Isa 51:9-10).

Thus, in the first reading, the baptism of Jesus is already seen as a struggle with, and victory over, Satan. Once again, the paschal mystery begins with the baptism of Jesus.

The Eastern liturgies make frequent use of Psalm 74:13-14 during the celebration of Epiphany: "It was you who divided the sea by your might, / who shattered the heads of the monsters in the sea. / It was you who crushed Leviathan's heads." The baptism of the Lord is a mystery of our salvation.

The second reading is from the Acts of the Apostles (13:25-33). Here St. Paul quotes John the Baptist, who speaks of the one coming after him, whose sandals he is unworthy to loosen. Paul then tells the Jews that the message of salvation was addressed to them, but they, fulfilling the prophecies, put Jesus to death. God raised Jesus up, however, and now the good news can be preached that "what God promised our ancestors, he has brought to fulfillment for us, [their] children, by raising up Jesus" (Acts 13:32-33).

The gospel is Matthew 3:1-6, where we see John the Baptist preaching repentance and the crowds confessing their sins and receiving baptism in the Jordan.

The reading of the gospel is followed by a *kontakion* (a liturgical song), which says, "The Lord went down today into the waters of the Jordan and said to John: 'Do not be afraid to baptize me, for I have come to save Adam, the first father.' " A *kontakion* is a *troparion* that sums up the theme of a feast. We can see, in this instance, how the *kontakion* emphasizes the paschal theme that has been sounded in the readings and earlier *troparia*.

Thus, beginning with the Vigil of Epiphany, the liturgy directs our attention to the Jordan, in which the mystery of our redemption is already underway. It would take too long to study each and every formulary connected with the Vigil, but we may at least note some passages from the Office.

In an *idiomelos* at Terce we find the same emphasis on the paschal mystery and on Christ's victory over the demon:

> You came in the flesh to the Jordan to be baptized as a human, O life-giving Savior, in order that you might enlighten us who were caught in error. . . . At the moment when you were freeing us from all deception and all the dragon's snares, you received a testimonial from the Father, and the divine Spirit descended on you in the form of a dove.[10]

At the baptism of Jesus, the Trinity revealed itself:

> To us, on this day, did the Trinity, our God, reveal itself as undivided: the Father in a loud voice bore clear witness to his Son; the Spirit in the form of a dove descended from heaven; the Son bowed his sinless head to the Precursor and received baptism. He freed the human race from slavery.[11]

At Sext, the theme of the struggle with Satan reappears in an *idiomelos*: "I have hastened to destroy the enemy hidden in the waters, the prince of darkness, so that I might free the world from his toils and give it eternal life."[12] The poem thus puts an expression of the paschal mystery on Christ's own lips: his struggle with the evil powers, followed by his victory and ours.

At None, an *idiomelos* gives voice to the theology of baptism: "He makes us children of God; in the realm of darkness he enlightens humanity through the water of divine baptism."[13]

The feast day itself, January 6, is marked by a very rich liturgy. In Vespers, celebrated on the eve, a beautiful idiomelic *sticheron* briefly states the theme of the celebration of Theophany: "By bowing your head before the Precursor you crushed the heads of the demons; you stood amid the waters and enlightened the universe so that it might glorify you, O Savior, enlightener of our souls."[14]

These Vespers have fifteen readings; among them are Genesis 1:1-13, which tells of land and waters being separated; Exodus 14, the water springing from the rock; Exodus 15, the springs of fresh water in the desert; Luke 3:1-18, John the Baptist preaching repentance and announcing another baptism. After the readings comes the blessing of water, a lengthy ceremony containing an opening song, four readings, a diaconal litany, and a long prayer followed by the lowering of a crucifix into the water. Then the crucifix is kissed and a mouthful of water taken.

In some churches of the Latin Rite, there used to be a blessing of water on Epiphany, in memory of the baptism in the Jordan. Pope Paul V authorized this custom wherever it already existed, and his Roman Ritual contains a formula for the blessing of water on the Vigil of Epiphany, although Pope Benedict XIV suppressed the formula in his revision of the Ritual; in any event, the custom had died out.

The Feast of the Jordan

At least one traveler has brought back an account of this ceremony:

> At St. Petersburg, on Epiphany, the feast of the Jordan is celebrated with great solemnity on the Neva, in front of the Czar's palace. A richly decorated chapel, open on all sides, is built, with a hole in the center of the flooring and down through the ice. At ten in the morning, the metropolitan of St. Petersburg celebrates in this temporary chapel a solemn Mass, at which all the great dignitaries of the Church and the troops of the Imperial Guard are present. After the divine service, the Emperor arrives with his entire court. Then the metropolitan blesses the Neva by lowering a cross in the open hole, while cannons are fired and the troops, kneeling and bareheaded, present arms. Everyone then tries to touch his lips with the water that has just been blessed and to get some of it for himself by making holes in the ice. In some provinces, the peasants make a hole in the ice in order to plunge into the water themselves; elsewhere, people are content to gather the water in containers.[15]

The themes developed in this festival of the waters are those of the Spirit, the water, the forgiveness of sins, and salvation.

Early on, a *troparion* inspired by Isaiah sings of the Spirit's gifts: "The voice of the Lord resounds over the waters and says: 'Come, all of you, and receive from the Christ who has manifested himself the

Spirit of wisdom, the Spirit of understanding, the Spirit of fear of the Lord.' " [16]

This is followed by two readings from Isaiah. The first (35:1-9) has already been read at Prime on January 5 and recalls the water springing up in the desert and the victory of the Messiah and the redeemed. The second (12:3-6) speaks of the wonderful things God has done for our salvation and invites us to draw water with joy from the fountain of salvation.

New Testament readings come next. The First Letter of St. Paul to the Corinthians reminds us that our ancestors were all under the cloud, crossed the Red Sea, were baptized by Moses, and drank from the spiritual rock that followed them, that is, from Christ (10:1-4). Finally, the Gospel of St. Mark (1:9-11) tells us of Christ's baptism and the Father's witness to his Son.

While the deacon chants a liturgical prayer, the priest prays in a low voice:

> Thus did you clothe yourself in our poor weak nature. Though you are King of all creation, you submitted to the bonds of slavery and deigned to be baptized in the Jordan by the hand of one of your servants so that, being without sin, you might sanctify the waters and open to us, through water and the Spirit, the way of rebirth and might restore us to our original freedom. [17]

Here we have the paschal theme of new life. The end of the prayer evidently recalls the words of Jesus in his conversation with Nicodemus: "Amen, amen, I say to you, no one can enter the kingdom of God without being born of water and Spirit" (John 3:5).

The priest then prays aloud a long and beautiful collect that has been attributed to St. Sophronius, patriarch of Jerusalem. It is possible, however, that this prayer, so archaic in style, is even older than that. It served as a model for the prayer for blessing the water in the Armenian liturgy. [18]

This long prayer of thanksgiving spoken aloud is really a continuation and amplification of the prayer said just before it in a low voice. It begins with an expression of gratitude: "Accept from us a thanksgiving worthy of your greatness for the wonderful deeds and magnificent works you have done since the beginning of the world and especially in these last times as you effect your plan of sanctification."[19] There follows a listing of these divine wonders, which the priest proclaims aloud and speaks of as accomplished "today":

> . . . Today the grace of the Holy Spirit descends
> upon the waters in the form of a dove.
> . . . Today the waters of the Jordan are changed
> into a remedy by the presence of the Lord.
> . . . Today the sins of humanity are wiped away in the
> waters of the Jordan.
> . . . Today paradise is opened to humankind, and the
> Sun of Justice shines upon us.
> . . . Today the kingdom of heaven has become ours. . . .
> This is the feast of the Lord that we see today in the Jordan; we see
> him casting into the Jordan the death due us for our disobedience, the
> stinging goad of error, and the chains that bound Adam; we see him
> giving to the world the baptism that saves.[160]

This conclusion of the prayer leads over to a second thanksgiving in which the whole of creation is associated with us in praising God for the wonderful things he has done for the sake of our salvation.

This long and beautiful prayer of blessing is in the line of the "Jewish blessing" and the early anaphoras, or eucharistic prayers, that we find in the third and fourth centuries. The themes developed in the prayer are the ones we have been seeing all along: Christ's baptism is the climax of God's various comings since the sin of Adam; it is the sign of our salvation and return to paradise.

Theophany

The same themes reappear in Matins for the feast of the Theophany. The *troparia* of the first Ode are typical in this respect:

> In the waters of the Jordan he creates Adam anew after he had undergone corruption; he crushes the heads of the dragons that have taken refuge there. So does the Lord, King of the ages, act, for he is clad in glory. . . . He who removes the filth from humanity by purifying himself in the Jordan on humanity's behalf has made himself like those who sit in darkness. So does the Lord act, for he is clad in glory.[21]

In this meditation on the paschal mystery, the last day and the return of Christ are not forgotten:

It is in the fire of the last day that Christ will baptize those who disobey him and do not believe that he is God. But it is in the Spirit and water that he renews through grace, and frees from their sins, all those who acknowledge his divinity.[22]

The celebration of the liturgy, that is, the Mass, has two readings. One is from St. Paul:

For the grace of God has appeared, saving all. . . . [It was] Jesus Christ, who gave himself for us to deliver us from all lawlessness and to cleanse for himself a people as his own. . . .
[H]e saved us through the bath of rebirth / and renewal by the holy Spirit. (Titus 2:11-14; 3:4-7)[23]

The other reading, Matthew 3:13-17, makes the baptism of Jesus the basis of our own purification: "Allow it now, for thus it is fitting for us to fulfill all righteousness." At the same time, it recalls the messianic anointing of Jesus: "This is my beloved Son, with whom I am well pleased."

This profusion of texts does not cause the real focus of the celebration of the Theophany to be overlooked. The celebration is of the baptism of the Lord, but, in and through this, it is of the paschal mystery. The baptism is the anointing of the Messiah for his mission of cleansing the world of its sins and destroying the evil powers. Once the baptism of Jesus has taken place, we possess the waters of salvation and new birth, and we are on the road that leads us back to paradise. Finally, the baptism of Christ is the mystery of our definitive union with him.

Epilogue:
A Journey into the Paschal Mystery

Thus far, we have been discovering the rich resources of Advent, Christmas, and Epiphany for our lives as we celebrate the liturgies of these seasons. As we end our survey, it will be worth our while to reflect briefly on the impressions we have derived from a study that was intended to make demands on us in our everyday lives.

We Catholics of today, unlike our predecessors of the first Christian generations, are in danger to some extent of having our attention and energies scattered. The early Christians celebrated only Sunday, including the special Sunday of Easter, and their attention was focused on the mystery of the death and resurrection of Christ. Breaking up the mystery of Jesus into several phases can indeed help in coming to grips with it, but only on one condition: that no phase is separated from the central paschal mystery. The Church has, of course, been aware of this condition, as we recognize by now. In her celebrations she frequently reminds us of the summit from which all grace flows and which is the source of all meaning for the life of the Church and for our individual lives. Advent, Christmas, and Epiphany are stages in a journey into the paschal mystery and from the latter derive their authentic effectiveness.

In a later section we shall be studying Lent from Ash Wednesday through to Holy Thursday morning and the reconciliation of sinners that used to be celebrated at Rome on that morning after a long period of conversion that was experienced, not only by sinners and by catechumens preparing for baptism, but by the whole Church as well. Once Lent begins, we are drawn more urgently toward the paschal mystery as presented to us in various liturgies that we shall later be studying more closely.

At every moment, then, we are journeying toward the definitive reconstruction of the world in accordance with the eternal plan of God.

Notes

Introduction to the Liturgical Year

1. CL 10. All citations of documents from the Second Vatican Council are taken from *Vatican Council II: The Conciliar and Post Conciliar Documents*, ed. Austin Flannery, vol. 1 (Northport, NY: Costello, 1998).

2. See *Foi et vie* 63 (1964): 49.

3. *Loc. cit.*, 57–58.

4. Ibid., and *Rivista Liturgica* 56 (1969): 576.

5. G. Thils, "Désacralisation et sécularité," in *Au service de la Parole: Melanges A.-M. Charue* (Gembloux, 1969), 395.

6. See H.-J. Kraus, "Gottesdienst im Alten und im Neuen Bund," *Evangelische Theologie* 23 (1965): 171–206.

7. For further discussion of these viewpoints, see Y. Congar, "Situation du 'sacré' en régime chrétien," in *Liturgie après Vatican II*, ed. J.-P. Jossua and Y. Congar, Unam sanctam 66 (Paris, 1967), 385–403; L. Maldonado, *Vers une liturgie sécularisée* (Paris, 1971); A. Nocent, *Le temps de la liturgie est-il passé?* (Paris, 1968).

8. St. Justin Martyr, *Dialogus com Tryphone* 12.3 (*PG* 6:499).

9. Origen, *Contra Celsum* 8.23, trans. Henry Chadwick (Cambridge, 1953), 468.

10. Abraham Heschel, in an article on time quoted by R. Aron in "La liturgie juive et le temps," *La Maison-Dieu* 65 (1961): 13.

11. R. Aron, *art. cit.*, 19.

12. See L. Maldonado, *op. cit.*, 170.

13. St. Leo the Great, *Sermo* 29.2 (*CCL* 138:148).

14. *Sermo* 36.1 (*CCL* 138:195).

15. *Sermo* 37.1 (*CCL* 138:200).

16. *Sermo* 26.1 (*CCL* 138:125).

17. *Sermo* 52 (*CCL* 138A:307).

18. *Sermo* 63.6 (*CCL* 138A:386).

19. See, for example, Th. Filthaut, *Die Kontroverse über die Mysterienlehre* (Warendorf, 1947); French translation: *La théologie des mystères: Expose de la controverse*, by J.-C. Didier and A. Liefooghe (Paris: 1954). L. Bouyer, *Liturgical Piety* (Notre Dame, 1955), 86–88, provides a good synthesis and a clear, constructive critique.

20. CL 5–7.

21. See Tertullian, *De resurrection mortuorum* 8.3 (*CCL* 2:931): *Cara salutis est cardo* ("The flesh is the hinge of salvation").

22. CL 7.

23. CL 7 and 33.

24. Paul VI, *Mysterium fidei*, encyclical, 29 (*AAS* 57 [1965]: 764; *TPS* 10 [1964–65]: 319).

25. S. Marsili, *Anamnesis 1: La liturgia, momento nella storia di salvezza* (Turin, 1974), see 92. This is the first volume of the seven-volume series by the professors of the Pontifical Liturgical Institute at Sant'Anselmo, Rome.

1. Waiting in Hope

1. This inscription was found at Autun in 1839 and can be assigned to the end of the second century. The text may be seen in, for example, the article "Abercius," in the *Dictionnaire d'archeologie chretienne et de liturgie* 1:83.

2. The *rudimenta gloriae* is an old expression from the 1962 baptismal ritual; cf. 2 Cor 4:18; Rom 8:24.

3. Isa 1:21-27; 2:1-5. *LH*, Monday of the First Week of Advent.

4. Isa 29:13-24. *LH*, third Sunday.

5. Isa 16:1-5; 17:4-8. *LH*, Thursday of first week.

6. Matt 3:1-12. Mass, second Sunday (A).

7. Isa 48:17-19. Mass, Friday of second week.

8. Phil 1:4-6, 8-11. Mass, second Sunday (C).

9. Heb 10:5-10. Mass, fourth Sunday (C).

10. Mark 13:32-37. Mass, first Sunday (B).

11. Matt 3:1-12; second Sunday (A). Mark 1:1-8; second Sunday (B). Luke 3:1-6; second Sunday (C).

12. Isa 40:1-5, 9-11; second Sunday (B). Bar 5:1-9; second Sunday (C).

13. Matt 21:28-32. Mass, Tuesday of third week.

14. Isa 39:19-21, 23-26. Mass, Saturday of first week.

15. Matt 9:35–10:1, 5a, 6-8. Mass, Saturday of first week.

16. Isa 35:1-10. Mass, Monday of second week.

17. St. Cyril of Jerusalem, *Catecheses* 15.1 (*PG* 33:870; W. K. Reischl and J. Rupp, eds., *Cyrilli Hierosolymorum archiepiscopi opera* [Hildesheim, 1967]).

2. The Hope and Expectation of the Ages

1. CL 10.

2. S. Pinckaers, "L'espérance de l'Ancien Testament est-elle la meme que la nôtre?" *Nouvelle revue théologique* 77 (1955): 785–99; A. Hulsbosch, "L'attente du salut d'après l'Ancien Testament," *Irénikon* 27 (1954): 1–20; J. Van Der Ploeg, "L'espérance dans l'Ancien Testament," *Revue biblique* 61 (1954): 481–507.

3. See C. Tresmontant, *A Study of Hebrew Thought*, trans. M. F. Gannon (New York, 1960).

4. See A. Gelin, "The Expectation of God in the Old Testament," in A. Gelin et al., *Son and Savior: The Divinity of Jesus Christ in the Scriptures*, trans. A. Wheaton (Baltimore, 1960), 22. [This volume is a translation of *Lumiére et vie* 9 (1953).]

5. J. Danielou, *The Lord of History: Reflections on the Inner Meaning of History*, trans. N. Abercrombie (Chicago, 1958), 341.

6. See L. Bouyer, *op. cit.*, chap. 15.

7. Invitatory for December 17–23. Responsory at Lauds on December 24.

8. St. Irenaeus of Lyons, *Adversus haereses* 4.14.3 (*PG* 7:1011; *SC* 100:546).

9. Rom 13:11-14. Mass, first Sunday (A).

10. See the Second Letter to the Thessalonians.

11. Teilhard de Chardin, "Modern Unbelief: Its Underlying Cause and Remedy," in *Science and Christ*, trans. R. Hague (New York, 1968), 115.

12. H. de Lubac, *Catholicism: A Study of Dogma in Relation to the Corporate Destiny of Mankind*, trans. L. C. Sheppard (New York, 1950).

13. *Homiliae in Ezechielem* 9.1 (*PG* 13:732).

14. See I.-H. Dalmais, *Introduction to the Liturgy*, trans. R. Capel (Baltimore, 1961), 58.

15. See L. Bouyer, *op. cit.*, 257–71.

16. Yves de Montcheuil, "Vie chretienne et action temporelle," *Construire* 12, 103.

3. Waiting for the Comings of the Lord

1. St. Augustine, *Epistola* 55 (*PL* 33:2–5; *CCL* 34:170).

2. *Sermo* 29.1 (*CCL* 138:148).

3. Th. Spassky, "La Pâque de Noël," *Irénikon* 30 (1957): 289–306.

4. Gregory of Tours, *Historia Francorum* 10.31 (*PL* 71:566; *Monumenta Germaniae Historica: Scriptores rerum merouingicarum* 3 [2nd ed.], 444–45).

5. See J. Hild, "L'Avent," *La Maison-Dieu* 59 (1959): 10–24.

6. See J. Audet, *La Didachè: Instructions des apôtres* (Paris, 1958).

7. *De bono patientiae* 13 (*CSEL* 3:406). *LH*, Saturday, first week.

8. *Constitution on the Church* 48. *LH*, Tuesday, second week.

9. *Enarrationes in Psalmos*, Ps 109:1-3 (*PL* 37:1446–47; *CCL* 40:1601–3), in *The Liturgy of the Hours*, vol. 1: *Advent Season, Christmas Season* (New York: Catholic Book Publishing Co., 1975), 228.

10. On "Blessed are the poor," see J. Dupont, *Les Béatitudes*, 3 vols. (Paris, 1969–73).

4. Introduction

1. Or: Joy for the saved of Israel; Isa 4:2-6.

2. Or: The Lord is in your midst; Zeph 3:14-18a.

6. Second Week of Advent: Prepare the Way

1. A. Lodts, *Histoire de la literature hébraïque et juive depuis les origins jusqu'à la ruine l'état juif* (135 après J.-C.) (Paris, 1950), 239; quoted in J. Steinmann, *Le prophete Isaïe: Sa vie, son oeuvre et son temps*, Lectio Divina 5 (Paris, 1955), 31.

7. Third Week of Advent: The Messianic Age

1. St. Irenaeus, *Adversus haereses* 4.20.5 (*PC* 7:1035; *SC* 100:638–40), in *The Liturgy of the Hours*, vol. 1: *Advent Season, Christmas Season* (New York: Catholic Book Publishing Co., 1975), 288.

2. *Dogmatic Constitution on Divine Revelation* 4. The words "as a man among men and women" are from the *Letter to Diognetus* 7.4. The text used here is from *Vatican Council II: The Conciliar and Post Conciliar Documents*, ed. Austin Flannery, vol. 1 (Northport, NY: Costello, 1998).

3. St. Augustine, *Enarrationes in Psalmos*, Ps 37, 14 (*PL* 36:404; *CCL* 38:382), in *The Liturgy of the Hours*, 303.

4. Origen, *Homiliae in Lucam* 4.6 (*PC* 13:1811; *SC* 8T 134).

8. Fourth Week of Advent:
The Annunciation of the Messiah's Coming

1. Paul F. Bradshaw, Maxwell E. Johnson, L. Edward Phillips, *The Apostolic Tradition: A Commentary*, Hermeneia (Minneapolis: Fortress Press, 2002), 1–6.

2. L. Bouyer, *The Seat of Wisdom: An Essay on the Place of the Virgin Mary in Christian Theology*, trans. A. V. Littledale (New York, 1960), 128–29.

3. St. Leo the Great, *Epistulae* 31.2–3 (*PL* 54:792), in *The Liturgy of the Hours*, vol. 1: *Advent Season, Christmas Season* (New York: Catholic Book Publishing Co., 1975), 321.

4. St. Irenaeus, *Adversus haereses* 3.20.3 (*PC* 7:944; *SC* 34:342–44), in *The Liturgy of the Hours*, 338.

The "O" Antiphons

1. See J. Guillet, *Themes of the Bible*, trans. A. J. LaMothe Jr. (Notre Dame, 1960), 25ff.

2. Ibid., 55.

3. See *The Jerusalem Bible*, note on Exod 3:14.

4. R. Poelman's *De la plenitude de Dieu* (Tournai, 1959), which is a selection of texts from St. Irenaeus, has a section titled "La divine extension des mains." Among other texts is the following: "By the divine outstretching of his hands Christ gathered the two peoples into the one God" (*Adversus haereses* 5.17.4, on p. 70).

5. Bradshaw, et al., *op. cit.*, 38.

9. Advent in the Liturgies of the Past

1. Edition of the lectionary: G. Morin, "Le plus ancient lectionnaire del l'Eglise romaine," *Revue bénédictine* 27 (1910): 41–74. For its history, see C. Vogel, *Introduction aux sources de l'histoire du culte chrétien au Moyen Age*, Biblioteca degli "Studi Medievali" 1 (Spoleto, n.d. [1965]), 308–10, 313–14, 322–23.

2. G. Morin, "Liturgie et basiliques de Rome au milieu du VIIᵉ s. d'après les listes d'évangiles de Wurzbourg," *Revue bénédictine* 28 (1911): 296–330.

3. Edition: A. Wilmart, "Le Comes de Murbach," *Revue bénédictine* 30 (1913): 26–59.

4. L. C. Mohlberg, ed., *Sacramentarium Veronense*, Rerum ecclesiasticarum documenta, Series maior: Fontes 1 (Rome, 1966), 166–70.

5. "Nativitatem panis aeterni" (Mohlberg, *op. cit.*, 168, 2.20–21).

6. L. C. Mohlberg, ed., *Liber sacramentorum Romanae Aeclesiae ordinis circuli (Sacramentarium Gelasianum)*, Rerum ecclesiasticarum documenta, Series maior: Fontes 4 (Rome, 1968).

7. A. Chavasse, *Le sacramentarie gélasien* (Paris, 1958), 442; idem, "L'Avent romain du VIᵉ au VIIᵉ siecle," *Ephemerides Liturgicae* 57 (1953): 297.

8. Gel. 1120: "Excita, domine, potenciam tuam et veni, et quod aecclesiae tuae usque in finem saeculi promisisti, clementer operare."

9. Gel. 1124: "Repleti cibo spiritali alimoniae supplices te depraecamur, omnipotens deus, ut huius participacione mysterii docea nos terraena dispicere et amare caelestia, adque omni nexu mortifere cupiditatis exutos regno perpetuae libertatis consortes efficias."

10. Gel. 1123: "Propiciare supplicacionibus nostris et aecclesiae tuae misericordiam tuam quam confitentur ostende, manifestans plebe tuae unigeniti tui mirabile sacramentum, ut in uniuersitate nacionum pemciatur quod per uerbi tui evangelium promisisti, et habeat plenitude adopcionis quod pertulit testificacio ueritatis."

11. A. Paredi, ed., *Sacramentarium Bergomense*, Monumenta Bergomensia 6 (Bergamo, 1962), 28–37; M. Ceriani, ed., *Missale Ambrosianum Vetus*, Monumenta Sacra et Profana 8 (Milan, 1912). See Vogel, *op. cit.*, 301–2.

12. *Sacramentarium Bergomense*, 51: "Deus qui in unigenito tuo novam creaturam nos tibi esse fecisti, respice propitious in opera misericordiae tuae et in adventu Filii tui ab omnibus nos maculis vetustatis emunda."

13. *Sacramentarium Bergomense*, 54: "cuius incarnatione salus facta est mundi et passione redemptio procurata est hominis procreati. Ipse nos, quaesumus, ad aeternum

perducat praemium, qui redemit de tenebris infernorum. Iustificet que in adventu secundo, qui nos redemit in primo."

14. *Sacramentarium Bergomense*, 60: "De cuius ventre fructus effioruit, qui panis angelici munere replevit. Quod Eva voravit in crimine, Maria restituit in salute. Distat opus serpentis et Virginis. Inde fusa sunt venea discriminis, hinc egressa mysteria salvatoris. Inde partus occubuit, hinc conditor resurrexit. A quo humana natura non iam captiva sed libera restituitur; quod Adam perdidit in parente, Christo receipt auctore."

15. P. Salmon, ed., *Le Lectionnaire de Luxeuil*, Collectanea Biblica 7 and 9 (Rome, 1944 and 1953). See Vogel, *op. cit.*, 291.

16. P. Cagin, ed., *Le sacramenta ire gélasien d'Angoulême* (Angoulême, 1918).

17. *Op. cit.*, no 1516: "Conscientias nostras, quaesumus, omnipotens deus, cotidie visitando purifica, ut veniente Filio tuo domino nostro paratam sibi in nobis inveniat mansionem."

18. *Op. cit.*, 1519: "Animae nostrae, quaesumus, deus, hoc potiantur desiderio, ut a tuo spiritu infiamentur ut sicut lampades divino munere saciati ante conspectum venientis Christi filii tui, velut clara lumina fulgeamus."

19. *The Bobbio Missal*, no. 363, p. 108.

20. See Vogel, *op. cit.*, 302–3.

21. J. Perez de Urbel and A. Gonzalez y Ruiz-Zorrilla, eds., *Liber commicus: Edición crítica*, Monumenta hispaniae Sacra, Series liturgica 2–3 (Madrid 1950–55).

22. See Vogel, *op. cit.*, 304.

23. Ibid.

24. M. Ferotin, ed., *Liber mozarabicus sacramentorum*, Monumenta ecclesiae liturgica 6 (Paris, 1912).

25. *Op. cit.*, 12: "O Verbum Patris quod caro factum es, tu habitares in nobis, praesta nobis, ut qui te venisse iam credimus, et venturum adhuc speramus, ab omni peccatorum eruamur contagione."

26. *Op. cit.*, 15–16: "Confortentur, quaeso, Domine Jesu Christe, in adventu tuo corda fidelium, tuoque in nomine genua roborentur debilium. Tua visitatione vulnera curentur egrorum, tuove tactu oculi inluminentur cecorum: tuo regimine vestigia firmentur claudorum, tuaque miseratione vincula absolvantur peccaminum. Quosque prospicis adventum suscipere, hos facito in secundum iudicii tui adventum ad te exsultantibus animis pervenire, atque in amenitate paradisi iucundaturos induce."

10. Christmas: A Charming Memory?

1. Bradshaw, et al., *op. cit.*, 38.

2. B. Botte, *Les origines de Noël et de l'Epiphanie* (Louvain, 1932), 105.

3. L. Duchesne, *Christian Worship: Its Origin and Evolution*, trans. M. L. McClure (London, 1903), 257–65.

4. C. Mohrmann, "Epiphania," *Revue des sciences philosophiques et théologiques* 37 (1953): 664. Article reprinted in C. Mohrmann, *Etudes sur le latin des chrétiens* 1 (Rome, 1961), 245–75.

5. *Art. cit.*, 644.

6. Botte, *Les origines de Noël*, 33.

7. L. Duchesne, in *Bulletin critique* 2 (1890): 41.

8. *Sermo* 187.1 (*PL* 38:1001).

9. *Epist.* 54.1 (*PL* 33:200).

10. See *Constitution on the Sacred Liturgy (Sacrosanctum Concilium)* 7, in *Vatican Council II: The Conciliar and Post Conciliar Documents*, ed. A. Flannery (Northport, 2007).

11. *Epist.* 55.1.1 (*PL* 33:205).

12. Ibid.

13. See J. Gaillard, "Noël: *memoria* ou mystere?," *La Maison-Dieu* 59 (1959): 43.

14. A. Baumstark, *Comparative Liturgy*, rev. B. Botte, trans. F. L. Cross (London, 1958), 156.

15. *Sermo* 190.1 (*PL* 38:1007).

16. *Sermo* 29.1 (*CCL* 138:147).

17. *Sermo* 28.1 (*CCL* 138:139).

18. *Loc. cit.*

19. *Sermo* 25.1 (*CCL* 138:117).

20. See Gaillard, *art. cit.*, 50–51.

21. H. Jenny, *The Paschal Mystery in the Christian Year*, trans. A. Stehling and J. Lundberg (Notre Dame, 1962), 32.

11. God and Human, King and Servant

1. *In vigilia Nativitatis Domini sermons* 3, 1–2.6 (*PL* 183:94–99).

2. J. Condamin, *Le livre d'Isaïe* (Paris, 1905), 58.

3. On all this, see A. Gelin, *The Key Concepts of the Old Testament*, trans. G. Lamb (New York, 1955); A. Robert, "Considerations sur le messianisme du Ps. 2," *Recherches de science religieuse* 39 (1951): 95.

4. Translated in J. Connelly, *Hymns of the Roman Liturgy* (Westminster, MD, 1957), 56.

5. The first, third, and fourth of these are translated in *The Hours of the Divine Office in English and Latin* (Collegeville, MN, 1963–64), 1:1166, 1249, 1253.

6. For example, Gen 24:27; Exod 18:10-11.

7. *Didache* 9.2. Text in A. Hanggi and I. Pahl, eds., *Prex Eucharistica: Textus e variis liturgiis antiquioribus selecti*, Spicilegium Friburgense 12 (Fribourg, 1968), 66.

8. St. Clement of Rome, *Letter to the Corinthians* 59.2. Text in K. Bihlmeyer, *Die Apostolischen Väter* 1 (Tübingen, 1924). The letter dates from the second half of the first century.

9. *Martyrdom of Polycarp* 14, trans. In H. Musurillo, ed., *The Acts of the Christian Martyrs* (Oxford, 1972), 13.

10. Anaphora of Serapion of Thmuis (Egypt) 1.3. Text in Hänngi-Pahl, *op. cit.*, 128.

11. See L. Brou, "Saint Grégoire de Naziance et l'antienne *Mirabile mysterium* des laudes de Circoncision," *Ephemerides liturgicae* 58 (1944): 14ff.

12. H. Denzinger and A. Schönmetzer, eds., *Enchiridion Symbolorum*, 32nd ed. (Freiburg, 1963). Translated in J. M. Carmody and T. E. Clarke, *Christ and His Missions: Christology and Soteriology*, Sources of Christian Theology 3 (Westminster, MD, 1966), 120. [Two words left in Greek in this translation have here been translated into English.—Tr.]

13. *Catecheses* 4.9 (*PC* 33:466–67).

14. *Sermo* 27.1 (*CCL* 138:133).

15. Translated in Connelly, *op. cit.*, 54, alt.

16. L. Cerfaux, "Le Fils né de la femme," *Bible et vie chrétienne* 4 (1953–54): 60.

12. The Christmas Pasch

1. *Adversus haereses* 3.19.1 (*PG* 7:939).

2. A paschal homily of St. Cyril of Alexandria, in the *Homiliaire patristique* (Paris, 1949), 121.

3. St. Cyril of Alexandria, *Quod unus sit Christus* (*PG* 78:1268).

4. See Th. Spassky, "La Pâque de Noël," *Irénikon* 30 (1957): 289–306.

5. Connelly, *op. cit.*, 54, alt.

6. St. Leo, *Sermo* 21.1 (*CCL* 138:85), in *The Liturgy of the Hours*, vol. 1: *Advent Season, Christmas Season* (New York: Catholic Book Publishing Co., 1975), 404.

7. Connelly, *op. cit.*, 56, alt.

8. *Sermo* 29.1 (*CCL* 138:146–47).

9. *Sermo* 21.3 (*CCL* 138:88), in *The Liturgy of the Hours*, 405.

10. The history of the text has been studied by B. Capelle, "La postcommunion de la seconde messe de Noël," *Questions liturgiques et paroissiales* 22 (1937): 298–308. For the text, see p. 308.

11. *Sermo* 25.5 (*CCL* 138:122).

12. *Expositio Evangelii secundum Lucam* 2.50 (*SC* 45:95).

13. *Expositio Evangelii secundum Lucam* 2.60 (*SC* 45:99).

14. *Sermo* 21 (*CCL* 138:88), in *The Liturgy of the Hours*, 405.

15. *Homiliae in Evangelia* 8.1 (*PL* 76:1103).

16. F. Mercenier and F. Paris, *La Prière des Eglises du rite byzantin*, 2 vols. (Amay, 1937–39), 2:119.

17. *Sermo* 62.1 (*CCL* 23:261).

18. See B. Botte, *Les origines de Noël*, 105. The text of the treatise *De solstitiis et aequinoctibus* is printed on pp. 93–105. See ll. 434–39.

19. See above, pp. 1–2, 6, 76.

20. *Homilia in Transfigurationem Domini* 18 (*PG* 76:573).

21. *Oratio in diem natalem Christi* (*PG* 46:1129).

22. "Le principe fondamental de la théologie morale," *Recherches de science religieuse* 42 (1954): 490.

23. *Ad Ephesios* 19.1–3 (*SC* 10 [3rd ed.]:89).

24. *Sermo* 22.5 (*CCL* 138:88).

25. *Adversus haereses* 3.22.4 (*PG* 7:958–59).

26. See p. 147.

27. *Hymn to the Blessed Virgin Mary* 1.2, in T. J. Lamy, ed., *Sancti Ephraem Syri hymni et sermones*, 4 vols. (Malines, 1882–1902), 2:522.

13. The Incarnation Today

1. See Exod 3:16; 4:31; 13:13; Ruth 1:6; Jdt 4:15; 8:33; Ps 79:16; Sir 46:16; Isa 29:6; Jer 29:10; Amos 3:2.

2. *Sermo* 21.1 (*CCL* 138:85).

3. *Sermo* 21.3 (*CCL* 138:88).

4. Christmas Preface I.

14. Meditative Celebrations of Christmas

1. Prayer over the offerings, January 1.

15. Christmas in the Liturgies of the Past

1. See C. Vogel, *Introduction aux sources de l'histoire du culte chrétien au Moyen Age*, Biblioteca degli "Studi Medievali" 1 (Spoleto, n.d. [1965]), 317–18.

2. Ibid., 310.

3. Ibid., 316.

4. L. C. Mohlberg, ed., *Sacramentarium Veronense*, Rerum ecclesiasticarum documenta, Series maior: Fontes 1 (Rome, 1956), section 40, nos. 1239–72 (pp. 157–63). Henceforth referred to as "Ver." with number of text.

5. See Ver. 1239.

6. Ver. 1242.

7. Ver. 1243: "Largire, quaesumus, domine, famulis tuis fidei et securitatis aumentum; ut qui de natiuitate domini nostril filii tui gloriantur, et aduersa mundi te gubernante non sentient, et quae temporaliter celebrare disiderant, sine fine percipiant: per."

8. Ver. 1258: "Deus, qui restaurationem condicionis humanae mirabilius operaris, quam substantiam condedisti: tribue, quaesumus, ut simul perficatur in nobis et quod creavit uerbi tui divina generatio, et quod eius hominis facti gloriosa natiuitas reformauit: per."

9. L. C. Mohlberg, ed., *Liber sacramentorum romanae aeclesiae ordinis anni circuli* (*Sacramentarium Celasianum*), Rerum ecclesiasticarum documenta, Series maior: Fontes 4 (Rome, 1960), no. 5. Henceforth, "Gel." With number of text.

10. Ver. 1241: "Uere dignum: quoniam quidquid christianae professionis deuotione celebratur, de hac sumit sollemnitate principium et in huius muneris mysterio continetur."

11. A. Paredi, ed., *Sacramentarium Bergomense*, Monumenta Bergomensia 6 (Bergamo, 1962).

12. The prayer is called the *Post pridie* and comes after the consecration. Text in M. Ferotin, ed., *Liber mozarabicus sacramentorum*, Monumenta ecclesiae liturgica 6 (Paris 1912), 116: "Haec, Domine, dona tua et praecepta servants, in altare tuum panis ac vini holocausta proponimus: rogantes profusissimam tuae misericordiae pietatem, ut eodem Spiritu, quo te in carne Yirginitas incorrupta concepit, has hostias Trinitas indivisa sanctificet; ut cum a nobis fuerint non minori trepidatione quam veneratione perceptae, quidquid contra animam male vivit intereat, et quidquid interierit nullatenus reviviscat."

13. Ibid., 195: "Qui ante tempus natus et te Deo Patre, tecum pariter et cum Spiritu Sancto condidit tempora, dignatus nasci et ipse sub tempore ex utero virginis Mariae. Qui tamen, cum sit sempiternus, statuos annorum decrevit decursus, per quos evolutus duceretur hic mundus. . . . Terram quoque fructibus repie; animas corporaque facito morbis delictisque carere; scandala remove; contere hostem."

16. The Epiphany: A Mystery of Plenty

1. See chap. 15, note 5, and corresponding text.

2. Ver. 1260.

3. Ver. 1250.

4. Ver. 1241.

5. Gel. 59, and J. Deshusses, ed., *Le sacramentaire grégorien*, Spicilegium Friburgense 16 (Fribourg, 1971), 89: "Quia cum unigenitus tuus in substantiae nostrae mortalitatis apparuit, in nouam nos immortalitatis suae lucem reparauit."

6. Gel. 57: "Corda nostra, quaesumus, domine, uenturae festiuitatis splendor inlustret, quo mundi huius tenebras carere ualeamus, et perueniamus ad patriam claritatis aeterne."

7. Gel. 60: "Inlumina, quaesumus, domine, populum tuum et splendore gratiae tuae cor eius semper accende, ut saluatoris mundi stella famulante manifestata natiuitas mentibus eorum et reueletur semper et crescat."

8. Gel. 65.

9. Gel. 66.

10. On this subject, see Botte, *Les origines de Noël;* J. Leclercq, "Aux origines du cycle de Noël," *ephemerides liturgicae* 60 (1946): 25; Mohrmann, *art. cit.,* 658.

11. Mohrmann, *loc. cit.,* thinks, however, that the early feast of the Epiphany in the East could not have been concerned solely with the birth of Christ; if it had been, how are we to explain the fact that once the feast of Christmas was introduced in the East, Epiphany should then have focused on the baptism of Christ? The answer is that, even in the early stage, the object of interest in the feast of the Epiphany was, as the word itself indicates, the manifestation of the divinity.

12. According to one view, the feast of Epiphany was introduced into Spain and came thence to Rome (Botte, *op. cit.,* 57). According to another view, it was introduced into Africa and passed thence simultaneously to Rome and Spain (Leclercq, *art. cit.,* 25).

17. The Magi of Old and the "Magi" of Today

1. See P. Benoit, *L'Evangile selon saint Matthieu,* La Bible de Jerusalem (in fascicles) (Paris, 1950), 31.

2. See *The Jerusalem Bible* (Garden City, NY, 1966), *New Testament,* p. 12.

3. See L. Cerfaux, *La voix vivante de l'Evangile au début de l'Eglise* (Tournai, 1946), 48–49.

4. Ibid., 54.

5. It provides the first reading in the Office of Readings in the new Liturgy of the Hours; it supplied the second and third of the nine readings in the older Breviary.

6. *Sermo* 31.1 (*CCL* 138:161).

7. *Sermo* 31.3 (*CCL* 138:163).

8. *Sermo* 32.1 (*CCL* 138:165).

9. *Sermo* 32.3 (*CCL* 138:171).

10. *Homiliae in evangelia* 10.2 (*PL* 76: 1111).

11. A. Feuillet, "La conversion et le salut des nations chez le prophète Isaïe," *Bible et vie chrétienne* 22 (1958): 5.

12. See J. Steinmann, *Le prophete Isaïe: Sa vie, son oeuvre et son temps,* 2nd ed., Lectio Divina 5 (Paris 1955), 129.

13. See Feuillet, *art. cit.,* 13.

14. *Sermo* 32.4 (*CCL* 138:176).

15. *Sermo* 33.5 (*CCL* 138:176), in *The Liturgy of the Hours,* vol. 1: *Advent Season, Christmas Season* (New York: Catholic Book Publishing Co., 1975), 561.

16. *Sermo* 35.1–2 (*CCL* 138:193).

17. *Sermo* 36.1 (*CCL* 138:195).

18. Connelly, *op. cit.,* 66.

19. See chap. 1, note 13, and corresponding text.

20. See the entrance antiphon for Epiphany.

21. Literal translation of the Latin antiphon for the *Magnificat* at First Vespers for Epiphany: "Hoc signum magni Regis est."

18. The Jordan: "Our Jordan"

1. The old but still valuable work of J. Corblet, *Histoire dogmatique, liturgique et archéologique du sacrement de Baptême* (Paris, 1881), gives a list of the representations of Jesus' baptism by John (2:524–50).

2. *Commentaria in Evangelium Joannis* 6.28 (*PG* 14:281).

3. *Homiliae in S. Lucam* 33.5 (*SC* 87:399).

4. *Commentaria in Evangelium Joannis* 6.27 (*PG* 14:281).

5. See J. Daniélou, *Origen*, trans. W. Mitchell (New York, 1955), 57–58; idem, *The Bible and the Liturgy* (Notre Dame, 1956), 99–113.

6. *Oratio adversus eos qui baptismum differunt* (*PG* 46:420–21), trans. in Daniélou, *The Bible and the Liturgy*, 102–3, alt.

7. F. M. Abel, "Exploration de la vallée du Jourdain," *Revue biblique* 10 (1913): 240.

8. On all this, see J. Bonsirven, *Le judaïsme palestinien au temps de Jésus-Christ: Sa Théologie* (Paris 1935), vol. 1.

9. See G. Vermès, *Discovery in the Judean Desert* (New York, 1956), who gives a translation fo the Rule edited by M. Burrows in 1951. On the baptism of the Essenes, see L. Cerfaux, "Le Baptême des Esseniens," *Recherches de science religieuse* 19 (1929), 248–65.

10. Isa 1:25; Zech 13:9; etc.

11. Isa 10:16-19; 30:27-33; 31:9; etc.; Jer 21:14; etc.

12. The last section (chaps. 55–66) of the book of Isaiah is not regarded as having been written by Isaiah himself.

13. There is a good study of the theme of God's fatherhood in L. Bouyer, *The Meaning of Sacred Scripture*, trans. M. P. Ryan (Notre Dame, 1958), chap. 21: "Our Adoption by the Father and the Gift of the Spirit."

14. Bouyer, *op. cit.*, 219.

15. A summary of the various interpretations, with bibliography, may be found in M.-E. Boismard, *Du baptême à Cana*, Lectio Divina 18 (Paris, 1956), 43–47. See also P. Joüon, "L'Agneau de Dieu," *Nouvelle revue théologique* 67 (1940): 318–21.

16. *Oratio 39, In Sancta Lumina* (*PG* 36:349ff.). Translation by Matthew J. O'Connell.

17. *Homilia de Baptismo Christi et de Epiphania* 3–4 (*PG* 39:368–69).

18. *Homilia 34, De baptism Christi homilia* 6 (*PL* 57:297–98).

19. Cana

1. See Boismard, *op. cit.*, 136; C. H. Dodd, *The Interpretation of the Fourth Gospel* (Cambridge, 1953), 300; L. Bouyer, *The Fourth Gospel*, trans. P. Byrne (Westminster, MD, 1964), 70.

2. H. Seemann, "Aufgehellte Bibelstellen," *Benediktinische Monatschrift* 28 (1952), 5–6. Boismard, *op. cit.*, 156, adopts this solution. But L. Bouyer, *The Paschal Mystery*, trans. S. Mary Benoit (Chicago, 1950), 37–41, and C. Charlier, "Les noces de Cana," *Bible et vie chrétienne* 4 (1953–54): 81, seem to come closer to the true solution of the problem.

3. Tertullian, *De baptism* 9.3–4 (*CCL* 1:284).

4. *Commentaria in Evangelium Joannis* 2 (*PG* 73:228).

5. *Epist.* 63.12 (*PL* 4:394–95).

6. *Catecheses Mystagogicae* 4.2 (*PG* 33:1098–99; *SC* 126:136).

21. The Baptism of the Lord

1. [The French lectionary has the variant reading that the author mentions at the end of this paragraph.—Tr.]

290 The Liturgical Year

22. Epiphany in the Liturgies of the Past

1. Gel. 65: "Uere dignum: te laudare mirabilem deum in omnibus operibus tuis, quibus regni tui mysteria reuelasti. Hancque enim festiuitatem index puerperal uirginalis stella praecessit, quae natum in terra caeli dominum magis stupentibus nuntiaret, ut manifestandus mundo deus et caelesti denuntiaretur inditio, et temporaliter procreates signorum temporalium ministerio panderetur. Et ideo."

2. *Sacramentarium Bergomense*, 189: "quia puerperio caelesti intulit mundo suae miracula maiestatis, ut adoranum magis ostenderet stellam, et transact temporis intervallo aquam mutaret in vinum et suo quoque baptismate sanctificaret fluneta Iordanis idem Iesus Christus."

3. *Sacramentarium Bergomense*, 199: "qui te nobis super Iordanis alveo de caelis in voce tonitrui praebuisti, ut salvatorem caeli demonstrares, et te patrem lumis aeterni ostenderes. Caelos aperuisti, aerem benedixisti, fontem purificasti, et tuum unicum filium per speciem columbae Sancto Spiritu declarasti. Susceperunt hodie fonts benedictionem tuam et abstulemnt maledictionem nostrum. Its ut credentibus purificationem omnium delictoru exhibeant, et Deo filios generando adoptive faciant in vitam aeternam."

4. See Corblet, *op. cit.*, 1:104–7.

5. Mercenier and Paris, *op. cit.*, 151.

6. *Commentaria in Evangelium Joannis* 6.46, quoted in Daniélou, *The Bible and the Liturgy*, 107–8.

7. *Oratio* 36 (PG 36:361), quoted in Daniélou, *op. cit.*, 55.

8. Ibid.

9. Mercenier and Paris, *op. cit.*, 151.

10. Ibid., 155.

11. Ibid.

12. Ibid., 159.

13. Ibid., 163.

14. Ibid., 166.

15. Blanchard, *Un hiver à Saint-Petersbourg*, in *Le tour du monde*, 3:206; quoted in Corblet, *op. cit.*, 1:111.

16. Mercenier and Paris, *op. cit.*, 170.

17. Ibid., 172.

18. A translation of the Armenian prayer may be found in J. Lemarié, *La manifestation du Seigneur: La liturgie de Noël et l'Epiphanie*, Lex orandi 23 (Paris, 1957), appendix 2, 525.

19. Mercenier and Paris, *op. cit.*, 172.

20. Ibid., 172–76.

21. Ibid., 185.

22. Ibid., 189.

23. The first part of the passage (2:11-14) is the epistle for the Christmas Mass during the Night in the Roman Rite.